NO ROOM FOR ERROR

BY BENJAMIN F. SCHEMMER

Almanac of Liberty

The Raid

U.S. Special Operations Forces
(forthcoming)

NO ROOM FOR ERROR

The Covert Operations of America's
Special Tactics Units from Iran to Afghanistan

COLONEL JOHN T. CARNEY JR.
AND BENJAMIN F. SCHEMMER

BALLANTINE BOOKS • NEW YORK

A Ballantine Book
Published by The Ballantine Publishing Group
Copyright © 2002 by Col. John T. Carney Jr., USAF-Ret., and Benjamin F. Schemmer

www.ballantinebooks.com

Library of Congress Cataloging-in-Publication Data
Carney, John T.
No room for error : the covert operations of America's special tactics units from Iran to
Afghanistan / John T. Carney Jr. and Benjamin F. Schemmer.
p. cm.
1. Special forces (Military science)—United States—History—20th century. 2. United
States—History, Military—20th century. 3. Special forces (Military science)—United
States—History—21st century. 4. United States—History, Military—21st century.
I. Schemmer, Benjamin F. II. Title.

U262 .C38 2003
356'.16'0973—dc21
2002028158

ISBN 0-345-45333-6

Book design by Holly Johnson

Manufactured in the United States of America

First Edition: November 2002

10 9 8 7 6 5 4 3 2 1

For the children and spouses
of the hundreds of "quiet professionals"—
the special operations warriors and scores of unsung heroes
whose feats we seldom hear of—
who have given their lives defending ours.

CONTENTS

CONTENTS

INTRODUCTION

I spent twenty-seven years in an Air Force uniform, traveling mostly by parachute and retiring in 1991 after fifteen years as a combat controller in "special tactics" units, the modern-day, far more versatile version of the Army's old airborne pathfinders. In 1977 I was picked to form the first such unit, which began as an ad hoc, six-man, classified team euphemistically called "Brand X." We were to work with other classified units that were just being formed to combat terrorism—principally airplane hijackings, in extremis hostage rescues and embassy seizures, and, potentially, recoveries of stolen nuclear weapons.

The missions were as varied as the places they took place in: the 1980 Desert One mission to rescue hostages from our embassy in Iran; the assault on Grenada to rescue six hundred medical students in 1983; the TWA 847 and *Achille Lauro* hijackings in the Mediterranean in 1985; the invasion that restored democracy to Panama in 1989; Desert Storm in 1991; Mogadishu, Somalia, in 1993; Haiti in 1995; the Balkans through the late 1990s; and, most recently, the war against terrorism being fought in Afghanistan.

Interspersed with these major events were smaller, clandestine, and often highly successful special operations, some of whose details

remain classified today. What isn't classified is the toll these missions have exacted. One hundred and three men from special operations were killed in action in those operations—37 percent of the
279 total combat casualties. Compared against their small numbers
(about 47,000 men and women—about 2 percent of a force totaling
2,249,000 active duty and reserve military personnel), America's
special operators have lost their lives in combat since 1980 at a
rate more than fifteen times higher than that of conventional U.S.
forces. Beyond these losses, another thirty-six special operations
men gave their lives during the same period on real-world missions
in seventeen other countries.

This story describes many operations conducted by many elite
units over the last twenty-two years, and the unique role that special tactics played in every one of these missions. So just what is a
"special operation"? A pioneer of special operations, retired Army
Lieutenant General Samuel V. Wilson, one of World War II's Mer-
rill's Marauders, put it best when he once said, "Special Operations
is a three-step dance: Get there, get it done, and get back!"[1]

Special operations encompasses every facet of unconventional
warfare, usually waged by clandestine forces that operate in small
groups against high-risk, high-payoff targets deep in hostile areas.
Those forces handle "direct action" counterterrorist missions (offensive operations) abroad, principally handled by the Army's Delta
Force and Navy SEALs, usually working with a small Air Force special tactics team. Special operations units also work with other
federal agencies on antiterrorist measures (defensive operations)
within the United States and overseas; lead the way in the war on
drugs in foreign countries; work to contain the spread of weapons of
mass destruction; and wage psychological warfare. Since the Vietnam War began, such units have led most forced-entry operations
and have usually been the first ones deployed to quiet transnational
unrest in places like Haiti, Panama, and the Balkans.

The units involved in these operations are all highly trained
and highly motivated.

Special tactics units are made up of small Air Force teams of combat controllers who are experts in airfield seizure in denied areas, controlling air strikes, and extricating friendly forces from harm's way. Embedded in their teams are pararescuemen (or PJs, for pararescue jumpers), combat trauma medics and rescue specialists who care for "precious cargo"—rescued hostages or wounded members of the special operations teams they support.

Special forces are Army units, long known as the "Green Berets," built around twelve-man A-teams in seven groups, each oriented to a different region of the world and each with fifty-four such teams. (Most of the teams fighting in Afghanistan came from the 5th Special Forces Group at Fort Campbell, Kentucky, which is oriented to Central Asia, and from the 3rd Special Forces Group at Fort Bragg, North Carolina, whose principal area of expertise has been the Middle East and Africa.) The teams are versed in local cultures around the world, functionally fluent in at least one of the languages spoken there, and able to recruit, train, and supply indigenous personnel or military units to operate more effectively on their own or to synchronize their work with either conventional U.S. forces or U.S. special operations units.

U.S. special operations forces also include the Army's 75th Ranger Regiment, the 160th Special Operations Aviation Regiment, two special operations signal battalions, and psychological warfare as well as civil affairs units.

Air Force special operations units include the 16th Special Operations Wing (still known as "Air Commandos") with its fixed-wing MC-130E/MC-130H Combat Talons, AC-130U gunships, and MC-130P refueling aircraft plus MH-53J Pave Low helicopters; the 919th Special Operations Squadron of the Air Force Reserves at Duke Field, Florida, with its MC-130E Combat Talons, plus two groups and similar squadrons abroad, as well as EC-130 Commando Solo aircraft in the Pennsylvania National Guard for psychological warfare broadcasts and electronic jamming.

The Navy's Special Warfare Command has eight *Sea-Air-Land* (SEAL) teams, two special boat and patrol craft squadrons, and several SEAL delivery units for clandestine insertions.

I was privileged to work with virtually all of these units during my active duty service; I have continued to work with them in one fashion or another since I "retired" in 1991; and now I arrange full college scholarships for the more than 325 children of special operations personnel killed on duty. I am deeply honored to have served with so many of their fathers.

Colonel John T. Carney Jr., USAF-Ret.
August 24, 2002

TUNGI, AFGHANISTAN

The first war of the twenty-first century quickly became America's first special operations war. President George W. Bush's "war on terrorism," triggered by the September 11, 2001, attacks on New York's World Trade Center and the Pentagon, began on October 7 when Bush and Defense Secretary Donald Rumsfeld announced the first U.S. air strikes against forces of the repressive Taliban regime and al-Qaeda terrorists in northern Afghanistan as part of Operation "Enduring Freedom." Within a few weeks they would announce the first two raids by American Rangers and other special operations forces in Afghanistan and acknowledge that small, clandestine teams of American special forces and special tactics units had begun operating directly with Afghan anti-Taliban tribesmen.

Air Force special tactics, Army special forces teams, and Army Rangers, Rumsfeld said, were targeting Taliban forces for long-range U.S. air strikes supporting Northern Alliance troops, gathering on-the-spot intelligence, and conducting unconventional hit-and-run raids on key targets. Soon after the Army–Air Force teams had infiltrated Afghanistan, Navy SEAL units also began operating there.

A brave young Afghan described the role that these special operators played in that war during a fierce firefight in eastern

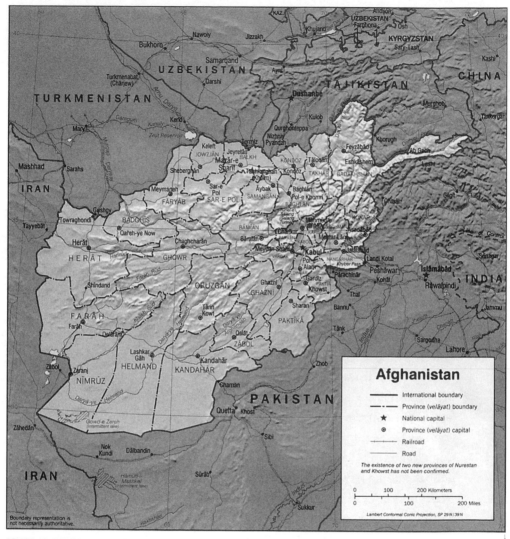

Afghanistan

- —— International boundary
- —·—·— Province (velāyat) boundary
- ★ National capital
- ⊕ Province (velāyat) capital
- +++++ Railroad
- —— Road

The existence of two new provinces of Nurestan and Khowst has not been confirmed.

| 0 | 100 | 200 Kilometers |
| 0 | 100 | 200 Miles |

Lambert Conformal Conic Projection, SP 29 N / 39 N

Boundary representation is not necessarily authoritative.

CENTRAL INTELLIGENCE AGENCY

2

Afghanistan in January 2002, when an American special forces and special tactics team leading anti-Taliban forces came under such withering fire that his comrades fled the battleground. Taliban and al-Qaeda fighters had depressed their antiaircraft guns on the hills and mountains surrounding the U.S.-led troops and were inflicting gruesome losses. But this particular Afghan stayed as the Americans held their ground and Sergeant William "Calvin" Markham, a special tactics combat controller, radioed for close air support strikes to suppress and destroy the enemy weapons. In the midst of this raging and bloody battle, the Afghan flung himself to the ground directly in front of the American sergeant to protect him from incoming rounds. Markham yelled at him, "What are you *doing?*" The Afghan replied calmly, "Sir, if they kill me, I'll be replaced. But if they kill you, the airplanes will go away."[1]

Except for such air strikes, however—blurred images of which appeared almost nightly on TV news for weeks after the president's and Rumsfeld's October announcements—little progress seemed evident in the war in its early days.

As American special operations troops in the country increased from "a few" to "less than a hundred" (actually, fewer than fifty by November 4) to "several hundred" (actually, fewer than three hundred of them), TV pundits and op-ed columnists complained that President Bush's war on terrorism had bogged down into a stalemate or "quagmire." TV screens were filled with images of precision-guided bombs—dropped from long-range B-2 bombers flying two-day, round-trip missions from the United States and B-1 and B-52 bombers flying twelve to fifteen hours and some 5,500 miles from and back to Diego Garcia in the Indian Ocean[2]—exploding on fuzzily pictured mud huts or barren, rugged terrain, but there was little sign and no word of progress against the Taliban. What would come to be known as "America's first special operations war" seemed to be off to an inauspicious start.

The *Washington Post*, for instance, headlined on November 2,

BIG GROUND FORCES SEEN AS NECESSARY TO DEFEAT TALIBAN;
BOMBING HAS LEFT MILITIA LARGELY INTACT

and reported, "The attacks have not eliminated any measurable number of Taliban troops. Northern Alliance forces have made no important gains against the Taliban . . . a major chunk of the 50,000 Taliban army and much of its arsenal are pretty much intact after three weeks of bombing."[3]

Dr. Andrew Bacevich, a West Point graduate and former armor officer who became director of Boston University's Center for International Relations, noted that ". . . the war's first weeks offer little cause for comfort" and complained about "inflated expectations about the efficacy of air power."[4] By the time Bacevich's article appeared in print, however, half of Afghanistan had fallen to the U.S.-led anti-Taliban forces, and it was clear that a new type of war was being fought.

Unfortunately, many observers did not, and could not, appreciate how special operations, special forces, and special tactics teams really operate. Once inserted into Afghanistan's inhospitable terrain, these troops had to make contact with the disparate tribal groups making up the Northern Alliance; establish some rapport in any one of a dozen or more languages—including Tajik, Uzbek, Pastun, Afghan, and twenty-two distinct dialects of Arabic; sort out which tribal leaders might prove reliable allies and which were ruthless warlords out to dismember their rivals and con their American suitors out of better arms and equipment for their own agendas; teach them how to scout out lucrative targets; prove their own ability to support Alliance operations by calling in effective air strikes to decimate opposing Taliban forces; and then persuade them to seize the moment and attack so as to incur minimum casualties. All in all, a difficult, dangerous, and time-consuming process.

That process took weeks. (In special forces training, men are taught that cultivating such bonding with indigenous forces can take months, possibly years.) The speed with which U.S. and Northern Alliance troops learned to rely on each other was all the more striking because special forces teams had not operated in Afghanistan since 1989, although there had been joint training exercises in other Central Asian nations since 1999, including the five "Stans" of the former Soviet Union—Uzbekistan, Tajikistan, Kazakhstan, Kyrgyzstan, and Turkmenistan. Furthermore, Afghan tribesmen (like the former Soviet republic of Turkmenistan) are notoriously hostile to foreign armies—as Soviet forces had learned from 1979 to 1989, when one hundred thousand of them were finally routed from the country by the Mujahideen after suffering close to thirty thousand casualties.

Although small pockets of resistance remained in most cities as Taliban forces either surrendered or tried to blend into the countryside, by late November all of the Taliban strongholds had fallen in quick succession to Northern and then Eastern Alliance tribal forces—Mazar-i-Sharif on November 9, Kabul by November 13, Kunduz by November 20, Herat, Bagram, and Jalalabad soon thereafter, and Kandahar by December 7.[5] Anti-Taliban tribesmen were often at odds with one another, but all were fighting to regain their country from Osama bin Laden's al-Qaeda terrorist network and the Taliban.

Whereas the U.S.-supported anti-Taliban had controlled only about 20 percent of Afghanistan in early November, mostly in the north, by midmonth they controlled half the country. A month and a half later, on December 22, a new interim government was established in the capital of Kabul.[6] Three months into the war, by January 2002, anti-Taliban coalition forces controlled virtually all of the country.

Such quick progress was remarkable given how only a few hundred American special operations forces were committed on the ground and the history of our past wars. After the December 7, 1941, attack on Pearl Harbor, for instance, four months passed before the United States responded with the Doolittle raid on Tokyo in April 1942. It took eleven months to start the land campaign against the Germans with the invasion of North Africa in November 1942, and two and a half years after Hitler declared war on the

United States before we landed in France on June 6, 1944—after the British and we had bombed Germany continually for nearly five years.[7]

The Pentagon didn't say so explicitly, but almost all of the early successes involved small Air Force special tactics teams helping to target air strikes against Taliban forces, welding together twenty-first-century technology with nineteenth-century tactics to bomb centuries-old caves.[8] Sometimes chasing terrorists on horseback or mules, American special forces soldiers and special tactics airmen used mobile phones and global positioning systems (GPS) to pinpoint targets for Air Force bombers and Navy strike aircraft. These planes dropped ordnance guided by laser designators or GPS to attack small concentrations of Taliban forces and al-Qaeda terrorists: 70 percent of all air strikes involved such precision-guided munitions, compared with only 8 percent for Desert Storm in 1991 and barely 35 percent in the Balkans.[9] Throughout the country, the Central Intelligence Agency (CIA) also had operatives on the ground, "tucked in very tight with the U.S. military" and—unlike many previous wars—reporting through the commander in chief of U.S. Central Command, General Tommy R. Franks, in a unified instead of split hierarchy.[10]

A few early engagements, however, involved "direct action" missions. By mid-November, U.S. special operations troops were taking the Taliban head-on. One classic operation took place in the dead of night on a rutted, mountainous road in the central part of Kandahar province, less than ten miles from the Pakistani border near the village of Tungi on November 22. News of that engagement barely made U.S. news dispatches—and with few details.

A Taliban convoy of two fuel trucks, a flatbed carrying eighty-five fifty-five-gallon oil drums, and several nondescript vehicles had stopped for the night near the Pakistani border, crudely camouflaged by tree branches and foilage. Its drivers were asleep behind their steering wheels, others on the soft, surrounding desert sand. Suddenly, the drivers were yanked out of their cabs by their feet, thrown on the ground, and quickly handcuffed by simple plastic restraints, as was everyone from the convoy. Some of the Taliban fighters noticed men sitting on the berms that lined both sides of the road, their weapons silently trained on the surprised and terrified convoy crewmen. The silent attackers wore military garb, helmets adorned with microphones and monocular night-vision devices, and flak vests, but no distinguishing insignia were apparent on this moonless night. Quietly, the convoy's crewmen were loaded onto oversized, jeeplike Humvees, driven a short distance across the berms, and ordered to sit on the desert floor. From out of the dark they heard the *whump, whump, whump* of two approaching but invisible helicopters and then scores of missiles and rockets launched toward the trucks. Massive explosions hurled oil drums and vehicles hundreds of feet into the air, all without one light illuminating the scene. Within minutes, the Taliban were loaded back aboard the Humvees and driven across the berms to the burning, smoldering wreckage that remained of their convoy. The mysterious soldiers cut off their plastic restraints, had them climb aboard a huge cart pulled by a few surviving donkeys and horses, and told its driver to transport them to the nearest village, about fifteen kilometers away. Almost in unison, the soldiers told the speechless convoy members quietly in "very bad Persian," "Have a safe trip. But spread the word."[11]

A Taliban commander in the border town of Spin Boldak permitted an American reporter and three Pakistani journalists to visit the site the next day, without Taliban guards. Plastic hand restraints were seen in the sand next to charred oil drums and the carcasses of three trucks and a burned-out tanker.

This was more than a week before anti-Taliban forces captured the capital of Kabul (on November 14) without a major fight. Three weeks later, the last Taliban stronghold of Kandahar fell as well, although the last al-Qaeda holdouts, who had hunkered down in the wings of a hospital there, weren't eliminated until the last day of January 2002.

Without naming the units involved, Deputy Defense Secretary Paul Wolfowitz quoted dispatches from two of the U.S. special operations teams involved in that operation during a major Washington policy address on November 14. He said, "Success in this campaign has come not just from our remarkable ability to fly bombers from bases in Missouri halfway around the world to strike targets with great precision. Success has also come from putting extraordinarily brave men on the ground so they could direct that air power and make it truly effective."[12]

Both dispatches, it turns out, concerned Air Force special tactics teams, small units of combat controllers and pararescuemen whose existence had been kept so secret since 1977 that they were not publicly acknowledged for sixteen years, until eight of their members were decorated following the October 1993 battle in Mogadishu, Somalia, in which eighteen Army Rangers, Delta Force members, and air crews from the 160th Special Operations Aviation Regiment died in the most intense firefight since the Vietnam War.

The first dispatch Wolfowitz quoted was dated October 25. Wolfowitz said he had removed all classified information. The message read:

> I am advising a man on how best to employ light infantry and horse cavalry in the attack against Taliban T-55s [tanks] . . . mortars, artillery, personnel carriers and machine guns—a tactic which I think became outdated with the introduction of the Gatling gun [in the Civil War]. [The Mujahideen] have done this every day we have been on the ground. They have attacked with 10 round AK's per man, with PK gunners [snipers] having less than 100 rounds . . . little water and less food. I have observed a PK gunner who walked 10-plus miles to get to the fight, who was proud to show me his artificial right leg from the knee down.
>
> We have witnessed the horse cavalry bounding overwatch from spur to spur to attack Taliban strong points—the last

several kilometers under mortar, artillery . . . and PK fire. There is little medical care if injured, only a donkey ride to an aid station, which is a dirt hut. I think [the Mujahideen] are doing very well with what they have. They have killed over 125 Taliban . . . while losing only eight.[13]

Wolfowitz said the American soldiers then went off and joined a cavalry attack on a Taliban position. (As Defense Secretary Donald Rumsfeld later quipped, "It was the first cavalry attack of the twenty-first century."[14]) Wolfowitz did not reveal that the Americans had included one request in their dispatch: The wooden saddles used by the anti-Taliban forces were uncomfortable, and they pleaded for tush-friendly leather models. (Secretary of State Colin Powell made sure these were quickly shipped to Afghanistan.)

The second dispatch Wolfowitz quoted was dated November 10:

Departed position from which I spoke to you last night . . . [We left] on horse and linked up with the remainder of [the element]. I had a meeting with [the commander]. . . . We then departed from our initial linkup location and rode into Mazar-e-Sharif on begged, borrowed, and confiscated transportation.

While it looked like a rag-tag procession, the morale into Mazar-e-Sharif was a triumphal procession. All locals loudly greeted us and thanked all Americans. Much waving, cheering and clapping even from the women . . . USN/USAF did a great job.

I am very proud of these men who have performed exceptionally well under very extreme conditions. I have personally witnessed heroism under fire by [two U.S. noncommissioned officers, or NCOs—one Army, one Air Force] when we came under fire last night, which was less than 50 meters from me. When I ordered close air support, they did so immediately without flinching even though we were under fire. As you know, a [U.S. element] was nearly overrun four days ago and continued to call close air support and ensured [Mujahideen] forces did not suffer a defeat. These two examples are typical of the performance of your soldiers and airmen. Truly uncommon valor has been a common virtue amongst these men.[15]

The same day, the Defense Department announced that eight humanitarian aid workers, two of them American, had been released by the Taliban southwest of the Afghan capital of Kabul, picked up by U.S. special operations troops, and flown out of the country. The dispatch also noted that over the preceding two days, air strikes "using anti-terrorist intelligence sources" on buildings near Kabul and in Kandahar had killed "some numbers" of Taliban and al-Qaeda's senior leadership, but that there was no evidence that Taliban leader Mullah Mohammed Omar or Osama bin Laden was present at either raid site. Within two weeks, however, unmanned Predator spy planes armed with Hellfire precision-guided missiles struck a small convoy one hundred miles from Kabul parked outside a three-story hotel near Gardez, an ethnic Pustan stronghold on the road into the Taliban mountain province of Paktia. Using intercepted satellite phone calls, British and later U.S. listening centers confirmed, as also did a further human intelligence source, that Mohammed Atef, the fifty-seven-year-old deputy to bin Laden and the terrorist group's senior military commander, had been killed in the attack.

U.S. forces first began fighting in Afghanistan with two simultaneous operations. One was a three-hundred-man Ranger parachute assault with eighteen special tactics troops on October 19 made from four MC-130 Combat Talons onto a military airfield in southern Afghanistan, code-named Objective Rhino, and the other was a raid on a Taliban command and control site near Kandahar, also involving special tactics personnel.[16] That raid captured a few mid-level Taliban leaders and brought home scores of documents whose intelligence value proved dubious. The chairman of the Joint Chiefs of Staff, Air Force General Richard B. Myers, said that the U.S. troops encountered only "light resistance," but in conjunction with those operations, two American soldiers were killed in a Black Hawk helicopter crash in Pakistan. A month would pass before Marines returned to the airfield and cleared it, providing a staging base for more special operations forces. They eventually turned it over to several thousand troops first from the Army's 10th Mountain Division out of Fort Drum, New York; then from the Army's 101st Airborne (Air Assault) Division out of Fort Campbell, Kentucky; and in July to the 82nd Airborne Division from Fort Bragg, North Carolina.

On October 30, Defense Secretary Donald Rumsfeld acknowledged for the first time that a "modest" number of U.S. special operations troops were on the ground—in northern Afghanistan only—supporting the Northern Alliance, although he added, "We've had others on the ground who have come in and gone out, in the south."[17] He was referring to the first of several twelve-man special forces A-teams who had been infiltrated first by parachute, usually with high-altitude, high-opening (HAHO) jumps that let the men glide tens of miles onto pinpoint objectives, then by helicopter, each accompanied by two or three Air Force special tactics troops. The first team joined up with Abdul Rashid Dostum, a war-callused Northern Alliance commander near Mazar-i-Sharif. Another team soon began working with Muhammad Fahim Khan from the Eastern Alliance, whose ragtag forces were fighting the Taliban near the city of Gardez, about eighty miles south of Kabul.

In just a few weeks, U.S. special operations personnel transformed the Northern Alliance into a force that was routing the Taliban army piece by piece, leaving it decimated and demoralized by the intense and precise bombing that special forces and special tactics teams on the ground had made possible.

By October 16, for instance, the director of operations for the Joint Staff, Marine Corps Lieutenant General Gregory S. Newbold, told a Pentagon press conference that "the combat power of the Taliban has been eviscerated."[18] His boss, the Joint Chiefs of Staff chairman, General Myers, tempered that assessment three weeks later on NBC-TV's Sunday-morning *Meet the Press*. When Tim Russert asked him if Newbold's statement was "still operative," Myers quipped, "I think if you'd ask General Newbold today, he would probably choose another term. In fact, we were surprised that a Marine even knew what 'eviscerated' meant." He cushioned that criticism by adding, "A lot of Air Force officers don't know what it means, either."[19] (But Newbold was not brought to appear before another Pentagon press conference for the next seven months.)

In early December, a wounded Air Force special tactics staff sergeant identified at the time only as "Staff Sergeant Mike" appeared on CNN's *Newsnight* to describe the recent fierce fighting at a prison uprising in a fortress outside Mazir-i-Sharif in which CIA agent Richard Spann was killed. He said of his comrades, "special tactics, the [the transcript says "unintelligible," but he said "pararescuemen"] in there, the combat controllers, the combat weathermen. It's—it's just that they're doing such an awesome job."[20]

The special operations work was so successful that it caused Pentagon planners and those from U.S. Central Command, co-located with the headquarters of U.S. Special Operations Command at MacDill Air Force Base in Florida, to reconfigure their initial plan for the first phase—Afghanistan—of the war on terrorism. That plan had called for the United States to "put in a large amount of American forces, hop them in by air," according to Air Force Brigadier General Richard L. Comer, vice commander of the Air Force Special Operations Command at Hurlburt Field in the Florida panhandle.[21] But by the time Defense Secretary Rumsfeld visited the home of special forces and special tactics at Fort Bragg, North Carolina, on November 21, he had reassessed the Pentagon's war plans and decided to let U.S. Central Command's commander in chief, Army General Tommy R. Franks, who has operational authority over the entire Persian Gulf region, horn of Africa, and

Central Asia, fight the war with special operations forces relying on surrogate troops from the Northern and Eastern Alliances. By then, two months from the time Franks had been ordered to deploy his first special operations teams in Afghanistan, there were still only about "a dozen" Special Forces A-teams on the ground there— "probably better than a dozen." As Rumsfeld told reporters accompanying him to Fort Bragg, "In an emergency, we dial 911 and ask for Fort Bragg." That was a remarkable accolade, given that the men Rumsfeld saluted were fighting a war for which the United States had no war plan on September 11, 2001, as Deputy Defense Secretary Paul Wolfowitz would acknowledge in congressional testimony late in June of 2002.[22]

Conventional forces from the 10th Mountain Division were also deployed to secure airfields in neighboring Uzbekistan and in Afghanistan as staging points for the unconventional warfare strategy that had evolved. (The Marines soon took over the Afghanistan base, called Camp Rhino.) In addition, small contingents of Britain's famed Special Air Service (SAS) and S.B.S., Special Boat Service, worked with U.S. special operations forces.

By December 22, after a weeklong meeting of tribal leaders in Bonn, Germany, a new interim government had been established in Afghanistan. Hamid Karzai, a forty-three-year-old chieftain living in exile in Pakistan since the mid-1980s who had infiltrated southern Afghanistan on October 8 and, riding a red motorcycle followed by his fighters on five similar bikes, linked up with special forces teams courting his mainly Pashtun tribesmen, was named prime minister. Karzai's men had been given the randomly selected code name "Texas Twelve" by the Americans supporting him. But he had barely escaped capture by the Taliban on November 1 when he convened a meeting of Pashtun tribal elders in Oruzgan province near Kandahar, the center of Taliban power. A special tactics and special forces team saved him by calling in devastating air strikes on the Taliban warriors trying to overrun his position.[23]

Late in January 2002, Karzai announced that the country's ruling body, the loya jirga or grand council, would meet in June to choose a transitional government after his six-month term expired, and that Afghanistan would hold free elections within two years. For the first time in two decades, Afghanistan began enjoying some semblance of civilized rule, although Taliban troublemakers were still roaming the streets of Kabul, the capital. More worrisome was the fact that Osama bin Laden had not been captured or even found, and Taliban leader Mullah Mohammed Omar was still at large as well (although both were possibly buried in the scores of caves and tunnels of Tora Bora and Zawar Kili that U.S. forces had searched and sealed or bombed to oblivion). But at least bin Laden was "a man on the run," as Deputy Defense Secretary Paul Wolfowitz described his plight in a Pentagon news conference on November 21.[24] (Although pundits never mentioned the issue, one reason why bin Laden may not have been captured or turned over by his confederates despite the "up to $25 million" price on his head is that the former Saudi multimillionaire could easily afford to pay even more handsomely to bribe his way to safe harbor.) Rumsfeld reiterated Wolfowitz's characterization late in January on NBC's *Meet the Press* when he said, "Right now, bin Laden and [Taliban leader Mohammed] Omar are not currently functioning effectively, [not] leading their terrorist networks; they are being driven. They are running, they are hiding, and we are after them."[25]

When Karzai paid his first visit to Washington on January 26–29, he told President Bush that America had "destroyed the Taliban regime and dismembered the al-Qaeda terrorist network in Afghanistan,"[26] and that he was committed to restoring Afghanistan to a representative democracy. But he asked the United Nations to beef up its twenty-two-hundred-man, British-led peacekeeping force in Kabul and deploy five thousand peacekeeping forces throughout Afghanistan's twenty-nine chaotic provinces, where Taliban pockets still exercised considerable influence and warlords with deep feuds held sway.

During the last days of January, the final two-day battle of the anti-Taliban era was fought over Gardez, a city of fifty thousand people living in medieval conditions where Karzai had named Padsha Khan Zadran to the post of governor of the region, Paktia province, having concluded that the incumbent, Saifullah (who goes only by one name), lacked enough political support to hold on to the job. But local tribal elders had refused to accept Khan's appointment, and when he moved to take Gardez by force, his fighters were defeated by Saifullah's.[27] (U.S. special operations troops purposely did not intervene in the fray, staying out of sight at their base south of the town. They had learned to be wary of such tribal rivalries after some Afghan leaders had tricked special forces teams into attacking competing warlords by identifying them as Taliban or al-Qaeda operatives, and extra wary after several "anti-Taliban" fighters even turned on them, wounding several American troops.) One prominent TV commentator, Bill O'Reilly of Fox News Channel's *The O'Reilly Factor*, said of the ebb and tide in the war, "Now we just seem to be waffling around."[28]

Nevertheless, within four short months a few hundred American special operations troops had virtually won the first phase of the war on terrorism. (As Secretary of the Army Thomas E. White pointed out, the United States had "more soldiers deployed on the ground in Utah [for Salt Lake City's 2002 Winter Olympics] than there are in Afghanistan today."[29]) But as Bush had emphasized in his State of the Union address on January 29, it was indeed only the first phase of a long struggle ahead:

> Our nation has . . . captured, arrested, and rid the world of thousands of terrorists, destroyed Afghanistan's terrorist training camps, saved a people from starvation, and freed a country from brutal oppression. . . . [But] what we have found in Afghanistan confirms that, far from ending there, our war against terror is only beginning. Most of the 19 men who hijacked planes on September the 11th were trained in Afghanistan's camps, and so were tens of thousands of others. Thousands of dangerous killers, schooled in the methods of murder, often supported by outlaw regimes, are now spread throughout the world like ticking time bombs, set to

go off without warning . . . [t]ens of thousands of trained terrorists are still at large. These enemies view the entire world as a battlefield, and we must pursue them wherever they are. . . . Our military has put the terror training camps of Afghanistan out of business, yet camps still exist in at least a dozen countries.[30]

President Bush noted that his war on terrorism was already targeting terrorists in those other countries. "Our soldiers, working with the Bosnia government, seized terrorists who were plotting to bomb our embassy. Our Navy is patrolling the coast of Africa to block the shipment of weapons and the establishment of terrorist camps in Somalia." About eighty-five special operations troops had also deployed to the Philippines with six hundred other U.S. troops and for six months would train local military units in counterterrorist operations directed against the Abu Sayyaf Muslim terrorist group on the southern island of Basilan in Zamboanga province, a cell that had once been linked to Osama bin Laden and al-Qaeda. In a speech at Winston-Salem, North Carolina, on January 31, Bush was able to claim, "We have totally routed out one of the most oppressive regimes in the history of mankind—the Taliban."[31] That same day, Defense Secretary Donald Rumsfeld, in a major policy address at the National Defense University, unveiled intentions to "inject American special operations forces as soon as possible into [other] conflicts."[32] Within weeks, small U.S. special operations teams were also training indigenous antiterrorist forces in Georgia and Yemen.

On April 18, Afghanistan's former king, Mohammad Zahir Shah, who had been in exile in Italy for twenty-nine years after being overthrown by a pro-Soviet cousin in 1973, returned with Karzai to Afghanistan under extraordinary security precautions that included decoy planes and heavily armed troops. He took up residence in a Kabul villa ringed by barricades and barbed wire and guarded by about 150 Afghan and Italian troops. Within two days of his arrival, British and Afghan troops foiled an assassination plot by Taliban and al-Qaeda fighters or other radical groups posing as journalists, detaining more than 550 people thought to be involved in the conspiracy. (Zahir's father had been assassinated when Zahir was only nineteen years old, and the plot against him resembled an earlier, successful assassination when two men posing as television reporters detonated a bomb hidden inside a camera in September 2001— shortly before the World Trade Center and Pentagon attacks— killing Ahmed Shah Massoud, the leader of anti-Taliban resistance in northern Afghanistan.)[33] At age eighty-seven, the king presided over the loya jirga, the June grand council called to form a permanent government and prepare his country for democratic elections in two years.

Nevertheless, the war on terrorism was far from over. Osama bin Laden and his top deputy, Mullah Mohammed Omar, had apparently escaped an American-led, twelve-day, two-thousand-man sweep, "Operation Anaconda," in early March 2002 against Taliban and al-Qaeda forces in hard-fought battles by U.S. special operations forces at Tora Bora, Shah-i-Kot, and Khost near Pakistan's mountainous 1,700-mile-long northwest border, which Afghanistan's anti-Taliban tribesmen were unable to seal off effectively.

A subsequent five-day foray throughout the region's caves and tunnels by five hundred soldiers from the 101st Airborne Division, accompanied by Federal Bureau of Investigation (FBI) forensic teams, failed to turn up any evidence that bin Laden or Omar had been killed there among the eight hundred Taliban and al-Qaeda fighters said to have died in the March fighting. But the sweep yielded helicopter loads of photographs, documents, dossiers, and vials containing an unidentified white powder that seemed to confirm that al-Qaeda was actively developing biological or chemical weapons of mass destruction. In early April, al-Qaeda's foremost recruiter and head of operations, Abu Zubaydah, was arrested in Pakistan during an operation in which American FBI and CIA officials participated (likely with a few men from Joint Special Operations Command). He was turned over to U.S. authorities for interrogation, taken to an undisclosed location, and soon claimed that al-Qaeda was close to building a crude nuclear device known as a dirty bomb, in which radioactive material is wrapped around conventional explosives.[34]

Thousands of British Royal Marine, Australian, and Canadian commandos entered the mountains of southern Afghanistan in mid-April, trying to ferret out remnants of Taliban and al-Qaeda forces thought to be readying a guerrilla warfare campaign against American-led coalition troops from sanctuaries in remote Pakistani tribal areas. Here, too, U.S. Air Force special tactics teams were playing a central role, since air support for the operation hinged on U.S. fighter-bombers, helicopters, and special operations AC-130 gunships.[35]

Afghanistan still had to constitute a new government, train its own army, purge rival warlords of Taliban leaders and Al-Qaeda terrorists hiding or trying to regroup in their midst, and get more help from Pakistan to deny the terrorists safety nearby. Still, it seemed the war was more or less won, a great victory with minimal friendly and remarkably few collateral casualties.

How did America's special operations forces come so far? These units had been virtual pariahs within their own armed services (and were largely being phased out of the active duty military establishment) in the late 1970s. Few people had even heard of them in the 1980s. And even in the year 2002 they were still being mislabeled as "special forces" instead of special *operations* forces.[36]

How did they make so much progress in a decade and a half that a few thousand troops from the forty-seven thousand men and women of the United States Special Operations Command, which didn't even exist until 1987, enabled U.S. Central Command to win, or at least look as if they were about to win, the first war of the twenty-first century?

Who *are* these shadow warriors? Where does America find men like these?

CHAPTER TWO

WHO *ARE* THESE WARRIORS?

Most of this book is about military units whose existence the U.S. government will not acknowledge. Asked anything about Delta Force or SEAL Team Six, the nation's premier counter-terrorist organizations, the Pentagon will respond only, "No comment." It neither confirms nor denies the existence of either unit.

In its public literature, the U.S. Special Operations Command at MacDill Air Force Base near Tampa, Florida, sometimes refers to "special mission units," but even that euphemistic term is used sparingly. The name *Delta Force* appears nowhere on unclassified organization charts of the U.S. Army Special Operations Command at Fort Bragg, nor is SEAL Team Six listed anywhere in the open literature of the U.S. Naval Special Warfare Command. Neither unit is ever mentioned in conjunction with the U.S. Joint Special Operations Command.

In his 1990 memoir, *An American Life*, former President Ronald Reagan scrupulously avoided mentioning Delta Force or SEAL Team Six in his ten-page description of the 1983 rescue operation on Grenada. Reagan's only mention of any special operations forces in conjunction with Operation "Urgent Fury," other than the Rangers, was that "the operation was scheduled to get started late that night [October 24] with the infiltration of commando teams to gather intelligence paving the way for the landing the next day." (The reference was to my special tactics unit, accompanied by Navy men from SEAL Team Six.) Reagan then wrote, "Early the next morning, after more than nineteen hundred Rangers and Marines had landed at two points on the island . . ." However, it was Delta Force and other groups from SEAL Team Six aboard helicopters from the Army's 160th Special Operations Aviation Regiment that led the assault. When writing of the 1985 attempt to free hostages aboard the hijacked TWA 847 jetliner, Reagan referred to Delta Force only as "a specially trained unit." Nor did he mention SEAL Team Six when recalling the 1985 *Achille Lauro* incident, only that the United States had "a plan for a crack team of Navy SEALs to assault the *Achille Lauro* and rescue the hostages from the terrorists," and that "after the airliner [carrying the fleeing hijackers] landed [at Sigonella], our team of Navy SEALs, who had been rushed to the base on Sicily, tried to arrest the hijackers."[1]

Thus, this book is mostly about men who live in official anonymity. Because the government's prohibition about identifying Delta Force and SEAL Team Six is probably breached more often than it is observed, however, I feel no compunction writing about these men or their units.

Both Delta Force and SEAL Team Six are what the government sometimes refers to as "special mission" units, the most elite ranks among America's 47,000 "quiet professionals" in our special operations forces.

Delta Force is more accurately known as the 1st Special Forces Operational Detachment—Delta. Both it and SEAL Team Six are so-called national assets.[2] They report through a special chain of command from the Joint Special Operations Command (JSOC) to the U.S. Special Operations Command—but more in an administrative sense than operationally. During real-world exigencies, JSOC most often works through the theater commanders-in-chief or the country ambassador they are supporting. They are never committed lightly, and they generally are used only on the most sensitive direct action missions or for in extremis counterterrorist or hostage rescue situations.

There are four other, less secret special mission units. These include the Army's 75th Ranger Regiment and its 160th Special Operations Aviation Regiment (first known as Task Force 160, whose existence was once kept strictly secret). They also include the Air Force's 1st Special Operations Wing (presently known as the 16th Special Operations Wing, but it may someday regain its coveted, original designation), and the Air Force's 720th Special Tactics Group, which I commanded but whose existence was never publicly acknowledged until 1993.

The work of most special operations units is conducted in support of and controlled by the regional or theater "war-fighting" CinCs—the commanders in chief of U.S. European Command, Pacific Command, Southern Command, Central Command, and what used to be Atlantic Command (now called Joint Forces Command). But most missions of the special mission units are controlled by the Joint Special Operations Command, as are all in extremis missions undertaken by Delta Force and SEAL Team Six. Most often, special tactics teams operate in direct support of those two units, although they deploy regularly with virtually all special operations forces.

Special operations forces represent the most frequently used but scarcest units wearing American uniforms. In late 1999, the Pentagon's Joint Staff listed thirty-one different types of units and weapon systems that were in such short supply that requests to deploy or engage them far outstripped their numbers or availability. Eighteen of the so-called low-density, high-demand assets— 58 percent—were from special operations forces.[3] (The other eleven low-density, high-demand assets were all highly specialized weapon systems such as the Patriot air defense system and the E-3A Airborne Warning and Control System.[4]) Thus, less than 2 percent of the force accounted for almost two-thirds of American military needs that exceeded the country's means.

Yet nothing was done to increase the numbers of those low-density, high-demand units until President George W. Bush's fiscal year 2003 budget, proposed in February 2002, to begin fixing the force mismatch. As Defense Secretary Donald Rumsfeld noted in his address at the National Defense University on January 31, the Department of Defense must look at "low density–high demand capabilities," explaining that this was a euphemism for "our priorities were wrong and we didn't buy enough." The department has known for some time, he said, that it does not have enough of "certain types of special operations forces."[5] The issue seems to have fallen off the radar screen, although Congress is weighing a proposed twenty-one percent increase in U.S. Special Operations Command's budget for the fiscal year beginning October 1, 2002. But most of that increase is for "operations and maintenance"—thus, the war in Afghanistan and training indigenous special forces troops in the Philippines, Georgia, and elsewhere. It is impossible to find in the thousands of pages of budget documents released as of August 23, 2002, any funds for or mention of new "low-density-high-demand" units and equipment to resolve the long-standing force-resource mismatches. Even at $4.9 billion, the new SOCOM budget would represent only one and one-third of one percent of the U.S. defense budget.[6]

While it is generally perceived that their work is dangerous, few people realize the hugely disproportionate casualties that special operations soldiers incur. As we've noted, in the past twenty-one years, special operations personnel have lost their lives on real-world missions at more than fifteen times the rate of their comrades in America's conventional forces. Their ranks account for only about 2 percent of all men and women in uniform, but they have suffered more than 37 percent of all combat fatalities since 1980. Special operations work is dangerous. One hundred thirty-nine men have been killed on real-world missions in twenty-five countries since 1980. Compare the number of special operations losses against total combat fatalities in America's principal military engagements over the past twenty-one years:

- Eight airmen died at Desert One in the 1980 Iranian rescue attempt; all of them were special operations personnel.

- Nineteen soldiers, sailors, and Marines died in the 1983 rescue of American medical students on Grenada; nine of them were from special operations units.
- Forty-eight percent of the twenty-three men killed in action in Panama in 1989 were in special operations units.
- In Somalia in 1993, 62 percent of the twenty-nine men killed in action were special operators.
- In Desert Storm, 17 percent of the 147 service members killed in action were from special operations.
- In Afghanistan, fifty-one American servicemen had been killed in action by the end of July 2002; thirty-two of them were special operations personnel.

Overall, special operations units suffered 37 percent of the 279 combat fatalities in those six operations; 35 other men have been killed in real-world operations in seventeen other countries since 1980.[7] The very nature of their missions makes their training even more dangerous: Another 232 men have died in training accidents.

Whatever their units may be, all the men (and now women) of American special operations forces have volunteered to live precarious lives and work at extraordinarily high operational tempos. Between October 1, 2000, and September 30, 2001, for instance, Special Operations Forces deployed to 146 countries or foreign territories with an average of 4,938 personnel deployed each week— while also conducting 132 Joint Combined Exchange events in 50 countries, 137 counterdrug missions in 23 countries, and humanitarian demining missions in 19 countries. That represents a 43 percent increase in country deployments in the ten years since Desert Storm, a 57 percent increase in the number of missions undertaken, and a 139 percent increase in the number of Special Operations Command personnel serving abroad in any given week—all with essentially the same number of people.[8]

This is their remarkable story.

CHAPTER THREE

"BRAND X"

A year after almost getting booted out of the Air Force, I knew we had arrived. Our five landing beacons came on in the middle of a pitch-black night deep in a North Carolina forest, and Charlie Beckwith burst out, "Well, I'll be damned. They did it!" We were near Laurinburg-Maxton, on an inactive military airstrip about a hundred miles inland from the Atlantic coast, on the South Carolina border forty-five miles southwest of Fort Bragg. The airfield once had an aircraft overhaul facility on it, but this had been closed down and there was nothing nearby. The five beacon lights were needed to guide a lumbering, four-engine C-130 transport onto part of a runway that was probably no longer than the deck of an aircraft carrier. Aboard the plane was Delta Force, just nine months old and sixteen months away from being validated as a "national asset" and America's premier counterterrorist force.[1] It was preparing for another live-fire takedown, one of innumerable such joint exercises that would lead to Charlie's moment of truth, the test of whether or not his Delta Force could be declared operational. It was August 17, 1979.

Just moments before, crouched down in the weeds beside that runway, I had watched Beckwith emerge from his car and complain scornfully to his intelligence officer, Major Wayne Long, "Bullshit! I told you they wouldn't make it. Let's just turn on the lights and get those planes in here so we can get on with this exercise."

Only days before, "Chargin' Charlie" had told me I was bald-ass nuts if I thought I could parachute six men from 12,500 feet of altitude—jumping "high," but opening our chutes "low," at only 2,500 feet, a so-called HALO (high-altitude, low-opening) jump meant to minimize time under canopy and thus the likelihood of being detected—assemble everyone into a small forest clearing on a moonless night; and, within thirty minutes, rig five infrared landing beacons in a T-box formation to mark a landing zone for the C-130. We would place four beacons marking the corners of a ninety-foot-square box at one end of a twenty-five-hundred-foot strip and center the fifth beacon at the other end of the runway. The box defined the area within which the plane's wheels had to touch down. We had to get all five beacons in place and turned on exactly sixty seconds before the C-130 was to land. *If* we could do that in the dark—meanwhile making sure the strip was clear of debris and obstacles—the pilots would risk landing without their lights on. They had worked with us before and had more faith in us than Charlie did—but not by much. There was no other way for Delta Force to reach this particular objective in time. Its men had no choice but to make that landing, and they knew that Charlie wouldn't allow the Air Force to send them on a suicide mission. Not on purpose, anyway.

The second I heard Charlie's surprised expression of approval, I tapped Master Sergeant Mitch Bryan on the shoulder and whispered, "We made it!" We didn't have a name then, but Air Force "special tactics" had arrived.

At the time, everyone called us "Brand X." We didn't exist on paper as an organization or formal Air Force unit. We were just a ubiquitous, small group of Air Force combat controllers cobbled together from all over the world and pressed into service for what were called "Emergency Deployment Readiness Exercises." That was a bureaucratic euphemism for "practice missions," usually "no-notice" exercises launched by the U.S. Readiness Command at MacDill Air

Force Base in Florida without prior warning to any of the participating units. They simulated hostage rescues, stolen nuclear weapons recovery, and counterterrorism direct action. They usually involved long distances and extreme weather—from Florida to Washington State and New Mexico or from Florida to small islands off Hawaii, to Death Valley in August, and to Wisconsin in December.[2]

For a year, up until that night, Brand X had seldom consisted of the same six men through any two consecutive exercises. I had to steal guys wherever I could find them and however I could get them to volunteer for temporary duty away from their parent units. And I had to recruit them without their unit commanders knowing what they were about to do (or had already done), or with whom, or where.

But at Laurinburg-Maxton, I finally had my own nucleus of six permanently assigned, highly trained combat controllers, all noncommissioned officers (NCOs). Mitch Bryan was the most seasoned—tall, handsome, full of mischief, willing to bet his last buck on any proposition, and well liked by the enlisted troops. He sported a mustache, as did some others on my team; they were later allowed to wear beards so they could blend in almost anywhere in the world. Like the men in Delta Force, we weren't supposed to strut around all spit and polished; some of us had to look like bums, airport ramp rats (baggage handlers, airplane refuelers, and latrine cleaners), or journalists recovering from bad hangovers. Mitch was my ranking NCO; he later became a lieutenant colonel in the Air Force. Vietnam experienced, Mitch was a competent combat controller and an excellent HALO parachutist whom I could count on to land on any airstrip anywhere to guide incoming aircraft. He had the night smarts of a fox: If there was one blown-out tire or piece of metal on that ninety-foot by two-thousand-five-hundred-foot rectangle, Mitch would find it, pitch black or pouring rain.

Technical Sergeant John A. "J.K." Koren was five feet eleven, medium frame, well proportioned, full of piss and vinegar, and always ready for a challenge. He had served with Mitch in Detachment One of the 56th Special Operations Wing supporting CIA operatives in Southeast Asia, as had two other men who soon joined our team. He had a quick mind and was always the next guy to volunteer after Mitch when the shit hit the fan. J.K. was always jovial with a good sense of humor even in the toughest of times. He was attached to Mitch's hip; they had been buddies from the beginning of their Air Force careers. J.K. was the more studious of the two. He displayed intuitive judgment and would have been my noncommissioned officer-in-charge—except that Mitch outranked him. J.K. later became an Air Force major commanding a squadron in England. Selected for promotion to lieutenant colonel, he turned it down to retire after twenty-seven years in uniform in order to spend more time with his wife, young son, and infant daughter.

One of the enlisted men I depended on most was Staff Sergeant David Wilson, a real nighthawk. He was our best spotter, the guy who looks out the C-130 or C-141 rear door or aft ramp and makes sure that we exit over the right spot. I used to tell David, "Your only reason for living is to make damn sure we land near the target area." At night, that was not an easy assignment. One amazing fact about David was that, although he was the smallest man in our team, he could eat more than anyone. He regularly ordered six eggs for breakfast.

On one particular night as David, the primary jumpmaster, was leaning out the side of the ramp of a C-141 aircraft preparing to give us the signal that only one minute remained before we would reach our release point, his main chute prematurely activated, violently extracting him into the darkness. The bottom pin on David's three-pin, twenty-eight-foot Para-Commander parachute had slipped out, allowing his pilot chute to catch the slipstream, thus inflating his main canopy. There was no way it could be stopped. As soon as he was under canopy, David faced an unusual peril: He observed a small general aviation aircraft violating our airspace. He had the presence of mind to wave orange and green chem lights to attract the pilot's attention to change his course. Chem lights are liquid-filled, plastic sticks; when snapped, they glow bright green or orange.

The team jumped a minute later. As procedures called for, we all checked in on our team radios as soon as we were under canopy. David, hearing us confirm that our parachutes were open, told us he had just landed on a tennis court. I told him to get to a major road, where we would pick him up after our mission was complete. David later told us that when he made the decision to go for the lighted tennis court, just as he was lining up to land, about five hundred feet from touchdown, the two ladies on the court quit playing and shut the lights off. David yelled and began throwing chem lights down onto the court. The startled ladies turned the lights back on to witness him make a perfect landing, and then drove him to a major road intersection.

Staff Sergeant Eddie Pound was an unassuming, short guy who wore bifocals and was the best radio operator in the business. He could fix any radio in our inventory. He was crucial to our team, making sure we could always communicate—and we always could. He was refreshingly enthusiastic, willing to try anything. Eddie had joined us from the Norton, California, combat control team with Mitch Bryan and John Koren.

We referred to Technical Sergeant Pete Holt as "Shoe Phone Pete" after Maxwell Smart, the secretive character in the TV series *Get Smart* who was always talking into his shoe and looking around corners. Pete loved intrigue and could scrounge anything. Large framed, six feet one or two, light hair, 210 pounds, affable, funny, Pete loved his beer and could drink most guys under the table. Pete could operate anything that was motorized, especially all the equipment on an airfield. Delta Force loved him. Whether they needed a generator or a truck to empty an aircraft latrine, Pete could operate it. An industrious guy with a great team ethic, he was a hands-on type who was always scheming.

We also had Technical Sergeant Ron Holder, a strong, compact ex-Marine who had been an instructor at the Combat Control

School, and Staff Sergeant Bud Gonzalez, a former rodeo bull rider who joined us from the Philippines' combat control team.

As for me, I was a thirty-nine-year-old major who had been passed over twice for promotion to that rank. That was a sad distinction: Roughly 80 percent of all captains were selected for promotion to major, and I had missed the cut twice. I had spent eleven years of notably undistinguished commissioned service as a personnel services officer, physical training (PT) instructor, and then football coach and recruiter at the Air Force Academy. This was my second year as a combat controller.

The night at Laurinburg-Maxton was a bit different from our previous exercises. There was more at stake, no room for error. We were leading Delta Force into one of its final tests before its "validation" exercise, the grueling four-day field exercise that late in 1979 would decide, under the strict scrutiny of dozens of skeptical generals, whether or not the top-secret elite unit, after two years of *very* expensive training, was ready for real-world counterterrorist operations. Little did any of us know on that August night that within months, on November 4, a mob of wild students would riot in downtown Tehran, seize the American embassy, hold sixty-seven Americans hostage (only fourteen of whom would be released over the next four and a half months), and throw us into action on a mission that for months did indeed appear suicidal. And it almost was: We lost eight men at Desert One trying to rescue the remaining fifty-three Americans in April 1980, and we failed.

The hostages didn't come home for 444 days. It was not a good harbinger for the other missions we would soon be sent on, and more than nine years would pass before we launched an operation that actually succeeded.

By then, special tactics had grown from a six-man team to the eighteen-man Brand X. Eventually it became an Air Force group of seven squadrons deployed around the world, composed of about 350 highly trained volunteers, all combat controllers and pararescuemen, "PJs." Moreover, I was promoted to full colonel in command of that group, selected "below the zone" (ahead of lieutenant colonels who were eligible for consideration), something unheard of for a former captain who'd twice failed promotion to major.

All this provided a striking contrast to my inauspicious beginnings in the Air Force. Like so much in life, this transformation started by accident . . . my fortune was often saved by men who stuck their necks out for me—and believed in me.

CHAPTER FOUR

JUMPING INTO COMBAT CONTROL

During my senior year in high school in 1959, my football coach had urged me to go to college instead of working in the submarine shipyard at Groton, Connecticut, which seemed like a preordained future for almost every player on the Fitch High School football team. I was a middle linebacker and fullback, and captain of the team. I was an indifferent, unmotivated, lazy student, however. Still, Coach Bob Anderson, one of our assistant coaches, a big, rugged lineman who had played at Duke, must have seen some potential that would take me beyond the Groton shipyard. He talked to my mom and dad in my junior and senior years and solicited their help to tutor me in math and English. I really didn't care about school, thinking I could always become a professional football player. But Bob said, "Let's send him to college." If it hadn't been for Bob Anderson, I'd still be in Connecticut hanging out in Sully's, one of the local beer parlors near the Navy housing project.

Bob's teammate at Duke, Ed Cavanaugh, who would later become head coach at West Point, put in a plug for me to a talent scout from the University of Arizona, and when the school expressed some interest in recruiting me, Coach Anderson insisted I go there to take its entrance exams. I flunked. He made me take the exams again after spending hour upon hour coaching me in academics and taking one practice test after another. Came time for the next entrance exam, I passed. The only reason I did so is that the coach had already tutored me on almost every question that appeared on the exam. He told me, "Next time, John, you might be on your own."

Before I went to Arizona, I had never been out of Connecticut and I had never seen a palm tree or so many beautiful women. The team captain, Tony Matz, took me to Nogales, Mexico, and introduced me to a prostitute (and later razzed me because I'd bought my mother a scarf on Canal Street). I used my fifteen-dollar monthly NCAA check (allowed for laundry) to party. I played fullback and defensive end, but I didn't study much, and my grades were so poor during my freshman year that it looked as though the school wouldn't renew my athletic scholarship. Coach Jim LaRue elevated me to the varsity my freshman year, so I was a good candidate, but I flunked every course I took except physical education.

I wanted to go home, marry my high school sweetheart, and did so, doing pick and shovel construction work and living in a trailer near the Navy housing project. In the middle of the summer I got a letter from Coach LaRue saying he was looking forward to seeing me back. He knew I didn't have the grades and sent along a couple of summer courses, one of which, of all things, was dairy science; since Groton, Connecticut, didn't have many cows, it was like a foreign language to me. But I studied the courses, filled out the lessons, and sent him back all the papers. I started to realize that my friends at the University of Arizona were encouraging me to study and get back into school, and they made out all the lessons for me. All I had to do was sign 'em and send 'em back. They even sent me the answers to the tests. Back at the University of Arizona, I had to take a final exam in dairy science; if I got a grade of B, I'd have just enough points to get my scholarship back. I showed up in the Agricultural College in August to start football practice. Two other freshmen were in the same boat I was—Donny Pallicelli and Fran Battista, both from Pittsburgh. The professor handed out the tests, and they finished answering the multiple-choice questions in fifteen minutes, way under the allotted time. I didn't get one answer right because the answers I had been coached to remember had nothing to do with that test, which was all about the genetics of cattle. The teacher could tell I was flustered: "You looked a little frustrated, Mr. Carney," he observed. It was an understatement. "This is a waste of time," I told him; I didn't know the answers and I had screwed up. "Don't worry," he said, "your two friends didn't pass either. I'm going to make a deal with you: What grade do you need?" I said, "I need a B." He replied, "I'm going to give you a B. And you're going to come back in the fall, take every class—and *earn* the B."

Twice in my life people have given me grades so I could succeed. Finally it dawned on me: It was a helluva lot easier to study than to go though what I was going through. My whole life, I've been able to point back to people who had absolute faith in me. People who would just "bridge" me until I finally woke up. A brush with failure and a teacher's generosity had jolted me awake.

From then on, I studied harder so my mom wouldn't be disappointed in me. Neither Mom nor Dad had gone beyond the fourth or fifth grade, and my dad couldn't even write cursive. My mom was really excited that I passed each year, and I was proud as could be when Coach "Gentleman Jim" LaRue welcomed me back each fall. Arizona ended up with a winning season every year I was there, racking up twenty-seven wins and thirteen losses. I wasn't a star player, but I loved being part of a winning team. As graduation neared, I wished more and more that my dad, who had died in my junior year in 1962, had lived to see me get my diploma. Arizona was a land grant college, which meant that I could take Air Force or Army ROTC. But I knew that as a former Navy Seabee and first class petty officer who'd been busted to able bodied seaman, Dad would be even prouder if I became an Air Force officer and earned my pilot's wings. Besides, someone pointed out that the Air Force ROTC cadets drilled only on Wednesdays, once a week, wore short-sleeved shirts, and usually carried books or field manuals instead of lugging rifles. The Army men drilled on Tuesdays and Thursdays and had to wear long-sleeved khakis, go to the armory almost every drill period, check out a rifle, and practice marching in formation with it. Picking the Air Force was a no-brainer.

Having flunked my freshman year, I had to work like hell to qualify for the Education College in my junior and senior years. ROTC became very helpful and got me my B to qualify for two more years of school. All you had to do was show up and say "yes, sir" or "no, sir"—plus you got paid thirty dollars every couple of months. That convinced me to stay in ROTC, where I ended up as commandant of cadets my senior year.

As soon as I was commissioned in 1964, I applied for flight school—but my eyes wouldn't cooperate. I had astigmatism and didn't get accepted. The Air Force wasn't about to entrust an airplane to someone who couldn't see the runway. The master sergeant at my ROTC unit—"Sergeant Charlie," as we knew him—had advised me to turn down a commission in the regular Air Force and accept only a reserve commission. His reasoning was simple: If I accepted the regular commission, I would not get the $350 allowance paid to reserve officers for their first uniforms; if I accepted the reserve commission, I would get the money *and* be offered a regular commission six months later. Like clockwork, the Air Force offered me the regular commission six months after I went on active duty. That was my first of numerous exposures to noncommissioned officers who knew how to play the game.

Disappointed as I was about failing the pilot-training eye tests, an NCO at Davis-Monthan Air Force Base outside Tucson told me I could apply for a medical waiver for flight training once I was on active duty. With the war in Vietnam heating up, I figured I would probably get one. I decided to try. I requested assignment to the East Coast so I could be near my mother, but while I was waiting for my waiver, they sent me to Oxnard Air Force Base in southwest California. My first claim to fame there was my ability to drink a yard of beer faster than anyone on the base. My less-than-thirty-second record lasted until I left for Vietnam. At Oxnard, I got ready for war with an assignment as a "special services" officer in the gymnasium.

The job involved running the recreation program—managing the gym and bowling alleys, loaning out basketballs and baseball bats, organizing boxing matches or softball games, and taking inventories of Ping-Pong sets, chess sets, Monopoly games, and Chinese checkers. Working for me was a master sergeant nicknamed "Chief Robinson," who happened to be a Hopi Indian.

Soon after I reported to the base, I received a set of orders signed by Colonel Robert Brewer, the base commander, to serve on a court-martial board with five other officers and a chief warrant officer named Smith. This was a so-called additional duty, something that was usually handled in an officer's free time. The orders said that Second Lieutenant Carney would be the court reporter, the lowest-ranking officer on the board. When I showed the orders to Chief Robinson, he said they were wrong. I outranked the warrant officer, Robinson noted; Smith should be the reporter. Armed with this knowledge, I went to the base commander's office that morning and requested an audience. I complained that I shouldn't be the reporter because CWO Smith was junior to me; Colonel Brewer said he would correct the mistake, smiled, and dismissed me.

That evening, I went to the officers' club for happy hour. CWO Smith, sitting with some friends, sent me a drink with his compliments. Then his group had a big laugh, and from the way they glanced at me, I surmised it was at my expense. The next day, Chief Robinson showed me a new set of orders. CWO Smith was no longer on the court-martial board, but I still was. Colonel Brewer had recut the orders: Now I was the junior member and still the court reporter. CWO Smith had just been thanking me for getting him out of court-martial duty. I learned one of my first lessons as an officer: Don't screw with warrant officers (typically with twenty or thirty years of service); befriend them at all costs.

Duty at Oxnard was a far cry from warring in Southeast Asia, but "someone has to stand on the sidewalk and clap for the heroes." A friend of mine from college had said that to me when I went to Oxnard. Indeed, my Air Force career began on the sidewalk. Oxnard was an Air Defense Command base flying F-101 Voodoos that frequently staged practice alerts at two or three o'clock in the morning. My job then, in defense of my country, was to show up at the mess hall and get two huge urns of coffee and about ten dozen cookies. I had a little blue Econoline truck that I drove to the flight line to distribute hot coffee and cookies to the crews and maintenance people. They called me the "Cookie Man." About the third time I was performing this crucial role, the security police barred me from approaching the flight line without the badge required for such access. They spread-eagled me and, after searching me, placed me in their truck, all the while pointing their weapons at me. The security police captain called the command post to announce that they had a second lieutenant in custody who claimed he was the "Cookie Man." The colonel on the other end of the phone line said, "Let him go. Give him back his coffee and cookies!" This was the first time in my Air Force career that I felt I really belonged; I was a first-stringer, serving cookies on a flight line.

My medical waiver for flight training did not come through. Instead, I was sent to Vietnam in 1965—still as a special services officer, first at Tan Son Nhut Air Base outside Saigon and then at a place called Ubon Air Base in Thailand. A serious war was unfolding around me, but I was on the bench handling "morale and welfare" at an obscure air base, still hoping for a waiver. My morale couldn't have been lower. The 8th Tactical Fighter Wing was at Ubon, flying F-4s to bomb North Vietnam every day. Me? I was not a first-, second-, or even third-string player; I was fourth-string. Not even in the game, like a water boy passing out Gatorade. About the only thing I learned at Ubon was at the bar in the officers' hootch. I heard some guys call themselves "combat controllers." I was intrigued: They weren't pilots, but they jumped out of airplanes, controlled airdrops, called in air strikes, and were excellent company.

In World War II, the Korean War, and the early days of Vietnam, part of what is now known as combat control had been handled by Army "pathfinders," paratroopers with a few extra days of training to judge when troops or supplies should exit an airplane; once on the ground, they measured wind velocity and sent up weather balloons to judge if winds were above or below the maximum for safe parachute operations. Directing close air support strikes from the ground was not handled by Pathfinders but usually by a two-man Army Air Corps or Air Force liaison or tactical control team attached to frontline units. Pathfinders fell out of favor in 1958 when virtually the entire 101st Airborne Division, then headed by Major General William Westmoreland, parachuted in an exercise in Kentucky and high wind gusts on the drop zone dragged eleven men to their deaths and injured scores of soldiers. To his credit, Westmoreland was the first person to jump from an airplane on the same drop zone the very next day.

Out of the blue, in 1966, just as my tour at Ubon was ending, a letter came from "Gentleman Jim" LaRue, my coach at Arizona, whom I had helped coach for a year. He said there was an opening on the Air Force Academy's football staff and suggested that I apply to Ben Martin, the coach there. So I wrote Coach Martin; LaRue wrote a strong letter of recommendation; and early in 1966 I got orders to join the Academy's athletic staff at Colorado Springs, Colorado.

LaRue was one of the early, great college coaches who believed in developing both football players and gentlemen. And he went the extra mile to help his ex-players become productive citizens. A handsome, dark-complected man at six feet tall with a medium frame, he was a running back or quarterback. He was soft spoken and conveyed a self-confident but not arrogant personality. He would say to his players: "Be a gentleman first; be a good student; and next be the best football player you can be." When my dad had died, I had no money to return home from Arizona to Connecticut for his funeral; Jim LaRue gave me the money out of his pocket. He was a caring coach, a warm and genuine man.

I spent the next eight years—1966 through 1974—at the U.S. Air Force Academy as a physical education instructor, freshman football coach, and, for my last six years, as an assistant varsity football coach, devoting most of my time to recruiting. It was a dream assignment.

As had Jim LaRue, Ben Martin became one of the great men in my life. I learned a lot from him. Although we had to play their teams on Saturdays, there was no way our recruiting program could compete with those of Notre Dame, UCLA, or any other big school. When we went out to recruit football players, we knew we were likely to get only high school players who were not highly sought after. Even that was difficult, for we were asking most of the young jocks to shave their heads, march to breakfast at five-thirty in the morning, and give us eight years of their lives—four at the Academy and four more on active duty. Consequently, we were lucky to get one, two, or maybe three highly motivated, first-rate, blue-chip athletes, the ones everyone else was wooing. Ben Martin's philosophy was to build our offense or defense around these "Blue Chippers." Hopefully, the other players would learn from them and try to better themselves. "What you've got as freshmen," Ben used to say, "is all you'll have as seniors." We didn't have junior college transfers like our competitors, because our recruits had to start college all over as freshmen. I locked Ben's idea away in the back of my mind: Build a team around one, two, or three all-stars. If the other team members had the raw capabilities, it would work.

Time flew fast. I was soon up for promotion to major. Then Martin called me into his office one day and told me I had been passed over despite my outstanding record. The Vietnam War was winding down, the Air Force was being downsized, and there was no longer room for captains or majors coaching football at the Air Force Academy. The following year I failed promotion again. This time the bad news came in a phone call from a major named Ron Fogelman at Lowry Air Force Base outside Denver, a short, stocky guy who always had a flattop haircut. He had an outgoing personality, a lot of energy, and displayed a lot of enthusiasm, and he was a great thinker and keen intellect. Thus, it caught my attention when he told me candidly that there wasn't much of a future for me in the Air Force and that perhaps I should press on with other plans. I was twenty-seven years old and already a failure. I ran into Major Fogelman twelve years later in a receiving line at the annual Air Force Association dinner in Washington to honor the twelve Outstanding Airmen of the Year, one of whom was Chief Master Sergeant Mike Lampe, then my senior NCO. Fogelman had risen to three-star general and was surprised to see me not only in the receiving line with him but also still in uniform, a full colonel with an impressive array of ribbons. He turned to me and asked, "What do we have to do to get rid of you, Carney? Drive a stake through your heart?" He eventually became the Air Force chief of staff and a much more enthusiastic supporter of special operations than his predecessors.

Atop Fogelman's bad news about my promotion, my wife asked me for a divorce. She had become fed up with my constant travels while recruiting Academy football players and left for California.

After Major Fogelman's phone call, I was ready to take off my uniform and try coaching professional football in the civilian world. But during a cab ride to the airport after an NCAA coaches' convention in St. Louis, Ben Martin and Charlie McClendon, the legendary LSU coach and later athletic director, talked me out of it.

The Academy's superintendent, Lieutenant General Jim Allen, gave me a pep talk also. A tall, blond, distinguished gentleman with a businesslike demeanor, he was someone you approached with caution; he could look right through you. But he was also extremely warm and sincere. He told me to quit being a jock and get into the "mainstream" Air Force. He said I had to get into the *operational* side of things or I'd never get promoted and would have to leave the service. "Up or out," they called it; three strikes and you were out. I didn't want to waste ten years and then have to start all over; I told General Allen I thought I'd try combat control. He turned to his aide, Major John Lorber (who went on to become a four-star general and commander in chief, Pacific Air Forces), and asked him, "What the hell is combat control?" It was obvious that combat control was not a known commodity in the Air Force. Allen's aide explained that combat controllers (by then part of the Air Force, replacing the Army's old pathfinders) set up landing zones for air-drops; cleared dirt strips for air assaults; checked the winds there and aloft so pilots would know when to drop cargo or tell paratroopers when to jump; kept planes on the right course, in the right intervals and sequences for landing; and sometimes guided fighter planes to their targets or directed fire for the side-firing AC-47 and AC-130 gunships used in Vietnam.

It was something I wanted to try. All *I* knew then was that besides parachuting a lot, combat controllers had to move and think fast and be blessed with both solid physical conditioning and sharp cognitive skills, more so than any other force involved with special operations. It sounded like a challenge, so late in 1974 I volunteered, but the staff officers who ran combat control and handled assignments in the Air Force personnel system made it clear: combat control didn't want *me*.

Rejection made me want the job all the more. General Allen made it happen: He called General Paul K. Carlton, commander in chief of Military Airlift Command, who had his own small combat control staff, and General Carlton instructed them to accept me. I reported to Air Traffic Control School at Keesler Air Force Base, Mississippi, early in 1975. Reliant again on a powerful benefactor, I felt like a complete failure as an Air Force officer with little or no future. I became obsessed with proving myself, determined to give my all, to master combat control skills and to succeed. Driven by a compelling need to belong, I had to prove that I had capabilities and could contribute. I didn't want to let down people who believed in me. Three months later I finished at the top of my class.

I was sent to Combat Control School at Little Rock Air Force Base in Arkansas. Again, I excelled—simply from fear of letting General Allen down. But by that time, combat control had become a dead-end career field, suffering from neglect, downsizing, and budget cuts. Like the Army's special forces after the fall of Saigon, combat control lacked an advocate. We were looked upon with indifference. In fact, in 1976, when I was going through the combat control qualification courses, its teams came under the aerial port squadrons of Tactical Air Command's and Military Airlift Command's airlift wings, and once a combat control officer made major, there was no further progression available in that career field. To get promoted, combat control officers had to cross-train and begin another career field. In 1977, all tactical airlift were reassigned to Military Airlift Command, but about the only training that combat control teams were getting was providing support for aircrews on the drop zone, marking D-Zs and scoring the drops, measuring distances from the intended point of impact for the TTBs—tactical training bundles or "titty [for T.T.] bundles." These simulated drops from the canister delivery system were used to resupply ground troops or support special forces teams in Vietnam and elsewhere. That was the worst part of the job: What we really needed was realistic training to hone our skills.

When I finished my training in 1975, I received orders to head a reportedly lackluster combat control team stationed at Dyess Air Force Base in Texas. Its eighteen team members were not enthusiastic about my arrival: They knew that the new guy in charge was a two-time loser for promotion to major. One of the last two officers who had served in the unit had been rif'd out of the Air Force (removed from active duty because of a "reduction in force"); the other had been passed over for promotion and resigned.

Dyess was anything but a plum assignment. Operational readiness for combat control teams had taken a big backseat to aircrew training. Everything we did was done on a shoestring. Funding squeezes meant aircraft weren't available for us to train adequately, so we did a lot of pencil training, keeping neat records and accurate counts of our parachutes. We were buried in an Air Force bureaucracy dominated by Strategic Air Command (SAC), Tactical Air Command (TAC), and Military Airlift Command (MAC), which focused on supporting conventional Army missions like large-scale troop deployments, and the Air Force hierarchy thought of combat control in terms of combat support rather than direct action combat operations. In essence, we were ground warriors, and there was an institutional Air Force reluctance to embrace a ground warrior ethic.

With standards low, promotions slow, and little realistic training, it was no surprise that we were short on what Ben Martin called Blue Chippers, outstanding airmen, noncommissioned officers, and officers who had a real future. I remembered what Martin used to say about the less-than-impressive football talent the Air Force Academy recruited: "This is what we have to line up Saturday against Notre Dame [or UCLA, or Navy, or what have you], so if you got turds in the lineup, you better start polishing them."

The team members at Dyess were sharp, dedicated men who lacked mission identity and direction. I knew that what I had to do was polish combat control at Dyess and pull the team together. I reminded myself that the power of a waterfall is nothing but a lot of drips working together. Buoyed by wry humor, I began the most energizing, rewarding work of my life.

I started by stressing physical conditioning. The kind of work we did required it: We jumped out of airplanes at freezing altitudes, lugged heavy radios, and ran up and down and all around rough landing strips. Sports were a natural way to get the unit in shape as well as build pride. We ran races, played pickup football games after duty hours, and staged wrestling, boxing, and tennis matches, overland map-and-compass marches, and even a few drinking contests. Mainly, there was a lot of "buffing." A few Blue Chippers began to surface: Master Sergeant Bill Winters was one of the first, a recruiting-poster noncommissioned officer. He impressed me at first glance and proved to be an excellent mentor for everyone from senior NCOs to captain. He's the one who really taught me the skills needed to be a good combat controller. He also paid me my first great compliment. During my first year at Dyess, he decided to retire. He told me he wished I had come along sooner because he would have liked to serve with me. Chief Master Sergeant James Howell and Master Sergeant Clyde Howard filled the void discreetly, keeping me on the right track, teaching me the ropes of everyday combat control duties, and emphasizing the do's and don'ts.

I watched for other men who were conscientious, dedicated, and believed that combat control done right was important to the wing's performance. Leaders had to work constantly to mentor, coach, and encourage their people, and I worked hard at that. As a football coach, I had learned that the difference between winning and losing is directly related to how well you prepare those who are responsible for performing. I had always believed that if you told people what to do, they might remember; if you told them and demonstrated what to do, they would remember more often; but if you involved them in the process of deciding why something had to be done, solicited their ideas and opinions on how it should be done, and demonstrated what could be done, they would almost *always* remember. Thus, I involved the whole team in everything I did. The Dyess combat control team started coming together.

For me, the chance to build a first-class team was a perfect marriage. In 1975, the C-130 wing at Dyess had its annual Operational Readiness Inspection (ORI), the Military Airlift Command test that could turn a colonel and wing commander into a brigadier general overnight or send him to the bench forever. For the combat control team, that ORI was the chance to show our stuff. We helped the wing through some tough exercises and set a new standard for combat control, indeed a new standard for the wing's performance. We were making a difference. We had proved our unit's worth, that we added real value to the airlift mission, and airlift is what MAC was all about. We received the highest rating MAC's inspector general staff could award, although the wing itself failed the ORI.

Word spread about how quickly and how much combat control at Dyess had changed. Late in 1977, I was summoned to MAC headquarters at Scott Air Force Base in Illinois and interviewed for a special assignment by a lieutenant colonel named John Gradowski and a colonel named Keith Grimes. In 1970, Grimes had been the weather officer for the Son Tay rescue mission. That November, fifty-six Army special forces volunteers had been flown into the heart of North Vietnam just ahead of a monsoon, landed twenty-three miles from downtown Hanoi, and raided a remote prison compound trying to free sixty-one American prisoners of war.[1] The camp proved empty, but not one man was lost on the mission, which was led by the legendary Army special forces colonel Arthur D. "Bull" Simons.

Grimes told me about a top-secret message that General George S. Brown, the chairman of the Joint Chiefs of Staff from 1974 to 1978, had just sent to the Pentagon's six "war-fighting CinCs"—the commanders in chief in Europe, Strategic Air Command, Atlantic Command, Pacific Command, Southern Command, and the Rapid Deployment Joint Task Force (then a three-star post that was the forerunner of U.S. Central Command). Brown told them to develop new contingency plans to cope with terrorism; that the military was training some new, highly classified special counterterrorist units formed at the direction of the president; and that each CinC should stand ready to support the new units during a forthcoming series of Emergency Deployment Readiness Exercises. Grimes told me that MAC needed a combat control team to deploy with the units, and he asked me if I would volunteer to lead the team. I jumped at the chance.

It was all an ad hoc arrangement, however. Grimes told me that the details would have to be worked out later. I would have six-to-eighteen personnel "slots" assigned to me, but nobody to fill them. I would have to negotiate with the MAC headquarters combat control staff and the numbered Air Force staffs about the availability of one individual or another as each deployment came up. It would be up to me to persuade other units to lend me the combat controllers I needed. That would be hard to do for two reasons.

First, tactical airlift (mostly the four-engine, turboprop Lockheed C-130s) had recently been transferred from Tactical Air Command to Military Airlift Command, and combat controllers were split into small groups that reported either to TAC's former aerial port squadrons (which ran conventional airfield operations), or to TAC or MAC headquarters staffs, or to the director of operations among various MAC wings which flew the larger C-141s and huge C-5s. The result was that combat contollers were tasked primarily to support day-to-day wing training and were given only two weeks a year to prepare for their wartime missions. They called it "dedicated training," but throughout this transition each team would use only a few men to support a wing's bundle training drops, and then the combat controllers had to cram a full year's worth of wartime training into two weeks. It was obvious to me that we were not creating a wartime-capable force: We were not organized, trained, equipped, or funded to go fight.

Second, there was no authorized "table of organization and equipment" and no designation for the unit I would lead, no station assigned for it, not even a name. Grimes warned me that most wings were undermanned and short of combat controllers, and they wouldn't want their people sent off on temporary duty assignments. I asked him, "What do I tell people when they ask me, 'You want to borrow Sergeant Jones for assignment to *what?*'" Grimes said it was all so classified the team would have no designation or name. Later, Technical Sergeant Pete Holt, better known as "Agent Orange" or Maxwell Smart's "Shoe Phone" Pete, who was stationed on the combat control team at Charleston Air Force Base and was one of the eighteen men we selected to participate from time to time, came up with the name "Brand X," and Grimes picked up on it.

It would be up to me to figure out how to build a team out of a nonexistent unit with different airmen assigned to it every time Brand X had to show its stuff—*and* to persuade headquarters jocks or the wings' directors of operations that our nebulous mission should take priority over chasing their training bundles.

I had always stressed to men on my combat control team that we had to be able to communicate, or we'd be useless. We had to be able to provide command and control. Without working radios, there could be neither. We had to be great air traffic controllers, up to speed on the latest procedures. We had to be able to shoot, move, and communicate. That meant reading maps and top physical conditioning. Once we hit the ground, we had to be able to reach our objective and do the job with whatever we carried in our rucksacks. The team agreed with me: "We had to out-Army the Army." We trained hard. There was nothing artificial about it. Among ourselves, we swore to never let our mouths write a check we couldn't cash. We developed some novel tactics and some standards against which to test everyone else. All the while, we also had to do our own housekeeping: We repaired our own radios, maintained our own vehicles, and packed our own parachutes.

Soon after I arrived back at Dyess, I was alerted to prepare for deployment to Alaska on a no-notice contingency exercise. It was the first test for Brand X, a grueling four-day test near Fairbanks, north of Anchorage, and it was cold. Once again, we really helped our fellow airlifters deliver the goods. Every airdrop landed right on time and right on target; not one paratrooper was injured because he'd been urged out the door too soon or too far from his landing zone and drifted into a cliff or some trees.

The scenario called for the 2nd Ranger Battalion commanded by Lieutenant Colonel Wayne Downing to fly to Alaska, where terrorists had stolen a nuclear weapon and were holding some hostages in a remote compound. Downing's unit was being validated as an "asset" under the Emergency Deployment Readiness Exercise program in a field test. (*Asset* simply meant that the unit was ready for counterterrorist operations under the direct operational control of the president and the secretary of defense.) The Rangers had to track down the terrorists, take them prisoner or kill them, free the hostages, and recover the nuke. During the planning session for the mission, Downing said he could handle it and wouldn't need us; in fact, he didn't want us. I shrugged it off at first, but then decided to call my new boss, Major General James "Bagger" Baginksi, who was MAC's director of operations; I told him, "They don't want to use us." Soon someone on Baginski's staff—probably Brigadier General Duane Cassidy, his deputy—called the Rangers and passed the word that if the Rangers wanted to use MAC aircraft to get to their target area, they absolutely *would* have a MAC combat control team with them. (This would prove only the first of three critical times the Rangers tried to deploy without us; we saved their bacon each time.)

We helped Downing's Rangers finish their plan for the mission. A few days later, on July 28, 1977, my team jumped from a C-141 into the Malmute drop zone near Elmendorf Air Force Base in Alaska to establish PZs (pickup zones for the assault forces) for three helicopters in the target area, where each would recover a Ranger platoon after they had assaulted the compound. But one of Downing's platoons became disoriented due to the large magnetic deviation between true north and their magnetic, GI-issued lensatic compasses. Master Sergeant Billy Slayton, whom I had borrowed from his job as commandant of the Combat Control School, conferred with the Ranger second lieutenant, and he and John Koren guided his men back to where they were supposed to be. It was just one example of our special tactics troopers taking the initiative and not being inhibited by rank.

An AC-130 gunship was to orbit overhead to support the Rangers if heavy fire was needed. Unfortunately, the gunship arrived ahead of schedule and was spotted by one of the bad guys. Tipped off that something was coming down, the terrorists jumped into a vehicle and took off. That presented some problems. Downing was having commo problems, his helos had left, and his Rangers were on foot while the bad guys were clocking down the road at about sixty miles an hour.

Slayton had been on previous exercises with us and said that I should tell Downing that we'd radio the gunship to get a fix on the vehicle and keep it in sight, then call the helicopters and have them return to pick up his platoons. Fortunately, each of Downing's platoons had one of our combat controllers with them, and we had our own radios, which *always* worked. (Every man on our team knew that if you wanted to stay out of the shithouse, your radio better work. We had a cardinal rule: Be able to communicate, or we are worthless.) Thus, we could pass the word to all the Rangers that we were going to make an impromptu air assault, literally on the fly. Downing liked it. We got on the horn to our controllers, who passed the word to the Rangers, who clambered back aboard their helos and, following cues from the gunship, flew ahead of the vehicles, landed, and set up an ambush. It worked; the Rangers freed the hostages and recovered the nuclear weapon.

From that day forward, Brand X controllers were attached to the Rangers wherever they went. We knew we were beginning to make a difference. But we celebrated our success with a bit too much exuberance. Before leaving Alaska, we had a pretty raucous celebration at a bar near Elmendorf Air Force Base.

I entered us into the bar's talent contest, and to my surprise, the men indeed had some talent. The act was a version of the "Full Monty," later made famous in the movie so named. The more the crowd cheered, the more clothes came off. We won the contest hands down—or, I should say, pants down. We put the $100 prize money on the table and invited the locals to join us as we drank into the night.

When I arrived back home, a message was waiting for me to report to the wing commander first thing Monday morning. I was certain word had gotten back about the talent contest and my ass was going to be on the carpet; the chance of me ever being promoted to major was zero.

The next morning I reported to the wing commander's office. When I was escorted into his office, there were several lieutenant colonels already there. I just knew they were from the JAG office ready to advise me of my rights. To my shock, the wing commander stood, smiled, and extended his hand to congratulate me on being selected for promotion to major. I couldn't believe it; my jaw dropped, and I could barely speak. I thanked the colonel for his support and left his office in a daze.

I was euphoric for a week—one that proved almost fatal for my career. The men had decided to have a combination promotion and farewell party for me at the noncommissioned officers' club. It was a great party—a party that almost got me court-martialed. Once again, the men displayed their talents. This time they performed a skit based on the ditty "Old MacDonald Had a Farm"—"with a chick, chick here and a chick, chick there." All went well until they decided there was going to be a bear on their farm. To emphasize and illustrate the bear, they dropped their pants, baring their butts. Unfortunately, just at that moment, the club manager rolled back the partition separating our room from the main ballroom being set up for the weekly bingo game. The men were caught with their pants down and singing "with a bear, bear here and a bear, bear there" by the bingo crowd scrambling for their bingo cards and favorite seats. Shortly before sundown the next day, the wing commander summoned me to his office. He had received a complaint over the "commander's hotline"; an investigation would follow.

Fortunately, I was already on orders to report to 21st Air Force headquarters at McGuire Air Force Base in New Jersey to head up its combat control office. Major General Thomas P. Sadler, a trim, scrappy airlifter and ex–forward air controller from the 1st Cavalry Division in Vietnam, was the 21st commander. He headed Military Airlift Command's biggest unit: 37,000 people in seventeen locations on five continents covering an area from the Mississippi River eastward through Europe to New Delhi, India. Given responsibility for my investigation, he turned it over to his judge advocate general with a wink: "How many officers do you know," he asked, "whose enlisted men throw a steak dinner and champagne party for him when he's transferred?" Unbeknownst to me, the JAG soon buried the report on the investigation or lost it in his circular file. Later I found out that Sadler had his JAG personally interview every one of the eighteen men on the Dyess combat control team. None of them could remember anything like what some puritanical bingo wife had reported. When I saw the general weeks later, he told me jokingly, "Carney, the only reason you're still around is because you had eighteen liars working for you." I was proud; certainly we were jelling as a team.

When I reported for duty at McGuire, Sadler wanted to send me to Rhein-Main Air Force Base in Germany to play football. But he told me I'd been picked for some spook business and that, while he didn't particularly like having to add a combat control guy to his staff, apparently it was important: MAC's commander in chief, General Robert E. "Dutch" Huyser, had called to tell him to get me into high gear fast, even though Sadler didn't have much of an idea where we were headed. Combat controllers were way down in his chain of command, but in my case, there would be no one in between. Sadler didn't seem too pleased about having a major reporting to him who had no unit and no men under his command. He told me he didn't really know what my job was about and didn't much care, but he told me that, if nothing else, I was to stay out of trouble at the officers' club and NCO club. I almost did.

Chief Master Sergeant Marty Shapiro, who worked for me in 21st headquarters, was retiring, and the combat control staff decided to throw a party for his retirement. They had me arrange for a female topless dancer to perform. Her name was "Nitro"; she just happened to hold the record in the *Guinness Book of World Records* for the longest topless dance. Sadler decided to drop in for a cocktail and to toast Marty. Nitro was a spectacular-looking woman, and when Sadler saw her in a sheer nightgown, totally nude underneath, he was determined to have her dance at the officers' club the following Friday during happy hour and had me arrange it. Nitro danced at the officers' club and was a smash hit.

But wives got word of her performance and complained up the chain of command past Sadler. The issue exceeded even Sadler's pay grade and made its way up the Air Force chain of command. That not only turned out to be Nitro's last appearance; it also ended topless dancing in Air Force clubs. Later, Duane Cassidy, promoted to major general, replaced Sadler as commander of 21st Air Force and decreed that Friday go-go dancing at the O' Club would have to go. Sadler would recall later telling me, "Carney, you get caught between the dog and the lamppost more than any shooter and looter I know."

I didn't have much time to miss the topless dancing. Within days of that flap, I began a whirlwind, nonstop cycle of four- or five-day temporary duty assignments all over the eastern United States.

Throughout the next year, I found myself hopping from McGuire to Charleston, South Carolina (where Sadler had a wing of C-141 transports), and from there to Little Creek, Virginia, Fort Bragg, North Carolina, Fort Benning, Georgia, or Eglin Air Force Base in the Florida panhandle, and sometimes overseas. My temporary duty orders said I was assigned to the 1701 MOBSS, which I think meant 1701st Mobility Support Squadron. In reality, I doubt the organization ever existed except on a piece of paper.

Years later Sadler would joke that "nobody knew what the hell the other was doing, it was all so secret." He said my work was so highly classified, I should be a SEAL or Army Ranger because no one in the Air Force had the foggiest notion what I was doing. He used to tell people, "John jumps to the sound of guns."

Egged on by his vice commander, then Brigadier General Robert B. Patterson, Sadler called me one day at Fort Bragg and asked me to parachute a team with the game ball and Olympic coin (for the pregame coin toss) into the National Collegiate Kickoff Classic football game in Giants Stadium at the New Jersey Meadowlands—at night. It would be on Saturday and on national television, Penn State versus Nebraska, the first game of the new collegiate season.

I owed a lot to Sadler for his support and told him I would do it if my boss, Major General Richard Scholtes, the Commander of Joint Special Operations Command, would let me do it. Scholtes gave me the go-ahead, with the understanding that I wouldn't let the stadium's announcers mention where we were from. I gave Sadler the good news and told him we would need the stadium on Friday for practice jumps and the airspace around it cleared. Since the stadium was in a high-traffic corridor for planes using La Guardia Airport as well as John F. Kennedy and Newark International Airports, I thought I had put up enough barriers that Sadler wouldn't be able to deliver. In fact, the Meadowlands was on the final approach path to Newark. In my mind I was convinced that Sadler had more than he could unravel to pull this off. Little did I know that Sadler had a Reserve officer on his staff who was the head of Federal Aviation Administration air traffic control for the area, and he arranged to have the airspace cleared for our Friday practice jumps. Sadler was also friends with the mayor, who arranged to have the stadium open for our Friday practices.

I selected four expert jumpers—Chief Master Sergeant Nick Kiraly, Sergeants Doug I. Brown and Billy Howell, and then First Lieutenant John Koren. Not having a stadium to practice jumping into, we rehearsed for the event at a drop zone near Raeford, North Carolina. We surveyed Giants Stadium and made ready for the Friday jump. Sadler had shown up by driving though the tunnel into the stadium with a few friends and city officials. He walked out to the center of the field, placed a dime on the fifty-yard line, and bragged, "My boys will land on a dime." But the Friday night practice was a disaster. The "spot," the point where the jumpmaster calculates we should exit the aircraft, was too far away from the stadium and a wind sheer of thirty miles an hour between 3,000 feet and 1,000 feet blew the men past the stadium. Billy Howell landed next to the interstate; Nick Kiraly landed at the parking lot next to the basketball arena, far from our target, about twenty yards from the security guards standing next to their pickup truck there. They asked him, "Where the hell did you come from?" but loaded him into their truck and drove him to Giants Stadium.

After a few minutes went by and I hadn't seen a trace of my jumpers, I knew something was wrong. Chief Kiraly radioed me that they had landed at the basketball arena. I told him, "Wrong place; wrong sport." Sadler asked me, "What's going on?" I told him we had miscalculated and landed in the basketball arena. He gave me a look of disgust, picked up his dime, and left. I did not hear from him again until after a successful jump into the stadium on national TV the next night.

By then, I had reminded the team that we had no room for error come Saturday night. The men used the close-by Teterboro Airport to take off in an H-3 rescue helicopter from the New York Air National Guard. But weather had started to move in, making the jump challenging, maybe even dicey. We had to synchronize with the marching band; the weather put that at risk, and the H-3 had to go around for a second pass. I radioed them from the stadium, "Go for it!" Billy Howell, a second-generation combat controller,[2] was the jumpmaster. He and Sergeant D. I. Brown nailed the exit point at 3,500 feet and, lit up by stobe lights on their helmets, landed precisely on time in and around the Penn State marching band to the roar of 77,000 people.[3] The band almost marched over the jumpers, but the effect was dramatic and the crowd was pleased. Sadler even walked onto the field to congratulate us. We then watched Penn State get trounced by Nebraska. Later that evening, we shared a hotel elevator with Penn's coach, Joe Paterno, and introduced ourselves. Paterno told us, "You guys were a big hit." The team was on cloud nine. The jump proved a big success on TV as well and paid my debt to General Sadler.

Flying back and forth from McGuire Air Force Base to Fort Bragg in North Carolina, Hunter Army Airfield in Georgia, Little Creek in Virginia, Hurlburt Field in Florida, or to Fort Lewis and McChord Air Force Base in Washington State, I met some *very* interesting units and real Blue Chippers, not just Air Force ones but Army and Navy too, and even a few Marines. They were all in newly formed (or forming) counterterrorist units—SEAL Team Six at Little Creek, Blue Light and Delta Force at Fort Bragg, the Ranger battalions at Hunter Army Airfield near Fort Stewart, Georgia, and at Fort Lewis, Washington, plus the Army's new Task Force 160, a special operations aviation unit at Fort Campbell, Kentucky.[4] That meant we would often need larger aircraft than the C-130s, and we began jumping from the C-141s at Charleston and Norton Air Force Bases that were training under newly developed special operations low-level tactics, SOLL II, meaning all flights were nap of the earth—flying below radar during every exercise. This gave me special respect for these consummately professional aircrews. Our work also involved the Air Force's 1st Special Operations Wing, the old "Air Commando" unit stationed at Hurlburt Field near Eglin Air Force Base in the Florida panhandle.[5]

Every trip brought a new challenge: jumping with the SEALs

off the coast of Hawaii near Barking Sands, in an uninhabited area with an airstrip surrounded by pineapple fields near the Pacific Missile Range launch pads; leading Rangers from Fort Lewis, Washington, out the door on a jump onto remote airstrips in the deserts of Nevada; and helping Blue Light rig its equipment for a make-believe assault on a terrorist training camp in the Everglades, resembling some makeshift Cuban camp in Central America.

Despite the newly forming counterterrorist units, special operations was reaching a nadir during this period. In the aftermath of post-Vietnam downsizing, funding for special operations forces had been cut by 95 percent. Reaching a low point in 1975, special operations forces constituted only one-tenth of 1 percent of the entire defense budget.[6] By 1977, Army special forces strength had dropped from seven robust active duty groups to three understrength ones; each of them was manned at only about half its normal level of one thousand four hundred soldiers. The prestigious 7th Special Forces Group was about to be relegated to the Army National Guard.

The Navy SEALs, who had won fame operating almost independently in the brown waters of South Vietnam's delta, were reduced to half their former strength and were struggling to convince fleet commanders of the blue-water Navy, all focused on the Soviet naval buildup, that SEALs could play important roles in open-ocean warfare. The Navy was spending little on SEAL modernization and was about to deactivate many more SEAL units and decommission the last of its special warfare submarines, capable of clandestinely inserting SEAL teams and recovering them from near an enemy coastline. None of the Air Force's special operations AC-130 gunships was to be funded for the active force beyond 1979, and all were scheduled for deactivation or transition to reserve units, a move that had signaled a near death knell for other units, like reconnaissance squadrons. The fleet of long-range MC-130 Combat Talons needed for deep insertions had aged severely; no funds were programmed for modifying them with new sensors or to extend their service lives, and all were programmed for transfer to the reserves. Air Force deep penetration helicopters were virtually nonexistent except in small Air Rescue and Recovery Service detachments. Promotions for people in Air Force special operations units lagged sadly behind their counterparts throughout Tactical Air Command, Strategic Air Command, and Military Airlift Command. Thus, Delta Force and SEAL Team Six proved to be anomalies, and conventional forces looked askance at these elite, supersecret units.[7] But the prospect that I had picked a career field with no career ahead never occurred to me.

Instead, I tightened the qualifications required of combat controllers picked to work with Brand X; they would have to undertake two special, voluntary training courses, and I became one of the first volunteers. The first course was the high-altitude, low-opening (HALO) parachute course at the Army's Special Warfare Center in Fort Bragg, North Carolina. A combat control staff officer called me, supposedly on the QT, and advised me not to go to HALO school. He said I wasn't experienced enough and could easily fall out. That would jeopardize my chances of remaining in charge of Brand X. I told him I'd take my chances and pressed on with my goals, which were to pass the course *and* to graduate first in the class. I won the so-called Iron Mike award, competing with Army Rangers, men from special forces, Navy SEALs, and Marine long-range reconnaissance specialists to become the number one student. All of it was hard work, but I learned the truth of what Vince Lombardi used to say: "The harder you work, the harder it is to surrender." Next came combat diving in a special Military Airlift Command combat diving/scuba school, with the academic portion at Charleston Air Force Base, South Carolina, and the dive work at Key Largo in Florida. My classmates included John Koren and David Wilson, both of whom would later join me with Brand X. The chief dive instructor was the affable but demanding combat controller and Vietnam/CIA veteran Michael Lampe, then a technical sergeant, who was working with Johnny Hall, John Karr, Tom Fagan, J. D. Burch, and Mort Freeman. I noted that Mike had a unique gift for motivating people to meet whatever standard he set, but I remember each of them because they helped me succeed in my goal.

CHAPTER FIVE

DELTA FORCE

Every mission given to Brand X involved some new, "special" tactics. We had to land planes with minimum lighting, infrared lights, and little or no communication. Compared to regular combat control work, everything had to be expedited: The whole idea was to use military airlift to deliver a select, small strike force anywhere in the world in the dark of night on the threshold of battle. Brand X was what the Air Force called "the air-to-ground interface"; we were the ones communicating with both the ground force and air component commanders. We handled not only the command and control but also the air traffic control, close air support, gunship firing, the drop zones, and the clandestine pickup zones. Without us, the operations simply were not possible. The use of air power in counterterrorist missions was primarily an airlift job; we made that work.

We were always under scrutiny from elite units in one of our sister services, waiting for us to screw things up, but we were driven to succeed. We were not going to let the units down, or each other. The combat controllers I had helped select and was now leading were determined not to bring shame to our small career field. The war against North Vietnam was history, so our focus was now on demonstrating what we could do to help in the war on terrorism. If anyone understood the importance of command and control, it was the units we supported—and us, a handful of overworked and undermanned combat controllers. We provided the communications they needed to get to the target, to lay close support or gunship fire on the target, to bring in the aircraft or helicopters that would haul them out of trouble. And we had to do it with whatever we could carry on our backs. My men wanted not only to serve their country, but to identify with and contribute to the frontline players. They knew they had been given a chance to become Blue Chippers, part of a first-string team, maybe America's most important one.

One of our toughest tests came in December 1978 at an exercise at Camp McCoy, Wisconsin. After isolation (a quarantine-like standard procedure to let the troops rest, settle down, perform their equipment checks, plan, and get fully briefed on their missions), we took off with Delta Force from Duke Field near Eglin Air Force Base in Florida and led a pitch-black assault into frozen Camp McCoy. Fourteen MC-130s were involved, led by Sadler's deputy, Brigadier General Robert B. Patterson. Once Delta Force was inserted, Patterson took the planes back to Pope Air Force Base, loaded hot chow aboard, and returned to Camp McCoy to bring Delta Force back home. But an Army general overseeing the exercise wouldn't let Patterson land because four of Delta's troopers were missing. With fourteen planes running out of gas, Patterson got me on the horn: I gave him permission to land his lead aircraft so he could convince the general that he needed to get his troops out of there. By then, Delta's troopers were so beat up, exhausted, and cold that the side of the runway was beginning to look like the Battle of Gettysburg. Patterson prevailed and stayed with the troops until everyone was accounted for. That exercise turned out to be a defining moment in choosing Delta Force over another unit that had been picked by Fort Bragg's commanding general and was competing for the job, Colonel Bob Mountel's Blue Light team.

After six or seven months of the merry-go-round all over the United States, I told Sadler I needed a home closer to Fort Bragg.

That's where the Delta Force commander, Colonel "Chargin' Charlie" Beckwith, wanted us, right under his thumb—something most people would shy away from, but I thought it was a great idea. I also told Sadler that the ad hoc pickup teams weren't going to cut it. We needed to build some synergy, develop some corporate memory, and get a real team going so we could support the Emergency Readiness Deployment Exercises properly. I stressed that we needed most of all to gain the confidence of Beckwith, a bruiser of a man, and that we had to be near him to do that. Beckwith was a skeptic, far from convinced that we would mesh with Delta's handpicked, hard-trained professionals. During our first encounter, he made that clear when he told me, "I'm not going to drag your combat control knuckles through the sand. You're not cut from the same bolt of cloth."

During its early formative years after 1977, Delta Force believed its niche was in low-visibility missions in non-permissive environments, and it spent little time working with the Rangers, special forces, and 1st Special Operations Wing. Its need for combat control support was not apparent because Delta expected to use commercial or covert aircraft to get to the scene. Yet it was understood that Delta would never be a totally self-contained organization. It *might* need Rangers to seize critical, nearby, threatening installations while Delta Force took down a particular target. At times, it might need the long-range MC-130 Combat Talons and MH-53 helicopters of the 1st Special Operations Wing, and possibly support from its AC-130 gunships. And it might need Military Airlift Command to get to denied trouble spots overseas. Brand X would be key to integrating most of these resources with Delta Force. Combat controllers could operate international air traffic control towers or set up unimproved landing sites, and they could deploy any way that special forces could—by HALO jumps, static line parachute drops, in small boats, on foot, or by swimming.

Charlie Beckwith was always circumspect; he would never throw out an idea until it had been evaluated, and he wouldn't adopt a novel idea until it was tested. Beckwith's attitude perplexed me at times. He didn't engage in extended conversations (leaving that to his staff), and he had a habit of asking flippant questions about how good we were, never bothering to wait for an answer. I had never been tested the way Charlie was testing me, but I knew I was being challenged. When I queried Charlie's staff about his standoffish attitude, they told me not to worry; we were doing fine. Charlie was gruff, aggressive, large-framed, a former University of Georgia lineman, but with a warm, gentle side. Most of the Army didn't want any part of him, and he liked it that way. At first sight, you'd never have believed he was the commander of Delta; there wasn't a lot of polish there, just a lot of smarts.

In due course, our team was deploying with Delta more often than any other unit, and then almost exclusively as its training intensified. But I needed to get close to Charlie, to get into his brain and win his confidence. At a meeting one day in the Delta compound, where I was trying to convince Charlie to include us in his plans and let us demonstrate on his exercises exactly what we could contribute, he remarked, "We're going to see if you've got any balls." Slightly miffed, I shot back, "And what makes *you* think, Colonel, that you have a corner on the market for balls?" Charlie turned to Bucky Burruss, the lanky, affable, but tough-as-steel major whom he had made Delta's first squadron commander, and said, "You know, I think I'm beginning to like this guy."

But we still weren't part of Charlie's team. How could we be? My "team" didn't exist. I'd show up with a different bunch of guys almost every time we worked with Delta. Atop that, wing commanders were getting tired of me robbing their best combat controllers for so many last-minute emergency exercises; they had missions, too, and drop zones to look after. So I had to call combat control teams or send messages to wing staffs all over the United States and often overseas to scarf up the needed people. It was an exhausting, divisive, unworkable setup.

In the fall of 1978, MAC's deputy for operations, Major General Bagger Baginski, and his assistant, Brigadier General Duane Cassidy, greased the skids to give me six dedicated (full-time), permanent combat controllers. Finally, my team would have some cohesion and corporate memory. With that authorization, I practically had carte blanche to choose people from anywhere in the Air Force, no questions asked.

But Beckwith still had his reservations. I decided that he and Cassidy needed to meet and set it up. Cassidy was a brigadier general who looked young enough to be Charlie's son, and Charlie allowed him only a polite but short discussion. Cassidy, however, made sure that Charlie understood one thing: Military Airlift Command would "lend" Charlie its airplanes for his forays only if Brand X was part of Delta's mission.

I picked Master Sergeant Mitch Bryan as my noncommissioned officer-in-charge, Technical Sergeants John Koren, Pete Holt, David Wilson, and Ron Holder, and Staff Sergeant Bud Gonzalez, relieved that at last Brand X would have some identity. Pete Holt, a Silver Star recipient from Vietnam and the Cambodian incursion, was a natural-born cheerleader who gave his all to everything. He broke a lot of bureaucratic rules to get the job done, like carrying a kit bag full of automatic weapons on a commercial airliner and blazing across the Charleston runway on one occasion to drop me off at the commercial air terminal just in time to catch a flight. (The only other person to get away with that was the vice president of the United States.)

Sadler also agreed to move me closer to Fort Bragg, but he decided Brand X should bed down at Charleston Air Force Base (where he had once commanded its airlift wing), since most of the missions we went on started aboard the C-141s sitting on the alert pad there. Besides, he thought we'd "blend in" better at Charleston because it already had a combat control team assigned to the base's 437th Military Airlift Wing. But that was just a cover for my real work heading Brand X. While we were a lot closer to Fort Bragg than we had been working from McGuire Air Force Base, I wasn't that keen about being co-located with the alert bird instead of with the team we would be supporting most of the time. To gain full confidence in us, Charlie and his staff had to live with us, eat and exercise with us, understand how professional we were, and know what we could bring to the table.

With my nucleus of six combat controllers, things started clicking better. We shared common goals—to be recognized, to show that we mattered. We worked diligently to make sure that if we said we had a capability, it would damn well be there when needed.

The next challenge was to start polishing our shooting skills. We didn't want to be a liability to Delta, the Rangers, or the SEALs. We would train to be very efficient with our weapons, although not to the level of Delta, whose men became renowned for their marksmanship. They should have been. Charlie had them on the firing range—in the shooting house, as he called it—at all hours of the day or night, practicing head shots until putting two bullets between the eyeballs seemed second nature. Charlie used three-inch by five-inch cards (the size of most foreheads) as targets, taping them all over stairwells and unlikely corners of his shooting house, and he had his men "aim" at them by gut feel, shooting from the hip or "snap shooting," as it were. After losing twice in matches against the Secret Service, whose help he enlisted in honing Delta's shooting proficiency, Charlie conceded that perhaps the Secret Service method worked best, at least getting the front sight on the target before pulling the trigger. He let his men try every weapon under the sun and let each man use whichever one suited him best. (Charlie preferred the old Army Colt .45 automatic: It had a big bullet and low velocity, so Charlie could eyeball the bullet all the way to its target.) Others were picked as sharpshooters—"long gunners," Charlie called them—exploding watermelons at up to a thousand meters away, sometimes more, using .50-caliber rifles.

And we were in shape. At this point, soon-to-be Master Sergeant Mike Lampe—the NCO who had run the Key Largo portion of the combat diving course when I was training in combat control—joined the team to replace Mitch Bryan, who had been selected for Officer Training School. Mike had earned a great reputation while assigned to the 1st Special Operations Wing at Hurlburt Field,

Florida, and with Detachment One of the 56th Special Operations Wing to support CIA operations in Laos at the height of the Vietnam War, for which he had been secretly decorated. Earlier, I had tried repeatedly to get MAC to transfer him from the Philippines into Brand X, but without success. He was a taskmaster with a great work ethic. PT was not fun for the troops when the "Bulb," as we nicknamed him, was leading the formation. Road marches, cross-country runs, and calisthenics became a way of life. Mike epitomized the person who can overcome lack of talent through sheer persistence and determination, although he had lots of talent. He always systematically evaluated options in terms of consequences and results. He was often stubborn and a pain in the ass, but I loved him.

We were determined that we would never fall behind on Ranger road marches or cross-country runs. So we started doing a lot of extra physical training on our own. Falling back on my days as a physical education instructor at the Air Force Academy, I introduced periodic aerobics and strength training. We didn't want to embarrass anybody; we wanted to be part of the team, not competitors. We were in shape, we could shoot, and Delta knew we were serious about helping where we could.

Beckwith began to trust us more. His unit, formally known as SFOD-D (for Special Forces Operational Detachment—Delta), was busy developing scenarios for the Emergency Deployment Readiness Exercises. I told him I wanted to provide combat control support for all his airfield operations, and that we should develop our tactics together as we went from one stage of training to the next. Charlie sensed that at some point or another, his men would have to land on a piece of dirt improvised as an airfield. He didn't want the landing gear sinking into the mud and knew that, besides communicating, we could get there undetected, reconnoiter the intended insertion point, and take soil samples to make sure the site was safe. We proved that in a desert exercise called Joshua Junction; it was Charlie's first exercise involving players from outside the Department of Defense, with teams from the FBI and Department of Energy. We jumped from 12,500 feet on a night as dark as it can get, hit our target of an old airstrip, set up communications and beacons in record time, and brought another C-130 to a safe landing in the middle of the night. Unfortunately, Charlie didn't get to see how smoothly we handled that gig. He had been called to San Juan, Puerto Rico, at the FBI's request to check on security preparations for the Pan American Games. I didn't know it until much later, but Charlie grilled Wade Ishimoto, his senior intelligence noncommissioned officer, about how we had handled things. We got a top-notch report card, but no feedback from Charlie.

As he was expanding Delta Force from one squadron to two, however, Charlie put us on his "bigot" list after an exercise at Camp MacKall, North Carolina, with a 727 from the Federal Aviation Administration (FAA). The bigot list was the list of people outside Delta's organization who worked regularly with Delta operators and whom Charlie allowed into its compound (at first, an old World War II barracks at Fort Bragg, and then a six-wing building that had once been Fort Bragg's stockade, located on a remote corner of the base). Unfortunately, the Air Force hierarchy didn't understand that our job was as important as we thought it was or as crucial as it was to become to Delta Force, the Rangers, and SEAL Team Six. For almost two years, Charlie Beckwith had been enjoying lackluster support from the Army, except for its chief of staff and its deputy chief of staff for operations, who had to intercede with Fort Bragg's senior commander to let Beckwith recruit top-notch candidates from special forces. Meanwhile, while Commander Dick Marcinko had the ear of the chief of naval operations about the need for SEAL Team Six, I was begging for two hundred dollars to buy six Casio scuba diving watches. To scrounge up even that amount of money, I had to appeal to a staff officer at wing level. Yet our ass was on the line every time we had to support an Emergency Deployment Readiness Exercise. We were the ones everyone pointed a finger at if something went wrong: no commo, no lights on the airstrip, no aircraft inbound on time. That's why I instilled in my men that we had no room for error. We were easy prey for anyone looking to assign blame for mistakes in timing or whatever.

That's why I felt so relieved, hunkered down in the weeds at Laurinburg-Maxton, North Carolina, after Charlie Beckwith gave up on us just before our beacons flashed on seconds later to prove him wrong. The same C-130 we had jumped from thirty minutes earlier hit the end of a runway on a very short airstrip, right in the middle of our box. Charlie's men scrambled out, took up their positions around an old Convair 990 on one of the parking aprons, and assaulted the damn thing with enough live ammunition and stun grenades going off to have the county sheriff complain about it the next morning. But it was all over in minutes. When Charlie and umpires from the Secret Service checked the dummies inside that 990, every "bad guy" had two holes in his forehead; not one passenger or crew member was hit.

Charlie's concept of an elite counterterrorist strike force, which he had first surfaced in a 1975 concept paper, was validated in a dual-target takedown at Fort Stewart, Georgia, in the early-morning hours of November 4, 1979, after one of the most complex, exhausting, and challenging live-fire tests imaginable. It had succeeded in winning the approval of evaluators not just from the Army's senior ranks but also from the Secret Service, FBI, CIA, FAA, as well as Britain's famous 22nd Special Air Service (SAS) regiment, Germany's GSG-9 counterterrorist unit, and France's equivalent, the GIGN. At about 7:00 A.M. on the Sunday morning the exercise ended, a radio message from the Pentagon alerted everyone that the U.S. embassy in Tehran had been seized during a demonstration by student militants, and that they were holding sixty-seven embassy personnel hostage.

CHAPTER SIX

DASHT-E-KAVIR

The seizure of the American embassy in Tehran triggered an international crisis that would last for more than fourteen months. For the United States, most of the repercussions involved Delta Force, which, within days, was tasked to come up with a plan to rescue the sixty-seven Americans taken hostage. (Three others had escaped and were hiding in the Canadian embassy.) It was precisely the kind of mission, but on a much more daunting scale, that Charlie Beckwith had long anticipated. He and Army Chief of Staff General Bernard W. Rogers and his deputy chief of staff for operations, Lieutenant General E. C. "Shy" Meyer, had long argued with the nation's military bureaucracy that America needed its own counterpart to Britain's counterterrorist strike force, the 22nd SAS, or Germany's GSG-9.

The Army chief of staff is only a chief of staff, not a dictator or an emperor, as Meyer would be reminded when he succeeded Bernie Rogers in 1979, promoted by President Jimmy Carter over more than forty-five general officers wearing three or four stars who were senior to him. Special operations was still anathema to many conventional officers. They shared little of Meyer's enthusiasm for standing up Delta Force or Task Force 160, the secret aviation unit he later formed to make sure there would never be a repeat of what became the Desert One tragedy and that Delta Force could get to the next war on time. As Meyer would recall the squabbling within his senior ranks about such units, long after he had retired in 1983, he said of his four-star generals, with whom he would meet annually at the Army commanders' conference (speaking here of their debates over which two-star generals should be promoted), "You would hear one guy who thought the candidate walked on water and another guy [who] thought he walked with nine inches of salt water over his nose."[1]

Asking Delta Force to come up with a rescue plan less than a week after its validation exercise was asking for a near miracle. The obstacles were formidable. Tehran was 11,600 miles from Fort Bragg. The American embassy stood in the very center of a city of more than six million people, and virtually all of them were hostile to the United States. Those two factors alone would make any rescue attempt extremely difficult.

In the ten months since the shah had fled and the Ayatollah Ruhollah Khomeini had returned from exile in France, the city had turned into a cauldron of unrest. Khomeini's supporters quickly overthrew the shah's recently established military government, and clashes erupted between religious factions; between religious parties and secular leftists; between the urban middle class and the disenfranchised poor.

Thousands were arrested and executed by Khomeini's religious militia forces. Khomeini's rule was proving more incompetent than the shah's, and he needed a scapegoat. He blamed all of Iran's troubles on the United States of America. Militant students had seized the American embassy for two days soon after Khomeini seized power in February 1979, but that crisis abated quickly. After November 4, however, nothing could mollify them, and it quickly became evident that the Iranian government could not control them. Khomeini's vitriolic rhetoric and religious fanaticism had incited mob rule. That would make a rescue attempt doubly difficult; Delta would be operating against a totally unpredictable, irrational adversary instead of the semi-permissive environment it had assumed for most of its rescue scenarios.

While Charlie Beckwith huddled with Delta's planners and whipped back and forth to Washington to brief the brass or get his latest instructions, Delta's training tempo increased brutally. Concurrently, Delta was trying to build up a second and third squadron and holding back-to-back source selection field exercises to find volunteers who could pass Beckwith's muster. In the first five groups, totaling 264 carefully screened volunteers—all seasoned soldiers and most of them combat veterans from Vietnam—only 73 men were chosen for the nineteen-week "Operators Course."[2] Others dropped out in the training it then took to become accepted as a Delta Force trooper.

It was obvious that a rescue was being planned, but the plan was so closely held for two months that no one knew what it was. In Washington, a special planning cell headed by Army Major General James B. "Hammer" Vaught had been set up in the Pentagon's Eighth Corridor near the River entrance and the office of the chairman, Joint Chiefs of Staff. Vaught, a tall, lean, scraggly, quiet, gravelly voiced but soft-spoken infantryman, was earnest and deliberate in conversation. He had no truck with bullshit, but appreciated everyone's views and invited everyone's opinion. Resourceful and well fitted to his job, he was a strong-willed patriot who showed little patience with naysayers. Vaught had spent a year in South America in the late 1960s tracking down the guerrilla terrorist Ernesto "Che" Guevara. Guevara was trying to foment a communist insurgency in Bolivia at the behest of Cuba. Vaught won't discuss it, but apparently he succeeded after a new Bolivian Ranger battalion that his special forces mobile training team, headed by Army Major Ralph W. "Pappy" Shelton, had equipped and trained, a band of six hundred Quechua Indian recruits who caught up with Guevara and his insurgents on October 8, 1967.[3] Vaught probably understood Delta's capabilities better than anyone in uniform: He had been one of the Army's senior evaluators during the unit's operational validation tests.

Before Vaught took over the Iranian rescue task force, Pentagon planners had come up with one cockamamy rescue scheme after another. Early on, they suggested that Delta Force parachute into the embassy compound. Beckwith called it a senseless suicide attempt. Delta Force would need some way to fly the freed hostages out of downtown Tehran, so why parachute them in to begin with? When the Joint Chiefs of Staff nevertheless expressed interest in pursuing the idea of a parachute assault, General Meyer uncharacteristically stormed out of the "tank," the room where the chiefs normally met, in a seething rage, telling the chiefs they were not going to send his soldiers to their deaths in that desperate a gamble. It took the JCS chairman, Air Force General David C. Jones, about fifteen minutes to talk Meyer into rejoining the meeting.

The solution seemed obvious; the planes extracting the hostages and Delta Force had to be the same ones used for Delta's clandestine or forced entry, the best spot for which seemed to be the Amjadieh soccer stadium immediately northeast of and across the street from the American embassy compound. It was only two blocks away from an Iranian military garrison immediately northeast of and across another street from the compound. But no transport plane existed that could take off and land vertically inside the stadium. There was only about 140 meters of flat ground inside it, one-third of the distance that a partially loaded C-130 would need to lift off. The only plan that seemed to make sense was to land Delta Force inside the stadium using large Navy RH-53D "Sea Stallion" minesweeping helicopters, which could then extract them and the hostages to an airfield outside Tehran and transfer everyone to larger, fixed-wing transports. But that meant a clandestine, intermediate refueling site or staging area would have to be found in Iran, since the helicopters couldn't make the nine-hundred-mile flight from an aircraft carrier in the Indian Ocean all the way to Tehran.

I was not privy to any of these proposals at the time. Early in December, Lieutenant Colonel John Gradowski, a thin, six-foot-tall, cigar-smoking helicopter pilot working at MAC headquarters in its XOZ office, a classified plans cell, told me to report to Washington.

I was to brief some people on our capabilities and on the different kind of beacons we had in our inventory. That was the first time I learned that a rescue attempt was in fact being put together.

Given how well my team had worked with Delta and the Rangers, I felt confident that we would be part of any such effort. That soon proved to be the case. I was next invited to a meeting at Fort Bragg in Delta's compound. There, all the leaders of forces that might be involved were brainstorming how to put a force into Iran. General Vaught was present, as were Jim Rhyne, a CIA pilot who had lost a leg flying in Laos for Air America, and Bud McBroom, another pilot from the CIA who had been a special forces communications noncommissioned officer and medic, and later, as a lieutenant, a member of special forces' famous "Mike Force" with Bucky Burruss. Their job was to hop, skip, and jump all over the country wherever a special forces camp or patrol found itself in deep kimchi and needed more muscle fast. Bud was humorous and good natured, but a pit bull when confronted. Colonel Tom Wicker, the director of operations for the 1st Special Operations Wing at Hurlburt Field, Colonel "Robbie" Roberts, the wing commander, and Lieutenant Colonel Sherm Williford, who commanded the 1st Battalion of the 75th Rangers, were also present.

We decided quickly that we had to find a place in Iran where we could stage our people, Delta and the Rangers; somewhere we could land undetected and position ourselves to mount a rescue if things started turning hostile—if, for instance, the Iranians started killing hostages.

During the meeting, I learned what pitifully little intelligence we had about our target. It seemed that we knew almost nothing about Iran, less about Tehran, and close to zero about the situation at the embassy. The Central Intelligence Agency, it turned out, had no agents left in Iran and no operatives. Its few men on the embassy staff had been taken hostage and were being held incommunicado. To make up for its lack of information, the agency had been flooding Delta's small intelligence staff with every scrap of raw data it came across. Most of it was irrelevant garbage and none of it was germane to the challenge before us. The more often Delta's small, overtaxed intelligence cell protested about the avalanche of unsifted "intelligence," the faster more of it arrived. Fortunately, Captain Wade Ishimoto, Beckwith's deputy intelligence chief, was able to get much better information from friends in the Agency through "back channels."

Eventually, the discussion focused on whether or not the "National Command Authority"—the president, the secretary of defense, and the chairman of the Joint Chiefs of Staff—was really serious about mounting a rescue. Talk turned to the need for some on-the-scene reconnaissance, "a set of American eyeballs," as Charlie Beckwith put it. I surmised that General Vaught wanted to get permission for just such a mission from the Joint Chiefs and the president as his way of testing whether or not they were really serious about a rescue attempt.

I soon found myself back in the Pentagon, where I was introduced to Vaught's planning staff. It was called the JCS Special Operations Division, located in a warren of specially secured vaults in the Pentagon basement. Almost everyone wore civilian clothes, but I found an unusually large number of Navy planners there— "Navy blue hiding in cheap thirty-five-dollar sports coats," one of my men would later joke of them. There were times when JCS Chairman General Davey Jones would review our plans right alongside us. I arranged special clearances for some of my men to join the planning cell and see the satellite imagery of various targets. Most of the early plans focused on seizing a hard-surface airstrip and killing the Iranian cadre force located there. That option involved a lot of bloodshed early in the mission, so we scanned overhead imagery for other possible and more isolated landing sites. One continued to stand out, on a huge plateau in the desert well south of the city of Tabas. Except for its altitude, five hundred to a thousand meters above sea level, the desert there looked like Death Valley.

It was now early March, and the hostages had been held captive for four months. I soon spent most of my time working with Central Intelligence Agency technicians trying to develop infrared landing beacons that could be remotely activated from a cockpit and worked with the CIA's pilots as well as some from the Air Force about what tactics we might use going into the desert. At that time, the only lights or beacons we had were so-called ELCO lights, named after the company that made them. They were bulky and cumbersome, they required a big battery inside, and they weren't very intense. We really wanted to devise some infrared lights that couldn't be seen by the naked eye and finally came up with some light-emitting diodes that weren't *very* visible to the eye and required night-vision goggles to detect them. Best of all, they could be activated remotely from a cockpit.

We had a prototype produced, flew against it, and found it successful. Next we started serious work with aircrews about how things might go down in the desert, what kind of landing zones had to be marked, and what kind of trafficability we needed for various loads aboard C-130s or C-5 jet transports. At that point, few in the Agency thought the mission would go. One member bet me the biggest steak dinner in Washington there would never be a rescue attempt.

Still, it caught me by surprise in early April when, trying to satisfy the skepticism of the wing commander and director of operations of the 1st Special Operations Wing about the Dasht-e-Kavir landing site, Charlie said, "We need to put our eyeballs on the target to check it out." He didn't want the Agency checking it out; he wanted someone who would actually have to land there. "You won't have any problem there if we send Carney in first." That put Wicker and Roberts on the spot, and they consented to using the site for planning purposes. I thought to myself, "Thanks, Charlie!"

It happened just like that. It was the first time in my thirteen-year Air Force career I had seen a big decision made that fast. That's how I became a "volunteer," as people would later describe my mission. Some volunteer! After all the "puffing" I had done previously to win Charlie's confidence that we could help him, Charlie knew I wouldn't say no.

All Charlie said to me after the meeting was "Get your bags

packed, boy." I loved the man's directness. He didn't give a rat's ass what I thought. To him, that was my job. His attitude was "Let's do it and see who the hell is serious about bringing the hostages home." Charlie wanted to get things moving. That's why they called him "Chargin' Charlie." Besides, he knew how much I wanted my team to be involved in the rescue. He had watched us perform and knew we were capable and willing to do whatever was needed to help Delta Force succeed. Charlie knew that I would go without hesitation. I told Colonel Bill Kornitzer, director of operations for the 437th Military Airlift Wing to which I was nominally attached, and my six guys that I was going to Washington on temporary duty for an extended period. I trusted those six men with my life, but it didn't bother me to lie to them; they knew what was going on, but never asked questions. All General Cassidy, the assistant deputy for operations at MAC headquarters, told the wing commander at Charleston was that I was to be supported with whatever I needed and that I was not to be asked about my activities. Even General Sadler, still my real boss, was kept out of the loop.

It was winter at Fort Bragg, North Carolina, and bloody cold. That time of year, the deserts of central Iran are hotter than hell. And hell is where Charlie sent me. Dasht-e-Kavir is one ugly place. Much as I might have looked forward to some warm weather, the prospect of visiting Iran was not enticing. I had three misgivings about the trip.

For one thing, everyone in the country seemed bent on killing "Yankee imperialists," and if you were an American, you were automatically a Yankee imperialist. There seemed to be a lot of extremists in the country, too. Students spent more time demonstrating around the embassy than they did in classrooms and enjoyed flagellating themselves in front of television cameras. Second, Iran is 11,800 miles and eleven time zones away from the East Coast of the United States, which would mean about twenty hours in the air each way. It was decided that I would fly from Dulles airport outside Washington to Athens, Greece, by commercial air on TWA—coach class, of course. This was government travel, after all, and that's how military people flying undercover for the CIA got to fly halfway around the world just before undertaking dangerous missions. TWA, however, was not my favorite airline since its planes kept getting seized by terrorists. (Even American ambassadors have to fly coach, I found out later, except for their inaugural trips to a new station and their farewell journeys home.) Third, the nine-hour coach flight to Athens would be the luxurious part of the trip. I would clear customs there and rendezvous with the two CIA pilots I had met at Fort Bragg, fly to Rome with them in a Twin Otter that had a large fuel bladder inside, refuel there, and fly on to Cairo to refuel again and get some overnight rest. We would fly to the British island of Masirah, off Oman, the next morning. The flights in the Twin Otter would prove the equivalent of a long trip in the back of a cement mixer.

Those were just a few of the reasons I thanked Charlie under my breath for sending me on this busman's holiday. From Oman, it would be another 550 miles to the center of the world's fifth-largest desert, the barren salt flat called Dasht-e-Kavir that Charlie and General Vaught had picked as the point where our MC-130 Combat Talons would rendezvous with the Navy helicopters. We called the site Desert One. There the helicopters would refuel from Air Force MC-130s and EC-130s, the latter being basically an airborne combat and control aircraft with an eight-thousand-gallon fuel bladder in its cargo compartment. The helicopters would then carry ninety-two men from Delta Force 275 miles onward to hills southeast of the city. There, retired Major Dick Meadows would be waiting at a hide site where Delta Force could regroup. Meadows was one of the first three officers Beckwith had picked for Delta Force. A seasoned special forces member and behind-the-lines operator, he had earned a rare battlefield commission in Vietnam; volunteered for Bull Simons's 1970 prisoner-of-war rescue mission into North Vietnam; and purposely crash-landed in an HH-3 helicopter into the cramped courtyard of the Son Tay prison so Simons's men could free the prisoners before the North Vietnamese might shoot them. Dick was now a government civilian in the grade of GS-13 (with a protocol rank somewhere between a major and a lieutenant colonel), and he was attached to Delta Force.

At the hide site, Delta Force would get some overnight rest and prepare to load aboard the trucks Meadows had obtained from a CIA operative for the trip to the embassy compound and, hopefully, from there to the Amjadieh soccer stadium with the freed hostages. There, the RH-53s would be waiting to start them on the long journey back home, rendezvousing with C-141 medical evacuation planes waiting at an airfield called Manzariyah, a large airstrip with high-speed taxiways but no infrastructure. It was barely more than large slabs of lots of concrete situated thirty-five miles southeast of Tehran. That field was to be secured by a company of Rangers. While Delta Force headed for the hide site and were taking down the embassy, my men and I would fly from Desert One to land at (or jump onto, if necessary) Manzariyah, set up the airfield for the Rangers to land there, await Delta's arrival with the freed hostages, and make sure everyone got out safely.

Smack in the middle of north-central Iran, Dasht-e-Kavir covered 18,000 square miles of the earth's most forlorn terrain, a featureless high plateau 250 miles southeast of Tehran that ran 240 miles east to west and up to 125 miles north to south. South of it lay another vast desert, Dasht-e-Lut, most of which we'd have to traverse, too. This last leg of my trip, however, would not even be in coach class; I'd be cramped with a motorcycle into the back of the noisy, twin-engine DeHavilland turboprop, and not even sitting down. Instead, my motorcycle and I would be lying atop the CIA's version of a water bed, a rubber bladder filled with the extra fuel the plane would need to make the nearly eleven-hundred-mile round-trip. The fuel was JP-4 aviation gas, which smells like kerosene. Rubber and kerosene generate a distinctive smell that becomes nauseating after about five minutes. We'd be in the plane for close to four hours each way while the smell would sting our nostrils and the fumes would burn our throats. We wouldn't have oxygen to relieve our noses because we'd be flying too low to need it, clearing the ground contours "nap of the earth," two hundred feet or less above the terrain, to avoid radar detection. And we couldn't carry oxygen because we needed to save weight for the gear we were lugging— five remotely activated strobe lights with long-life batteries to mark a makeshift airfield in the sand plus the paraphernalia I needed to calibrate the California Bearing Ratio, a measure of how much weight or force a surface can withstand without collapsing or rutting. That involved a penetrometer, which measured the density of the soil. I had also lugged along what looked like a thin posthole digger, about two and a half inches in diameter with a big screw on one end, with a handle that broke down into foot-long sections much like a lot of fishing rods. With it, I would take soil samples so a geologist with special security clearances could later independently test them to make sure the desert floor could handle the weight of our heavily laden C-130s. To do all this in the short hour allotted, I had a motorized dirt bike cuddled up beside me on the CIA's water bed.

I'd get to do all this in a week. More than two days of the week—forty to fifty hours, I figured—would be spent riding airplanes, the last thing on earth I needed more of. For this, I was getting paid about $40,000 a year, not including my jump pay or hazardous duty pay, which added $110 a month. I called the whole trip "my week to hell and back," although it turned out to be rather uneventful, a piece of cake compared to the things we normally did. Uneventful, except for the things I screwed up in the desert and details the Agency screwed up getting me home.

I was armed with a nine-millimeter Heckler & Koch automatic that had a silencer, more to bolster my confidence, I thought, than to ward off capture if we were discovered. In that case, we'd claim we were geologists who'd gotten lost trying to find an oil survey team. I was dressed in black jeans, a black sweater, and a black watch cap, having taken it as a matter of faith that the CIA knew what geologists wore in the field. I spent the long flight listening to CIA transmissions from Europe in Morse code on a high-frequency radio. The reconnaissance at Desert One during the night of March 31 and April 1 came off pretty much as we had planned it.

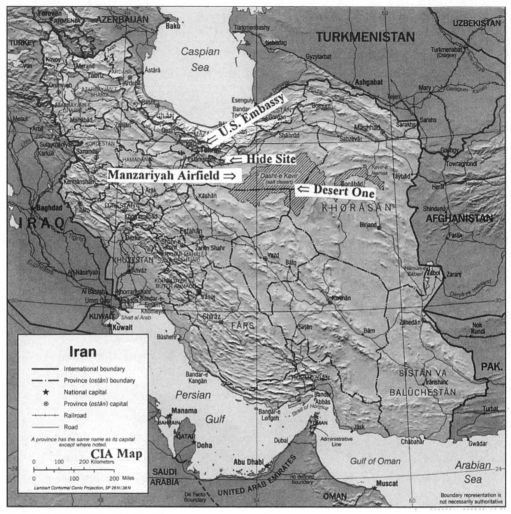

CENTRAL INTELLIGENCE AGENCY

The glitches were small ones. For one thing, we landed on the wrong side of a road through the area. The road went from the holy city of Qom, seventy-five miles south of Tehran, to Meshed, near the Afghanistan border in northeastern Iran. We were supposed to land to the south of the road, but landed north of it by mistake. Worse, we had agreed to land near where the road was straight, but the pilot decided it would be better to land near the point where the road made a sharp bend. As a result, I spent a lot of time trying to get oriented and find the spot on the road that was supposed to be my starting point for pacing off a landing strip. We had planned to be in the area for only about an hour, but I lost most of that time because I couldn't get my bearings. I walked back to the aircraft and asked the pilot to help me out. Jim Rhyne was a large man, about six feet two inches tall and 230 pounds with a round, Irish-looking face. He was a take-charge guy who expressed his views strongly. Jim told me nonchalantly, "Oh, yeah. I landed north of the road, not south of it." He said it so casually you'd have thought he was a bartender who had poured a Miller Light because he was out of Bud Light. To me, it was like landing upside down: It left me totally disoriented. As a result, the starting point I had picked for my survey was ninety degrees off, and I had wasted forty-five minutes laying out the wrong T-box.

The moment we had landed, I started laying out a landing zone, using my K-bar knife to dig holes deep enough so the top of each beacon, the "beehive" with the bulb and the lens, would barely poke above the desert surface. With no time to reset all the beacon lights, I raced hundreds of yards on my motorcycle to move the beacon that would signal the end of the improvised "runway" so it would line up with a diamond-shaped box instead of the standard square one. Other things had eaten into what little time we had. As soon as I got out of the airplane, for instance, some vehicle lights had appeared on the road to the north of us and swung directly at us when the vehicles came around a bend in the road. That caused some consternation about whether or not we had been compromised, so we moved the aircraft farther into the desert so the

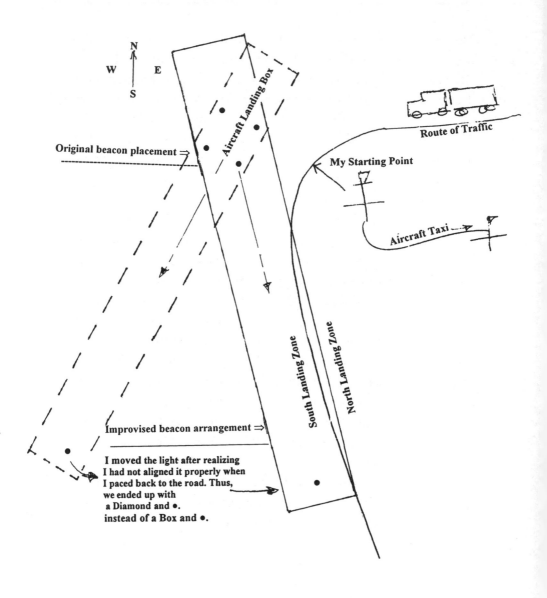

How my T-box ended up as a diamond at Desert One because the CIA landed on the wrong side of the road near the bend instead of far away from it on the straightaway.

headlights wouldn't hit the aircraft skin while they were passing by. Every once in a while a vehicle would slow down, and I worried that the aircraft would leave me fending for myself. We had to finish the job in time to get out of Iran before dawn, and we were way behind schedule.

Bud McBroom, the unflappable copilot, came out to help me align the new light setup. I couldn't turn them on, so I had to be able to look down the imaginary runway to see someone standing where the light was. Bud was like the guy holding a stadia rod on a road survey team. Bud was a character, full of wit and courage, a wonderful human being. He kept trying to introduce some levity into the situation, singing, "Pardon me, Roy, is that the cat that ate your new shoes?" Every time a car came around the bend, the two of us would hit the desert floor and lie as flat as we could, pretty close together. The second time we did this, Bud started his song again. It happened over and over. The man was a stitch; he really knew how to break the tension, and he had more balls than a pinball machine. He personified the statement "Dynamite comes in small packages." (I learned later that he was usually upset with the Agency; he thought it was cheap and too controlling. But he retired with the Agency's highest award, the Intelligence Star, and then apparently was re-called for other missions abroad.)

The minute we had the beacons implanted, we ran for the aircraft, took off, and headed out of Iran. We got out of the country uneventfully, but a telex message awaited me in Oman saying I was to get back to the States as quickly as possible. The Agency had tickets ready for me to fly to Cairo, Rome, Greece, and then to London, where I would finally head home. I have to hand it to the Agency; it had things pretty well greased. My bags were full of soil samples in cylinders that looked like pipe bombs, plus about five thousand dollars in old, small, South African gold Krugerrands, my backup "passport," if you will. (In today's dollars, that would be worth about ten thousand dollars.) But I went through one airport after another with no problems. No one asked any questions or searched my bags.

Things changed in London. At Heathrow Airport, I would be more or less on my own before catching a TWA plane to Dulles International Airport outside Washington. En route to my flight, however, I was intercepted by two Agency people who walked up to me and called me out by my real name, not the alias I had been using. That alarmed me a bit until I remembered I was in London, so it couldn't be that big a deal. They had been sent to find me and get me back to the States pronto. Instead of heading for my TWA flight, they took away that ticket and said I'd be flying home on the Concorde. They started hustling me to British Airways' Concorde lounge. By now I had been up for forty-eight hours straight, I hadn't had a bath in three days, and I was very tired. I didn't know what the Concorde was; it didn't register with me, and apparently I resisted their hospitality a bit, so they had to get a little forceful.

My presence in the Concorde lounge offered quite a contrast to the Concorde's normal passengers. I was in dirty Levi's, smelling somewhat ripe, surrounded by petits fours and champagne and being waited on by a butler while people were looking askance at me. It was a bit embarrassing. I couldn't help but think about how slickly the Agency had handled my travels to London but how ineptly it had fallen short once I got there. Just a quick change of clothes in a lavatory would have helped a lot, but herding me into a first-class lounge didn't seem very smart. I stood out like a diamond on a goat's ass. I think the only reason British Airways didn't throw me out was that I looked like I was part of a rock band. I was glad when we boarded the plane, a slender tube of supersonic luxury with soft, deep leather seats—much more like *my* idea of a water bed. Three hours and forty-five minutes later we landed in Washington, and within an hour I was in Vaught's office.

Vaught started right off asking me about all the truck traffic at the landing site. Apparently word had reached Washington about all the vehicles that had passed by, and some factions in the chain of command were insisting that we scrub any plans to operate at Dasht-e-Kavir. Since I hadn't talked to anyone about our desert foray, the reports about truck traffic had obviously come from the

Agency, end-running or preempting Vaught and the Joint Chiefs of Staff. Given the kind of stonewalling we had encountered before, it didn't surprise me that CIA's brass would go out of its way to scoop us, to finally give someone some useful intelligence and do so as if *it* had come up with pay dirt.

After my meeting with Vaught, I sat down with the Combat Talon crew from the 8th Special Operations Squadron that would lead Delta Force to Dasht-e-Kavir. Lieutenant Colonel Bob Brenci, the squadron commander, would be the lead pilot, Major George Ferkes his copilot. I told them that after being interrupted by so much truck traffic, I had decided to change the landing box to a diamond, afraid that if someone stumbled across the beacons, they might recognize the box pattern for what it was—the touchdown point for a clandestine landing. Brenci thought that was a great idea—"Good thinking, John." Actually, my "good thinking" was the result of the screwup I had made in heading off ninety degrees from the bend in the road instead of from the straight stretch where we were supposed to land.

Delta Force consisted of two understrength squadrons, only about eighty shooters at the time.[4] (Another squadron was in training but wouldn't be ready for four to six weeks.) As Delta's troopers trained for the real thing, more and more people got added to the rescue force. Air Force Colonel Jim Kyle had been named the on-site commander for Desert One and became my nominal boss; and he told me that because so many people—nineteen in all—had been added to the operation, we would need two landing strips, not just one. That made things pretty exciting, but I had walked or ridden over the whole area and assured him that it would be no sweat: Once we landed, we could establish a second strip north of the road that would mirror the one I had marked out to the south of the road. Each of my combat controllers would be lugging sixty to seventy-five pounds of radios plus our GAU-5 rifles, 9-millimeter automatic pistols, and a good load of ammunition. To make sure we could set up the second runway expeditiously, so the second plane formation wouldn't have to circle around, I decided we'd all use motorcycles. The first C-130 would begin lowering its rear loading ramp as it approached touchdown,[5] and as soon as the plane stopped, my team would speed down the ramp on our bikes and establish the second strip within seconds. Charlie Beckwith liked the idea so much he added some other motorcycles to speed a few of his men out to set up perimeter security and establish a roadblock at the bend in the road.

As the clock brought the Iranian mission closer and closer, Delta Force was rehearsing its embassy takedown—ninety-two times—at sites all over the country. Having proved ourselves to Beckwith's troops, we were almost left out of the rescue mission early on because the Rangers decided they didn't need us for their airfield seizure at Manzariyah. Instead, they wanted to use their own radio operators. Lieutenant Colonel Sherm Williford, commanding the 1st Ranger Battalion, and Captain David Grange, the company commander in charge of the seizure, had us removed at the last minute from a rehearsal at Indian Springs, Nevada, in January 1980. Their radio operators had no UHF equipment to direct the AC-130 gunships that might have to be called in, but tried to rely on their FM radios relaying messages through the MC-130 Combat Talons.

The rehearsal became a goat rope, a fiasco witnessed by Air Force Lieutenant General Richard Gast, who had been assigned as an adviser to General Vaught because of his prior service heading the U.S. military assistance mission in Iran. Gast scrubbed the remainder of the exercise for safety reasons and summoned everyone to a meeting at the Delta Force compound in Fort Bragg's former stockade. There, he made it clear that "airmanship will be handled by *airmen*," and we were reinstated as part of the rescue force. This meant that, true to the two-night scenario called for, we flew eight hours from Fort Bragg to Indian Springs, rehearsed the Desert One landing in the dead of night, flew home eight hours, and then flew back to Indian Springs the next day for the airfield seizure rehearsal, and home again. But at least we had won our missions back.

It was a struggle that would recur time and again over the next twelve years—even in Afghanistan in 2001 when the colonel in charge of a major Special Forces operational detachment said he had no need for special tactics members to be attached to his teams and that his men could direct their own close air support; but he later *directed* that special tactics teams be deployed with him. It undoubtedly will happen again until the commander in chief of U.S. Special Operations Command stipulates that air traffic control and close air support are primary functions of special tactics, not secondary roles for men with other urgent missions.

Meanwhile, the powers that be in Washington continued to vacillate over whether or not to even mount the rescue attempt. At the top of the food chain, Secretary of State Cyrus Vance resigned in protest over the issue, although he withheld his resignation until after the operation.[6] The national security adviser, Zbigniew Brzezinski, was hesitant and inclined to side with the State Department. Stansfield Turner, the CIA director, was too busy refocusing the Agency to provide more strategic intelligence from platforms in space and at sea rather than from human beings. The kind of intelligence Delta Force needed had to come from human sources—human intelligence, or HUMINT, as it's known—but Turner had decimated the Agency's HUMINT ranks, and there was almost no human intelligence coming out of Iran.

CHAPTER SEVEN

DESERT ONE—OPERATION "EAGLE CLAW"

E verything that could go wrong, did. Eight men died when we had to abort the mission because the richest nation on earth ended up short one helicopter. Tragically, nothing had been learned from the 1970 Son Tay rescue mission, when similar helicopters were led by MC-130s almost equivalent distances into the heart of North Vietnam. Contrary to many reports, President Jimmy Carter did not micromanage or interfere with the Iranian operation; the military hierarchy bungled it.

There is little about the mission that hasn't already been widely reported, especially in the so-called Holloway Commission report[1] and a book, *The Guts to Try*, by retired Air Force Colonel James Kyle, who had been the site commander at Desert One. Five aspects of the mission, however, bear more scrutiny: intelligence sharing; the unescorted helicopter missions; an unexpected thick layer of sand and dust on the landing site; loss of unity of command; and the failure to stage a full dress rehearsal.

Eighteen years after the rescue attempt, some of us learned that the CIA had received a covert communication that detailed some of the most important information we needed—the exact location of three hostages being held in the Iranian Ministry of Foreign Affairs.[2,3] The CIA claimed that it had stumbled, only by providence, on similarly detailed information on almost all the other hostages who were being held in the American embassy compound when a Pakistani cook named Luigi, who was really Italian, and his wife, who had been working in the embassy, happened to be on the last leg of a flight from Tehran to Frankfurt and found himself seated next to a CIA officer. The story about Luigi has been viewed with some skepticism over the years. White House press files located in the Carter Library in Atlanta show that an Italian cook was released from the embassy on or about November 16, 1979.[4] The CIA apparently fabricated the Pakistani cook story in order to protect its source inside the embassy and gave up its information only after it was absolutely certain that the rescue mission would be launched.

The only other "human intelligence" out of Iran came in snippets that added up to the belief that all but three of the hostages had been moved back into the main embassy compound. In addition, representatives of the International Red Cross were able to visit the embassy compound and see most, but not all, of the hostages on April 14.[5] Brief clips of the visit that were broadcast on Iranian TV the next day suggested that most of the hostages were being detained on different floors in the Chancery building, one of seventeen buildings inside the compound.

Still, that was good news for Delta Force, because four foreign nationals had been allowed to visit the embassy compound back in mid-November and seen most of the hostages. They reported that the hostages were spread about in six different buildings, none of which was the Chancery, where most of them had been seized. A few days later, the Iranians had released three women hostages and then ten black males, most of them Marine guards, who confirmed suppositions about the initial hostage detention sites. Much of our last-minute information came from our own people, special forces men who sneaked into the country with Dick Meadows to set up the hide site for our helicopters and to reconnoiter the outside of the embassy without tipping off that a rescue would soon be under way.

Sheer luck blessed us with an update on the hostages' location just before we left Wadi Kena for Oman. The stepmother of the youngest Marine hostage, Kevin Hermitage, had traveled to Tehran as a private citizen, against the advice of the State Department; she managed to gain access to the compound and visit with her son on April 22. At the conclusion of her visit, she made a short, televised announcement expressing her gratitude for being allowed to visit. The announcement was shown on TV around the world. The site of her visit was the Chancery building.[6]

The Joint Chiefs of Staff backed the rescue attempt, but were too busy squabbling over which service would play what role to oversee detailed planning for the operation. As a result, while there were seven so-called rehearsals, each involved only a few components of a rescue force that had been cobbled together from four services and at least six different units. Few of us got to do all the rehearsals. I got to go through only two of them. Brand X had six men assigned at the time, all of whom (except me) made most of the rehearsals; but we had to add a lot of men at the last minute, and they got involved in only one rehearsal. There never was anything remotely close to a *full* dress rehearsal.

In mid-April, General Vaught informed the commanders that we were going to deploy to Germany and therefore needed to get our troops ready to move from Fort Bragg to Charleston Air Force Base. From that point on, everyone was scrambling to get their people back to home plate and pack up for the mission. We had arranged for Mike Lampe to be transferred permanently into the unit from the Philippines, instead of reporting to the 7th Special Operations Squadron in Germany. He came aboard on November 1, just three days before the embassy was seized. In April, he was with Mitch Bryan in Yuma, Arizona, on one of the compartmented exercises when a helicopter picked them up and took them to Yuma Air Station. From Bragg, we drove to Charleston, climbed aboard a C-141, and left for Rhein-Main Air Force Base near Frankfurt. We refueled there and left for Wadi Kena, Egypt, where an annual JCS exercise was under way, thus making our presence less noticeable.

We stayed there several days, practicing motorcycle operations prior to flying on MC-130s to the island of Masirah, off the coast of Oman. At that point, I couldn't believe there were still skeptics, thinking and stating aloud that the mission wouldn't go. In fact, Charlie Beckwith got upset with one strap-hanging colonel, as he called him, who stated flatly that the mission would likely be canceled. Charlie asked to have the "nervous Nellie" amputated—removed from his area. That evening, April 23, we were given the go-ahead.

Amid all this consternation, the one person who had stood fast and was the biggest supporter of a rescue effort was President Jimmy Carter. Like most other members of the rescue force, I was absolutely confident—110 percent sure—that we could rescue the hostages. In retrospect, our odds weren't that good; knowing what I do today, I'd have given us a 50-50 chance of succeeding, losing maybe seven of our own men but with none of the hostages harmed. Some of the men were less sanguine and thought we might lose five to ten hostages. However, I am convinced to this day that America could not have asked for any better-trained or more dedicated, committed individuals to bring the fifty-three hostages home. I am not easily impressed, but I must admit that I was highly encouraged by the determined and confident looks on the faces of Delta's men.

Brand X had a great team of seven guys ready for the rescue. Mitch Bryan would accompany me at the control point with Air Force Colonel Jim Kyle, who was in charge of the Desert One site. Mitch's job was to handle the air traffic control and ground control, should it be necessary, since the operation was handled under radio silence. John Koren, Mike Lampe, and Bud Gonzalez were in charge of setting up the second landing strip north of the road by rigging the landing strip in another Box-in-One pattern along with lights in an inverted Y for the helicopters, with the throat of the Y being their touchdown point. Staff Sergeant Dick West set up our portable TACAN (Tactical Air Control and Navigation) system. Airman First Class Rex Wollmann from the 1st Special Operations Wing handled the TEMIG beacons (tactical electromagnetic impulse generators) for the gunships to read azimuths to their targets. I was at the control point by the TACAN with a radar transponder for a reference point, a ten-pound SST-181 X-band radar beacon, and a handheld FM radio for intrateam control. Our radios, however, were all hand-me-downs from Delta Force, not the best models, and communications on the desert would prove sporadic and garbled.

We were each lugging forty-five to sixty pounds of radio gear or beacons plus our weapons, ammo, and rucksacks—but we almost never made it to Desert One. At the last minute, Major Jesse Johnson, Beckwith's operations officer, tried to have us taken off Charlie's plane, the lead Combat Talon, to make room for more Delta Force shooters. A heated discussion erupted. Even at that critical juncture, we had to fight to get onto the playing field; Johnson lost the argument.

We set down at 10:15 P.M. local time after aborting an earlier attempt because we spotted a truck barreling down the road past our landing site. Just as we were touching down on the second pass, we saw a bus almost directly below our wing. At least we had planned for such a contingency. Wade Ishimoto would race off the rear ramp on a dirt bike to create a roadblock on the road, with Johnson setting up a second one. At the same time, my men would charge off on their bikes to set up the second landing strip north of the road.

The last C-130 was due to land about an hour and forty-five minutes later and the helicopters twenty minutes after that. Refueling the helicopters and reboarding Delta Force was supposed to take about forty minutes, after which the rescue force would head for its hide site near Tehran.

It is impossible to describe the harsh, nerve-racking conditions we endured at Desert One as we waited hours for the helicopters to arrive. It had been decided that the MC- and EC-130s would keep their engines running for fear that some engines might not restart. Even with their flaps extended to deflect heat and sandblast for those off-loading ammunition, takedown gear, and camouflage nets from the planes' aft ramps, our "Welcome to Desert One" was a painful experience. The high-pitched, earsplitting whine of those twenty-four engines, even at idle power, was eerie amid an otherwise silent desert. This would eventually grow to eight C-130s on the ground with thirty-two engines screaming and blowing sand and dust.

At the time I had surveyed the landing site, it was hard-packed sand, like a pool table. By the time we landed there three weeks later, Desert One was covered in ankle-deep, soft sand from dust storms that had passed through the area in the interim. Movement was difficult, exhausting, and even painful. The MC- and EC-130s could barely taxi, and we immediately fell behind schedule because Delta Force and the Rangers had to struggle to unload everything that would have to be wrestled back into the helicopters expected to arrive soon. Given their lousy intrateam radios, J.K. Koren, Mike Lampe, Bud Gonzalez, and Dick West lost communications from the second landing site with the control point that Kyle and I had set up south of the road with Mitch Bryan. The noise, moreover, was deafening. Visibility was measured in tens of yards; at times it was zero.

Delta's troopers were still trying to unload all of their gear and ammunition from the first MC-130 on the north landing site when Mike Lampe realized that the second plane due there was about to land. Unable to reach me or Kyle by radio to find out if the landing sequence had been changed, he trudged through the sand to the nose of the Combat Talon and signaled its pilot with his chem-light marshaling wands to "Move, *now!*"—instantly!—off the landing strip and into the desert, leaving Delta troops and some of their gear tumbling out the rear of the airplane. Within about thirty seconds, the second MC-130 landed on its original schedule, narrowly missing the plane Mike had just moved.

No one had anticipated that the helicopter linkup would take so long, but we shouldn't have been surprised. They had never shown up on time once in any of our rehearsals and, in one instance, had landed at the wrong place. As soon as planes landed and had moved onto their parking aprons, their cargo ramps and doors were opened and crewmen, Rangers, and Delta Force members looked out to see a foglike effect, as if a bag of flour had been thrown into the air. Their tire tracks had left deep grooves in the sand, which was blowing behind them like a scene from the dust storms that suffocated the midwestern plains in the drought of the early 1930s. At least one plane's belly dragged over some bumps in the sand and bogged down as it was taxiing, until the pilot throttled maximum power to force it moving again. That raised a thick new cloud of dust, obliterating the landscape. But even that didn't obscure a brilliant explosion on the horizon. It turned out to have been a fuel truck barreling down the road between the two landing strips, a tanker one of the perimeter security teams had stopped with a light antitank weapon mounted on the handlebars of one of their motorcycles. The tanker exploded into a mushroom cloud on the horizon as another plane was approaching our makeshift airfield, leaving aircrews to wonder if one of their planes had just blown up.

Throughout the long wait for the helicopters to arrive, the C-130s' crews, Rangers, and Delta Force members continued to off-load gear. Loadmasters from the EC-130Ps deployed their refueling hoses behind their aircraft, knowing that time was critical. Somehow, their "hose draggers" set up each of their refueling points within the allotted six minutes. These men were barely more than kids, all unsung heroes, not hard-core commando killers but everyday airmen wearing only one or two chevrons on their sleeves. They spent endless hours drudging along to pump fuel into "war chariots" so the "heroes" could go fly and complain about bad flight lunches. They were unrecognized faces, like finance clerks and administrative types who get yelled at for others' mistakes. The hose draggers had been pulled off the flight lines or out of their trucks to "volunteer" for the trip to Desert One. One day they were pumping gas in the hot sun at Hurlburt and the next they were given goggles, masks, and gloves and flown to a blacked-out strip of desert and told to drag 340 pounds of hose, then put it all together in six minutes in the middle of a sand blizzard. Then, like the rest of us at Desert One, they waited for the helicopters. To one of the loadmasters, it seemed that "enough time had passed to have landed the entire 82nd and 101st Airborne Divisions, as well as a new government."[7]

The first helicopter didn't arrive until after we had been on the ground for almost two and a half hours; another half hour passed before the last, the sixth one, made it, seven and a half hours into our mission. That still left enough time for the helicopters to refuel and make it to the hide site forty-five minutes before sunup.[8]

There were now ten aircraft at Desert One, all with the engines running. The Combat Talons' propellers and high-velocity downwash from the helicopters' rotor blades blew sand and dust for hundreds of yards, singeing our faces and blinding us. There was no place for us to hide from it. But there was one memorable sight that one man at Desert One would still recall, twenty-two years later:

> Each combat controller stood alone with us, wands in hand, trying his best to brace himself against the fury of the rotor-wash and sand pummeling his body. I did not see a single one hunker down or try to run away from the approaching helos. Each stood his ground until his charge was safely on the ground and ready for refueling. Imagine standing in the middle of a parking lot at two in the morning, blindfolded, in the middle of a tornado, with a raging bull coming at you. You had to have been there.[9]

Desert One became a scene from hell itself. None of the principals on the scene (Kyle and Beckwith, for instance) was wearing any distinctive clothing or markings, and Kyle kept dashing from one plane to another and then among the helicopters. Some confusion ensued about who was in charge, because General Vaught had elected not to delegate authority but instead to relay orders over his command net. There were, in effect, four mission commanders on the ground at Desert One: Beckwith, Kyle, Lieutenant Colonel Bob Brenci, in charge of the Combat Talons and tankers, and Marine Lieutenant Colonel Ed Seiffert, the helicopter flight leader.[10]

We lost unity of command, a paramount principle of war. Since I had at least *some* radio contact with every pilot on the landing zone, I should have strongly urged that Kyle stay in one place, a command-and-control point or tactical operations center where we could relay his questions and instructions through my combat controllers on our short-range intrateam radios or even by messenger on our motor bikes. (I later learned that the satellite communications, or SatCom, radio that Kyle was looking for had been placed on the wrong aircraft.)

The Marine helicopter pilots had been briefed that Desert One would be like a parking lot—no loose sand. That posed a special problem for the helicopters, with their smaller nose wheel tires, some of which were damaged and deflated on landing. In addition, we discovered after landing at Desert One that an EC-130 loadmaster had arbitrarily removed fifty feet of hose from the forward-area refueling system to make room for all the troops and gear crammed aboard his plane. This required that the helicopters move that much closer to the refueling EC-130. Their pilots had to perform what Seiffert would describe as a "wounded frog" technique, a combination of air and ground taxiing, holding their nose wheels off the ground. My controllers had to park the helicopters with their rotor tips a mere twenty feet from the C-130s' tails and wings.

Seiffert's pilots were physically and mentally exhausted after flying blind through two suspended dust clouds, one 45 miles deep beginning 230 miles from the *Nimitz*, the second area about 95 miles deep and lasting to within 100 miles of Desert One. Wearing night-vision goggles and fighting off vertigo, the pilots had to slow from 130 to 80 or 90 knots to maintain visual contact with the other helicopters, which proved impossible for some. Their copilots were riveted on the cockpit instruments, especially the radar altimeters since they were flying one hundred to two hundred feet above the ground, which they couldn't see for extended periods. All of this took place while approaching ninety-eight-hundred-foot peaks as they neared Desert One. In the MC- and EC-130s, we had flown into the same phenomena, but with better radars and instruments, and simply eased our planes above the problem.

One of the six helicopters that made it to Desert One from the eight that left the *Nimitz* had a second-stage hydraulic system failure, and it had to shut down. Seiffert reported to Kyle that the aircraft was unsafe—"If the controls lock up, it becomes uncontrollable"—and grounded it. Kyle asked Beckwith if he could handle the mission with five helicopters by cutting down on his force by about twenty men. Beckwith said, "No way—I need every man I've got and every piece of gear. There's no fat I can cut out." Kyle radioed Vaught and recommended an abort. Twenty minutes later, almost eight hours into the mission, the word came to proceed withdrawing the rescue force.[11] Kyle and Beckwith ordered everyone to reboard their MC-130s and EC-130Ps.

By then, one of the MC-130s was short about three thousand pounds of fuel to make it back to Masirah. Because two other helicopters were blocking access to the EC-130 bladder aircraft, Kyle ordered the two helicopters out of the way. Jockeying the two planes into position stirred another blizzard of sand. One of the helicopters couldn't taxi into position. Its nose gear tires were askew, probably from a hard landing and trying to taxi in what seemed like dry quicksand, and the left tire was cocked off its rim while the right one deflated. Moreover, there were at least six inches of loose sand beneath the nose gear, so the pilot elected to lift off and air-taxi. About twenty-five feet off the ground, it disappeared in dust when Kyle heard a loud *whack*, then an explosion, and saw an inferno engulf the tanker commanded by Air Force Captain Harold L. Lewis Jr. The helicopter had drifted sideways and slammed into the top of the EC-130's inner left wing. Three Marine helicopter crewmen and five Air Commandos from the EC-130 perished.[12] Forty-five other C-130 crewmen as well as Rangers and Delta Force operators were sitting in the back of the EC-130 on near-empty and leaky fuel bladders.[13] They were crowded next to approximately eight thousand pounds of ammunition plus several thousand pounds of takedown gear they had loaded aboard to take back to Masirah. A fireball blew from the front to the rear of the aircraft, blowing the galley floor down onto the flight deck steps. The aircraft was a man-made bomb waiting to detonate.

Ammunition at the front of the plane started to cook off—explode—as the fire moved aft, and the survivors aboard raced to the rear exit doors. The plane's three loadmasters—Technical Sergeant Kenneth Bancroft, Technical Sergeant Wesley Witherspoon, and Sergeant James W. McClain Jr.—remained calm amid this chaos. They took command of an impending disaster, calmed the panicked troops, and forcibly pushed many of them away to operate the handle that would open the only usable, right-side door. Sergeant Bancroft saw one of the junior fuel specialists being trampled underfoot by terrified troopers, forced his way to the man, bodily picked him up, carried him out of the aircraft, and then directed a number of troops away from the exploding ordnance to the safety of another tanker.

Technical Sergeant "Spoon" Witherspoon found about twenty men pressing him against the only usable exit for those trapped inside, called upon his inner strength to force the crowd away just far enough to get a hold on the exit's handle, and managed to get the door open. As the troops started to exit, he noticed dazed men turning to run toward the plane's still-turning propellers or heading for the abandoned helicopters. He somehow maintained order, then leaped out and shepherded the confused troops safely to other aircraft.

Sergeant James W. "Banzai" McClain Jr., a second-generation Air Commando whose father had served in Southeast Asia, helped Bancroft open the left paratroop door, but when he found it unusable due to structural damage and intense heat and flames pouring into the cabin, he calmed panicking soldiers there and began to forcibly push unresponsive personnel out the right exit that Witherspoon had managed to open. He heard a troop commander shouting that the right exit was being closed; terrified troops were using the door's handle to swing out of the exit and had pulled the door loose.

Realizing that if the door were to close, men bunched up there would be trapped, McClain pushed his way to the aft cargo ramp, reached down and pulled the troop door up, locked it in place, and directed the remaining troops to safety. Seeing that the cabin was finally empty, McClain began moving forward to the cockpit, but another explosion flared and blew him out the right troop door onto the desert floor. McClain extinguished his burning flight suit and decided to move away from the explosions when he observed a dazed force member by the plane's right wingtip, unable to move. He picked the specialist up and carried him half a mile through the dry-swamp-like quagmire of thick dust and sand to a waiting aircraft. He organized a group of disoriented personnel and led them to safety amid explosions from detonating munitions and aircraft wreckage, incurring both burns and shrapnel wounds.[14]

To the best of the authors' knowledge, none of the courageous loadmasters' feats have ever before been publicly acknowledged. The summaries noted here are based on the unabridged official recommendations for the Airman's Medals each received for extraordinary heroism. But the official citation accompanying each award was six lines long and spoke only of "heroism involving voluntary risk of life outside of the continental United States." There was no mention of the year 1980, of Iran, or of a rescue mission, and not one detail of the circumstances warranting the awards.

Their medals were belatedly awarded at an almost impromptu ceremony *two years later* in a parking lot at Hurlburt Field, Florida— by an Air Force general who flew in for the occasion late one afternoon after the men had been made to stand at parade rest for an hour. The general was still dressed in his flight suit; none of the men recognized him, no one remembers his name, and he left fifteen minutes later. The men were given the rest of the day off. They had all been recommended for a significantly higher decoration, but it was decided the decoration had to be for "non-combat" heroism—due to political considerations and so as not to focus undue attention on the failed Desert One mission.

Without realizing it at the time, Banzai McClain had also

broken his back when he was blown out of the exploding EC-130P. When he complained after the mission of stiffness and backache, doctors at Eglin Air Force Base, Florida, X-rayed him and told him he was fine. McClain continued to have problems and reported to the hospital so often that Air Force medics not only labeled him a malingerer but also complained formally that he was exceeding the base's annual budget for visits per patient. (The seriousness of an illness or injury had nothing to do with the criteria for the frequency of consultations or emergency room visits.) They told McClain they suspected he was just trying to qualify for an "early out" retirement for disability.

McClain handled it stoically, giving full credit to dedicated flight surgeons, but despairing of military medical care that was a sick bureaucratic "system." When the invasion of Grenada unfolded in 1983, McClain's adrenaline kicked in and he flew as the mission loadmaster aboard the lead Combat Talon MC-130E commanded by Colonel Jim Hobson, who received the coveted MacKay Trophy for Airmanship.

Seven years after Desert One, after volunteering for flight testing the new MC-130H (Combat Talon II) at Edwards Air Force Base in 1987, McClain came upon a flight surgeon, Major "Doc" Leckie, who had been a former special forces medic and had a gift for diagnosing chiropractic problems. Leckie recognized immediately that something was indeed wrong with McClain's back and scheduled him for tests at Travis Air Force Base Medical Center in northern California, where a neurosurgeon tested him at 8:00 A.M. one morning and at 1:00 P.M. asked him when he had broken his back. He found that McClain had been walking around since 1980 with several herniated discs and numerous spinal fractures in his lower back. He was scheduled for surgery within a month, which was a success—but the damage had been done. McClain flew with Leckie on a flight evaluation and professionally hoodwinked his way through the exam so he could keep flying. He worked, parented two children, and tried to manage the pain. In 1994, with the downsizing of the military that became one of William Clinton's legacies, McClain was retired (along with thousands of other experienced special operators and servicemen and -women) after twenty years of service instead of the twenty-two years that had been a standard for men with his service.

There is a fourth noncommissioned airman who earned the Airman's Medal after the collisions at Desert One, and he warrants special mention because of his actions in the disarray that ensued after the helicopter destroyed the EC-130 tanker. This was Technical Sergeant "Radio" Randy Gingrich, the radio operator and communications specialist on the EC-130 that was adjacent to the one hit by the RH-53. He was preparing for takeoff when the accident happened. Without regard for his own safety, Gingrich rushed to the wreckage that was now a blazing inferno. Observing that one of the RH-53 pilots was on fire and struggling to free himself of the conflagration, Gingrich leaped into the flames, put out the pilot's burning flight suit, and dragged him to the safety of his own aircraft, where the pilot received lifesaving medical attention. While doing that, Gingrich also stopped to grab the wounded copilot of the RH-53, who had been unable to move because of wounds.

Due to exploding ammunition and fuel from both aircraft, Gingrich's aircraft suddenly started taxiing with the crew entrance door open. Knowing the aircraft could be damaged and made unflyable, Gingrich moved forward, leaned precariously out the entrance, managed to grasp the door cable, and pulled the door shut. He saved the lives of the two helicopter pilots, prevented the loss of his own aircraft and crewmen, sustained burns and injuries from his actions, and did all this at night in hostile territory under conditions the U.S. government considered peacetime, not combat.

Throughout these minutes in hell, men all over the Desert One site scrambled for their lives as ammunition and fuel exploded all about them. The Marine aircrews left highly classified documents aboard their helicopters—many of which they should not have been carrying. It was decided the aircraft had to be abandoned as several were riddled with shrapnel. But those horrible minutes represented the most courageous performance imaginable by my combat controllers. With Kyle they made sure every survivor got aboard a C-130, and the combat controllers even policed up their TACAN gear and all the remotely activated beacons the CIA had developed. The Agency could not believe we had retrieved it all.

According to the after-action report, under the charge of former Chief of Naval Operations Admiral James L. Holloway, twenty-one different problems ("issues") crippled the Iranian rescue mission. Yet the report glossed over what I considered to be the simplest and most important problem. MC-130 Combat Talon "guide dogs" or pathfinders should have led the eight Navy RH-53s from the carrier *Nimitz* on their 800-mile journey to Desert One, just as Talons had led the HH-53s that flew the 676-mile, nighttime round-trip to Son Tay prison in 1970. If this had happened, Delta Force might not have ended up one helicopter short of the number needed to bring home the hostages and their rescue team. Indeed, there were thirty-four special mission aircraft (RH-53s, MC-130s, EC-130s, AC-130s, and so forth) and twenty support aircraft (C-141s, KC-135 tankers, EC-135 electronic warfare aircraft, and C-130 airborne command and combat control systems) bound for Desert One, Tehran, and Manzariyah. One or two MC-130s leading eight helicopters could have made all the difference.

Most of the helicopters bound for Desert One got lost in thick, suspended chalk-white dust clouds called "haboobs," a not uncommon occurrence in Iran. Incomprehensibly, no one from the CIA or DIA (Defense Intelligence Agency) had bothered to mention the phenomenon to any of the pilots, even though weather (an unexpected typhoon) had been the determining factor in deciding when to launch the 1970 Son Tay raid. Worse, because of over-restrictive "operational security" compartmentalization, experts from Military Airlift Command's Air Weather Service, who were familiar with the haboob phenomenon, weren't allowed to talk with any of the mission's pilots. Apparently the planners of the Iranian mission had been too busy to study why previous rescue missions failed.

What is most ironic is that en route to Desert One from their base at Masirah, the Combat Talons passed within sight of the Marine helicopter formation;[15] thus, they could easily have guided the helicopters to Desert One. Alternatively, the Talon crews (who flew into the same haboobs) could have radioed the helicopter crews in a short burst of code to simply climb a few hundred feet and overfly the haboobs or to just press on and soon bypass them. (One helicopter aborted only fifty miles from the rendezvous site, and one more helicopter is all that was needed.) The aircraft that needed the sophisticated navigation gear the most—the helicopters—removed almost all of it (unnecessarily) *and* their secure radios *and* their forward-looking infrared (FLIR) to reduce weight. Thus, they were literally flying blind, and could not advise one another of actual weather conditions, which were much more benign than the pilots believed. Furthermore, the pilots lost sight of their objective—to rescue hostages. They should have broken radio silence for a second or two to query the Combat Talons, regain their bearings, and find better weather.

Many critics of the failed mission have blamed a Marine helicopter crew that turned back to the *Nimitz*, saying, for instance, in one case, that it should have simply ignored indications on the instrument panel of impending rotor blade failure. But none of those critics flew for four to six hours through the disorienting haboobs and experienced the navigation system failures that the Marines did. That six of the eight helicopter crews made it to Desert One is, in fact, a tribute to their airmanship, perseverance, and courage. One can legitimately ask why Marine pilots so inexperienced in low-level night flight over treacherous terrain were picked in the first place to fly the Navy RH-53D minesweeping helicopters. Although too few of the Air Force's new MH-53 Pave Low helicopters were yet available to mount the rescue, it turns out that the Air Force had more than one hundred special operations–qualified HH-53 rescue pilots on its rosters and nearly one hundred more MH-53 special operations pilots who could have been requalified on the Navy RH-53Ds in short order. Many of them had extensive combat experience in Southeast Asia flying search and rescue missions deep into Laos and North Vietnam. An earlier Air Force special operations project had proven that it is far easier to train such pilots to transition from one variant of a helicopter to the other than to give special operations training to non-special-operations pilots who are already qualified on the desired aircraft.[16] Thus, one has to blame the Joint Chiefs of Staff themselves for letting the Marines fly, just so that each of the four military services could be part of the action.

The second blunder at Desert One was overcompartmentalization in the name of "operational security." That's what kept the Marine pilots in deep trouble from alerting the mission commander (General Vaught) to the blinding and disorienting dust clouds they unexpectedly encountered, or from letting the Combat Talon crews at Desert One (who had already flown safely through, and above, the haboobs) radio the helicopters that they should simply climb to a higher altitude—and that as they neared Desert One, they would soon be through the phenomenon in any case. (Similar preoccupation with operational security would lead the Joint Chiefs of Staff not to alert the Defense Mapping Agency that maps of Grenada would be needed in 1983; the same error sent no agents to infiltrate and reconnoiter the island, even while the State Department was warning Cuba that we intended to invade and trying to persuade Cubans on Grenada not to resist.)

The third fatal error of the Iranian rescue attempt was that no full dress rehearsal took place. Disparate groups of different units cobbled together in haste attempted to synchronize their work literally on the fly. Virtually all of the twenty-one causes of the tragedy at Desert One would play pivotal roles in Grenada three years later—even after the Joint Chiefs of Staff recommended and the National Command Authority established a new, permanent Joint Special Operations Command to plan such missions, properly integrate and train the multiservice forces executing them, and be responsible for conducting in extremis crisis responses worldwide.

DESERT TWO—OPERATION "HONEY BADGER"

"There is no failure in failing, only in failing to try."[1] We readied another Iranian rescue attempt, one that would be far more difficult. One of the reasons was that, contrary to all operational security considerations, the Marine helicopter crews had carried classified plans for the April mission aboard their aircraft—and left them in the wreckage strewn about Desert One. After the mission was aborted, the Iranians meticulously pieced the charred documents back together (as they had thousands of shredded papers seized with our embassy) and even published most of them. Thus they had a telling preview of our modus operandi as we tried to devise another rescue mission, an operation that became known as Honey Badger. Worse, the Iranians moved the hostages about so often that locating them proved near impossible (although most were eventually brought back into the American embassy compound). The Central Intelligence Agency's newest case officer—a thirty-two-year-old neophyte who spoke not a word of Farsi—was moved blindfolded to at least twelve different locations between November 1979 and January 1981, and held in solitary for 425 of the 444 days that passed before the hostages were finally released.[2]

Those twelve moves included frequent ones within the twenty-seven-acre embassy compound, where he was shifted back and forth among the embassy's three floors and to five different rooms in its Chancery as well as to the ambassador's residence, and, after the rescue attempt failed at Desert One, to Evin prison, Komiteh prison, back to Evin prison, and, days before he was released, to the Iranian foreign minister's guest house.[3]

The Army had been forming its own secret, mini air force—Task Force 160—just in case the other services couldn't or wouldn't get us to the target again. As for Brand X, we were still fighting to stay on—or get on—the playing field. The Rangers had decided once again that they didn't need combat controllers to handle their airfield seizures. Instead, they would have their radio operators handle the air traffic control just as the Army's pathfinder paratroops had once done, and even have them call in AC-130 gunship strikes. They asked us to train their people in how to set up TACAN navigational beacons. Thus, we were competing with pathfinders throughout Honey Badger over who would control the helicopters and the forward-area refueling points, and who would marshal aircraft on the landing zones.

At least the Holloway Commission caused a new joint headquarters to be established—the Joint Special Operations Command at Fort Bragg—that we would report to operationally and that was charged full time with integrating all of the services' special mission units, standardizing operating procedures, and conducting sanity checks of all our exercises and rehearsals. We finally were working as a truly joint team, but the realistic training exercises took a sometimes deadly toll on our special mission units.

The first mishap involved a crash Air Force experimental program to equip MC-130s with JATO bottles for an ultrashort "jet-assisted takeoff"—just like what Strategic Air Command's B-47 nuclear bombers had used for more than a decade to take off from short European and Southwest Asian airfields around the periphery of the Soviet Union. Called "Credible Sport," it reconfigured three

C-130s with scores of JATO bottles encasing the bottom half of the rear of each airplane (the empennage) and space-age computer technology from NASA's moon mission to give the planes unbelievable short takeoff and landing performance. The first plane wasn't even ready for its maiden test flight for months. In front of a gaggle of high-ranking observers, the plane crashed on its first flight when the Lockheed pilot decided that he was better than computers at firing the retro rockets. He wasn't, but the "crash" program proved that that scheme would have been a questionable option.[4]

Meanwhile, our unit grew to twice its previous size, and Brand X was finally given an official Air Force designation, "Det 1 MACOS"—Detachment One, Military Airlift Command Operations Staff. The 21st Air Force finally decided to let us move from being a covert, part-time component of the 437th Military Airlift Wing's combat control team at Charleston Air Force Base to Pope Air Force Base and into a new facility at Fort Bragg adjacent to JSOC, where we were at home with Delta Force and could focus full-time on our real missions. The name Det 1 MACOS was picked to be deliberately unrevealing and to hide manpower spaces for us. The commander of Joint Special Operations Command said we had the best cover of any of his six special mission units because no one could figure out what our name stood for.

We ended up woefully undermanned for the tasks given us, with just ten men: myself; Captain Craig Brotchie; Chief Master Sergeant Nick Kiraly, my noncommissioned officer-in-charge; two tactical team leaders, Master Sergeant Mike Lampe and Master Sergeant Wayne Norrad; Technical Sergeants Dave Lillico, Johnny Pantages, Dick West, Rick Caffee, and Rex Evitts; and Staff Sergeants D. I. Brown, Jerry Bennett, Chuck Freeman, Fran Oste, and Doug Phillips. The Air Force promised us more personnel but wouldn't let us fill our authorized billets.

In August 1980, we had our validation test for a second rescue attempt at Reese Air Force Base west of Lubbock, Texas, which had a runway similar to that of the Mehrabad airport near Tehran, and we passed with flying colors. But the Desert Two rescue mission was canceled when the Iranians released our hostages the day Ronald Reagan was sworn in as president.

During the next two years our team grew slowly. We worked hard, making several mistakes along the way but doing our best to avoid errors—which I looked upon as mistakes we didn't learn from.

Let me illustrate my philosophy with a real exercise mistake. In 1982, Staff Sergeant John "Mac" McReynolds had a key responsibility on a Ranger exercise that counted heavily on our reliability as a significant special operations asset. He was to parachute with the Rangers seizing an austere airfield, set up the box lights on the approach end of the runway, and turn them on after he received word the runway was clear of debris. Once the lights were on, the MC-130s with the rest of the Ranger force and others in trail would land without any radio transmissions to clear them in. For some reason, Mac didn't get the lights on, and the main assault force had to break off their landing approaches, go around, and come in again. I was furious, but not given to public floggings. I simply told Chief Master Sergeant Nick Kiraly to put Mac on a flight back to Fort Bragg just as soon as possible. I wanted him separated from his teammates, with time to reflect on the cause and effect of not getting his lights on as briefed. And I wanted the entire team to understand that a serious mistake had been made in a business where we had no room for error.

Once back at Fort Bragg, I met with Sergeant McReynolds privately. He was mortified by the episode and understood the magnitude of his mistake. Had that been a real-world mission, I told Mac, many people might have lost their lives—our teammates on the ground and the small Ranger airfield-seizure team were all exposed. Meanwhile a gaggle of C-130s with hundreds of Rangers aboard were circling over hostile territory and vulnerable. Finally, I told him, I—your commander—had to stand up in front of a hotwash debrief and explain to an entire Ranger battalion why our combat control team had failed its crucial mission. Mac got the picture: His action, or lack of actions, had set us back in the eyes of our own community, and his teammates could not tolerate this ever happening again.

Mac never let us down again. He was benched for a while, but after he returned to duty we never had a problem with the box lights being turned on exactly as planned.

Before I ever heard the buzzword *empowerment*, I understood the importance of making sure that each man on our team understood our whole mission and why his role in it was so important. That made my job relatively simple; the men decided the best way to accomplish a mission. My job was to train them, equip them, and make them understand our role. Then I had to support them any way I could to let them perform in a way that would allow us *all* to succeed and become a team everyone could count on.

General Cassidy, who had always looked after us while in MAC's operations directorate, was promoted to major general and replaced General Sadler as commander of 21st Air Force. Thus began an entirely new, unique relationship, a personal and professional bond that I treasure to this day. Not one to be outdone, Cassidy surprised us all by showing up one day in 1983, unannounced and by helicopter, at our training site for water jumps, the Key Largo Ocean Diver's Shop. He caught me even more off guard by announcing, "Thought I'd make a few water jumps with you, Major Carney."

For reasons I no longer recall, I had anticipated just such an eventuality by asking John Koren, then a captain and commandant of the Combat Control School at Pope Air Force Base and Fort Bragg, to devise a basic airborne course for VIPs. We called it Operation Blue Fin, planning to use water jumps that wouldn't endanger neophyte jumpers with the hard landings and the physical conditioning for parachute landing rolls required in the Army's three-week regular airborne course. This lessened the potential for broken legs but raised the risk of drowning if the jumper couldn't get out of his parachute harness quickly and got dragged under by a waterlogged chute.

Cassidy was a command pilot with more than eight thousand cockpit seat hours to his credit, but he had never bailed out of an airplane, much less gone through parachute training. We put him through a crash three-hour course at a remote corner of the Homestead nuclear power plant, where we had set up a "death slide" into a holding pond to practice water landings, and late that afternoon Major General Duane H. Cassidy made the first of five parachute jumps from twelve hundred feet of altitude out of a perfectly good helicopter into an inlet patrolled by more than its share of sharks. As soon as he hit the water (with his face to the wind, as we'd taught him, so he could lean back and ride the water as the wind blew his chute toward the shore), Mike Lampe and Rick Caffee raced up in a Zodiac. Cassidy barely had time to get damp before Mike made a beautiful swan dive from the Zodiac's prow to collapse Cassidy's billowing parachute, helped him into the rubber craft, and then raced him to a nearby fifty-five-foot recovery boat. Once aboard, Cassidy enjoyed a cold Coke and told us he wanted to jump again. "Why, sir?" I had the audacity to ask. "Because I want to earn my parachute wings," the fifty-year-old major general replied. Turns out he had done his homework: Technically, all one needed to do to qualify for jump wings was to make five parachute jumps. There was no requirement in Air Force regulations specifying the weeks of jump school that Army paratroopers had to go through at Fort Benning. We jumped Cassidy once more that day as dusk fell and three times the next morning. Celebrating over a cold beer on the dive shop's terrace, where we checked all our scuba gear and repacked our parachutes, I took special pleasure in watching Colonel Bill Foley, the director of the Airborne Board, pin on Cassidy's jump wings—pounding them through his flight suit into his chest hard enough for their clip-on pins to draw a trace of blood. (Thanks, Bill: You almost got me fired.) But Cassidy was really proud of those wings.

Soon after his water jumps, my mother took ill and was in the hospital. I took a break from being at her bedside one day and went out to the parking lot to continue reading a book entitled *Solo*, by Jack Higgins.[5] I came across a vignette about a soldier wearing a Red Beret attending a funeral and knew that my mother had died. I ran up to her room, and as I had expected, she was gone. I buried my Red Beret with her. To this day, I believe that book conveyed a message from her about how proud she was of me and my earning my Red Beret.

And knowing how proud Cassidy was to be "one of *us*" made *me* all the prouder to wear that headgear. I knew his support would help us make an even bigger difference as Brand X grew in size, transitioned through the first of many different unit designations,[6] and trained for the unknown missions that lay ahead. Our next major operation would involve a crisis that President Ronald Reagan grew to take very seriously, but to which the Defense Department hierarchy and the Joint Chiefs of Staff inexplicably paid little heed.

CHAPTER NINE

GRENADA—"URGENT FURY"

At daybreak on Tuesday, October 25, 1983, Delta Force, Navy SEALs, Army Rangers, and U.S. Marines launched a full-scale invasion of the small Caribbean island of Grenada, more than two thousand troops in all. They were soon joined by eight hundred paratroops from the 82nd Airborne Division—and eventually by about six thousand of them. All told, it took more than eight thousand American soldiers, sailors, Marines, and airmen to seize the island.[1] It was America's biggest military operation since the Vietnam War.

The invasion, called "Urgent Fury," was supposed to be a quick, surprise *coup de main*, a one-punch knockout to prevent a Marxist takeover of the island and to evacuate some six hundred American medical students. Instead, problems caused by constantly changing scenarios, superficial planning, security overkill, lack of service interoperability, service parochialism, and routine "fog of war" screwups turned it into a bloody, six-day fight and nine-day operation that President Reagan later termed a "textbook success."[2] It succeeded because of good old American ingenuity, can-do spirit, realistic prior training, and remarkable courage by young American troops, most of whom were undergoing their first test on a battlefield.

We achieved our missions, but took heavy casualties. Nineteen men were killed in action and 123 wounded. The enemy was a hastily organized force of about fifty Cuban military advisers, over seven hundred Cuban construction workers, and one thousand two hundred members of Grenada's People's Revolutionary Army.[3] Many of the casualties were from friendly fire. Nine of the fatalities were U.S. special operations forces.[4]

To this day, I doubt that any one person knows how ineptly Urgent Fury was planned and executed. In the long run, however, the operation proved a defining moment for special operations, for it led directly to the creation, by congressional mandate three years later, of the U.S. Special Operations Command, when special operations finally came into its own.

I had a ringside seat at the initial planning for the military intervention in Grenada. I was supposed to lead a pre-invasion reconnaissance and surveillance mission two nights before the initial assault. Instead, I watched the invasion take place, called in naval gunfire during the worst day of fighting, and listened to the operation unfold on virtually every radio channel used by American soldiers and Marines as they were clawing desperately to take control of an island nation comprising only 133 square miles, measuring roughly 35 miles long and 10 miles wide.[5]

American forces deployed for Urgent Fury outnumbered the enemy by almost four to one. Our odds were nearly ten to one against *trained* military forces, Cuban and Grenadian, amounting to fewer than eight hundred personnel. Conventional military wisdom says that an attacking force typically needs a three-to-one superiority to prevail. Our touch-and-go performance despite a ten-to-one advantage shows just how poorly the operation was conceived, especially considering that most of the opposing force consisted of construction workers with only rudimentary small-arms proficiency.

Part of the problem the U.S. military had in planning the October operation stemmed from the swiftness with which the Grenada crisis unfolded in late 1983. The fact that a crisis *would* unfold should have surprised no one. In the twelve days leading up to the invasion, moreover, there were almost daily indicators that significant military action would be required. There was ample time to plan the operation, but the planning was confounded by a cascade of overlapping, often contradictory orders from Washington. The military units involved were not informed of what the overall operation might entail or how their missions would mesh with those of other forces. And the national security hierarchy failed to provide any maps of the island or to obtain the most basic intelligence needed to execute combat missions.

Barely twice the size of Washington, D.C., Grenada is the southernmost island of the Windward group in the West Indies. It lies only one hundred miles north of Trinidad, just off the coast of Venezuela, and about one thousand six hundred miles from Miami. Its population was a little over one hundred thousand at the time. With a per capita income of less than three thousand dollars, the island was economically dependent on tourism and exports of nutmeg, bananas, and cocoa.

In 1979, five years after Grenada had won its independence from Great Britain, the leftist New Jewel[6] Movement seized power in a bloodless coup and allied itself with the Soviet Union and Cuba. It invited Cuba to build a ten-thousand-foot-long runway at Point Salines, near St. George's, the island's capital and only city, with a population of thirty-five thousand, suburbs included. Ostensibly the airfield was to boost Grenada's tourist industry. The existing runway at Pearls on the opposite side of the island was too small for intercontinental aircraft and, because of nearby mountains, could not be lengthened. The United States became concerned because the new runway could also handle fighter-bomber aircraft that Cuba or Russia might use to interdict American air and sea routes to Europe or the Middle East. Eighty-five percent of Army tonnage bound for Europe or the Middle East originated in ports on the Gulf of Mexico and had to transit the Caribbean through one of only two exits to the Atlantic.[7] The United States feared the Jewel government would invite Cuba to use the new runway as a refueling site for its operations in Africa, especially Angola, or as a launching pad for the same kind of Marxist adventurism in the southeastern Caribbean and northern coast of South America that was causing so much bloodshed in Nicaragua and El Salvador. On March 10, 1983, during a major Washington speech, President Reagan cautioned, tongue in cheek, that the building of a naval base, new airfield, and areas for military training on the island of Grenada were no doubt "simply to encourage the export of nutmeg."[8]

Thirteen days later, Reagan was more explicit. During a nationally televised address from the Oval Office (in which he proposed his Strategic Defense Initiative), he held up overhead photos of Grenada and pointed to construction of the runway at Point Salines. Reagan warned Americans,

> As the Soviets have increased their military power, they've been emboldened to extend that power. They're spreading influence in ways that can directly challenge our vital interests and those of our allies. . . .
>
> Grenada doesn't even have an air force. Who is it intended for? The Soviet militarization of Grenada, in short, can only be seen as power projection into the region.[9]

Seven months later, on Saturday, October 12, 1983, as the runway neared completion, another military coup took place on Grenada. Maurice Bishop, the island's Marxist leader, who was close to Fidel Castro but had begun courting the United States the previous spring, was removed from office and placed under house arrest. That coup was led by even more radical Marxists, Bishop's two closest deputies, Deputy Prime Minister Phyllis Coard and General Hudson Austin, commander in chief of Grenada's armed forces.[10]

On October 13, the U.S. ambassador to Barbados, Milan Bish—who was also responsible for Grenada—alerted the State Department that the political situation on Grenada was deteriorating and recommended that the United States be prepared to evacuate its citizens if conditions worsened. About six hundred American medical students were studying there at the American-owned St. George's Medical College, and several hundred American tourists were thought to be visiting Grenada.

The next day, a State Department interagency group asked the Joint Chiefs of Staff to review its contingency plans should an evacuation be necessary. This prompted a call to U.S. Atlantic Command (LantCom) in Norfolk asking how it would evacuate U.S. civilians from the island.[11]

The cascade of events in the diplomatic and policy arenas that followed made it clear that the situation on Grenada was serious, unstable, and unpredictable. Multiple options for U.S. military intervention surfaced fast.

On October 17, when the president was first briefed on the unfolding crisis, followers of the popular prime minister freed Bishop from house arrest and accompanied him to the main military barracks at Fort Rupert. Two days later, armored vehicles fired into a crowd of Bishop supporters. Bishop was assassinated, as were three members of his cabinet, one of whom had been viciously beaten, and fourteen other Grenadians were killed when they marched to protest those atrocities. General Austin seized power, and the island's rogue government ordered a shoot-on-sight, twenty-four-hour-a-day curfew.

Late that afternoon, October 19, the JCS sent Atlantic Command its first warning order, requiring that plans for an evacuation be ready within twenty-four hours. By 3:47 A.M. on the twentieth, the warning order had been passed on to Military Airlift Command headquarters at Scott Air Force Base, Illinois. A crisis action team was activated there at 4:58 that afternoon, and a response cell was activated at 21st Air Force headquarters at McGuire Air Force Base in New Jersey at 8:00 P.M. JCS orders arrived at McGuire two hours later to ready two of the five options contained in the warning order. Both required that 21st Air Force have seven C-141s carrying personnel and twenty-seven C-5As carrying heavy equipment to be airborne in less than thirty hours.[12] Twenty-first Air Force was now commanded by Major General Duane H. Cassidy, a good-looking, dark-haired officer with an infectious smile and personality and a no-nonsense approach to problems. During this period, October 20–23, however, Cassidy was at Scott Air Force Base in Illinois for Military Airlift Command's annual commanders' conference, and his vice commander, Brigadier General Robert B. Patterson, a soft-spoken officer with a wry sense of humor, was running the show at McGuire. He kept asking to be allowed to take some of his planners to Norfolk, but he was turned down until Sunday, the twenty-third.

Also on October 20, Prime Minister Tom Adams of Barbados sent a message to the State Department urging military action to restore a legitimate government on Grenada. The State Department said that a formal written request would be required before any such action could be considered. However, Secretary of State George P. Shultz and the Joint Chiefs of Staff chairman, Army General John W. Vessey Jr., warned the White House Special Situation Group, headed by Vice President George Bush, that the Grenadian military might resist an evacuation and that armed Cuban construction workers might intervene. Vessey recommended that the mission be expanded to include neutralization of Grenadian forces and armed Cuban workers and reconstruction of the island's government. The group approved.

From October 14 to October 20, a State Department–led interagency group had been meeting periodically with the Special Situation Group, which instructed the Joint Chiefs of Staff to ready various evacuation alternatives. Secrecy was deemed paramount; operational security was an overriding consideration. Vessey imposed a "special category" restriction on all message traffic about planning for the operation as the JCS worked with a crisis action group at U.S. Atlantic Command in Norfolk to assess options.[13] Planning for the operation was so tightly restricted—"compartmentalized," in military parlance—that not even the National Security Agency, the Defense Mapping Agency, or even the Joint Staff's Deputy Directorate for Politico-Military Affairs was alerted.[14] Those restrictions would have a devastating impact on the rescue operation.

During a visit General Vessey happened to be making in Nor-folk on October 20, the commander in chief of Atlantic Command, Admiral Wesley McDonald, briefed the JCS chairman on possible courses of action. Because of uncertainty about the likely opposi-tion, one option included a large joint task force. The JCS warning order sent to LantCom the day before had focused on a noncombat-ant evacuation, a mission for which Marines were often used. Thus, it was natural that Atlantic Command and the JCS had been think-ing of using Marine Amphibious Ready Group—One, which was then in the Atlantic north of Bermuda with the 22nd Marine Am-phibious Unit (MAU), a nineteen-hundred-man force headed for Lebanon on a routine rotation of the Marine battalion landing team there.

Late that day, after the message arrived from Prime Minister Adams of Barbados urging military action, planning began for full-scale intervention. That night, the 22nd MAU was ordered to head south and take up station five hundred miles north of Grenada. No reason was given for the change in destination, but it could not have been hard to surmise: News stations were reporting regu-larly about upheaval on the island; rumors were circulating that the Grenadians were mobilizing two thousand reservists to augment one thousand five hundred regular soldiers and six hundred armed Cubans; and the Joint Chiefs of Staff began pressuring McDonald to use both sets of forces, Marines and Major General Richard Scholtes's special operations teams from JSOC.[15]

The MAU commander, Colonel James P. Faulkner, guessed that his unit might be committed in a "permissive evacuation," but he had no information regarding the number or location of the poten-tial evacuees, nor did he or the amphibious squadron commander have any maps of Grenada.[16] Shortly after midnight, Atlantic Com-mand also directed the Second Fleet flotilla built around the aircraft carrier *Independence* and its battle group to steam for Dominica.[17]

At about four o'clock the next morning, October 21, George Shultz and National Security Adviser Bud McFarlane, who had assumed his job only four days before, had awakened President Reagan and urged him to consider military intervention. Reagan ratified the order to divert the Marine flotilla toward Grenada.[18]

Early the same morning on Barbados, an emergency meeting of the Organization of Eastern Caribbean States (OECS) voted to ask Barbados, Jamaica, and the United States to send a multinational peacekeeping force to Grenada. Sir Paul Scoon, the governor general of Grenada (which technically was still a member of the British Commonwealth), asked the organization to free his country from Grenada's new Revolutionary Military Council.[19] The OECS sent its request and Scoon's to Charles A. Gillespie, the ranking U.S. diplomat in the Caribbean, who dispatched both messages from Barbados to the State Department.[20]

Also on the twenty-first, Military Airlift Command told 21st Air Force to forget one of the options it had been working on and concentrate on two others, which entailed an initial assault by JSOC forces with the Rangers to be followed by an 82nd Airborne contingent on October 24. MAC also notified the 21st of a CINCLANT meeting at 1:00 P.M. on the twenty-second. MAC made clear that no aircrews were to be put on standby alert yet. General Patterson immediately sent four officers to Norfolk to work with LantCom's planning staff. They arrived in Norfolk at 2:30 A.M., October 22.

There was only one secure telephone in the 21st Air Force command post at the time. Patterson recalls that "most of the information between Norfolk and McGuire had to be transmitted via off-base telephone booths [using] lots of quarters."

In the early-morning hours of that Friday, McFarlane and Shultz awakened Reagan again to inform him that six nations from the Organization of Eastern Caribbean States had asked the United States to intervene militarily and restore democracy to Grenada. Reagan quickly acceded and asked McFarlane how long the Pentagon would need to prepare a rescue mission. McFarlane said the Joint Chiefs of Staff believed it could be done in forty-eight hours. Reagan said, "Do it."[21]

I was not privy to any of this turmoil until the night of October 20. No after-action reports or official histories of Urgent Fury agree on just what happened in the following thirteen days, or exactly when various events occurred, or who did what. Autobiographies by some senior participants are at odds in significant details as are the two official histories from the Joint Chiefs of Staff Historical Office, even though both were published in the same year. I believe I have reconstructed the operation as faithfully as can be done from the historical records now available; by cross-checking my own recollections with key players; and through access to the unpublished, handwritten, or tape-recorded after-action notes of many of those at the center of the operation. But it was a chaotic sequence of events, so convoluted and entangled that getting it all straight seems impossible. Operation Urgent Fury became the military equivalent of a Japanese Kabuki dance created by three or four choreographers speaking different languages, all working independently of one another.

When the Joint Chiefs began contemplating military action, I was at home resting up from the semiannual Capabilities Demonstration which the Joint Special Operations Command at Fort Bragg—formed in 1980 to command missions of all of the nation's special mission units—puts on for the U.S. military brass, senior State Department officials, and select higher-ups from foreign governments or their embassies in Washington. I was watching Thursday-night football on TV the evening of October 20 when I got a phone call from the operations desk saying that Major General Dick Scholtes wanted to see me as soon as possible in Joint Special Operations Command headquarters. I arrived about 10:00 P.M. at the JSOC secure compound. General Scholtes was huddled with several of his planners, looking at some maps of the Caribbean and one of the overhead photos of Grenada that Reagan had shown on TV the previous spring. I was surprised that JSOC didn't have more current imagery of an island that the president only months before had called a threat to the security of the Western Hemisphere. Headquarters also had a real-time readout facility for our reconnaissance satellites, which can easily find a soccer ball or read a license plate from outer space,[22] but the island was too covered by clouds on October 20 to provide a good look.

Scholtes told us he had received a call on the secure phone in his quarters at 9:00 P.M. from Army General Jack Vessey, chairman of the Joint Chiefs of Staff. Vessey had ordered him to be in Washington at six o'clock the next morning with a plan to capture Grenada, establish a new government, rescue some six hundred American students of a medical school on the island, and evacuate four hundred other foreigners. Vessey had told him the operation would be launched in four or five days. JSOC, the chairman added, would be the "supported command." We would not only lead the parade, but would actually be in charge of it. There was no mention of Atlantic Command.[23]

In short order, I was huddled with the key planners and commanders—Army Colonel Bill Palmer, JSOC's head of current operations, and his deputy, Lieutenant Colonel Dick Pack; Marine Corps Lieutenant Colonel John Blankenship, head of JSOC's J-5 or plans section; and Navy Commander Andy Anderson, who worked in JSOC's current operations section; Colonel Sherm Williford, Delta Force's commander; Lieutenant Colonel Wes Taylor, commander of the 1st Ranger Battalion from Hunter Army Airfield, Georgia, and Lieutenant Colonel Carl Hagler, commanding the 2nd Ranger Battalion from Fort Lewis, Washington; plus Navy Captain Robert A. Gormly, commander of SEAL Team Six.

The plan we drafted was simple, the way we always tried to keep things. Men from my combat control team, accompanied by a few men from SEAL Team Six, would make the preliminary reconnaissance and surveillance. JSOC would use the 1st Ranger Battalion with a combat control team attached to seize Point Salines, the main airport on the southwest end of the island; and the 2nd Ranger Battalion would seize Pearls airfield on the opposite, northeast side. Delta Force would rescue precious cargo, our euphemism for hostages, from Fort Richmond prison. We set H-hour, when the operation was to commence, for 2:00 A.M. That was standard JSOC doctrine, to conduct all its operations in the dark of night. By 6:00 A.M. our work would be completed, and conventional forces flown in from the United States would take over as we disappeared from the island.[24]

The plan began to come unglued within hours. At 2:00 A.M., the director of operations or J-3 of the Joint Staff called to tell General Scholtes that the commander in chief of U.S. Atlantic Command (CINCLANT and LantCom) would be the supported command and that JSOC would support him. The J-3 also told Scholtes that the operation might be launched a lot sooner, in seventy-two hours. He was ordered to be in Norfolk in the morning with his planning cell, instead of going to the Pentagon, and to brief Admiral Wesley L. McDonald, CINCLANT, on our concept of operations. Scholtes told me I should get to Norfolk in his place with Pack, Blankenship, and Anderson. We flew there on a CH-47 helicopter from Fort Bragg's Simmons Army Airfield.

At 2:30 A.M., JSOC notified Delta Force's deputy commander, Lieutenant Colonel L. H. Bucky Burruss, that the unit would rescue the medical students at True Blue campus near the end of Point Salines airfield. At 3:00 A.M., Lieutenant Colonel Wes Taylor was told that his men from the 1st Ranger Battalion would seize Point Salines airfield and assist in rescuing American citizens. He was told the operation might go in seventy-two hours, but not to advise anyone of the forthcoming mission. Both Taylor and Hagler were allowed to return to their home stations that evening.

At 7:00 A.M. on Friday, October 21, our planning cell began our meeting with Admiral McDonald and McDonald's staff. This was the first time JSOC and Atlantic Command had ever planned anything together. Problems surfaced immediately.[25]

For one thing, LantCom had almost no intelligence about the military situation in Grenada—only wildly conflicting information that was useless. Over the next three days the Joint Staff and Defense Intelligence Agency would supply seven different estimates of the size of the threat and five different estimates of likely enemy resolve, from "the Cubans are not likely to interfere militarily" and "the People's Revolutionary Army on Grenada is ineffectual" to "the Grenadians will mount a determined resistance but there will be little resistance from the Cuban construction workers." The DIA's final assessment was that the Cuban "military advisors are lightly armed and a poorly trained adversary."[26] Atlantic Command, and especially Admiral McDonald, were even more blasé: The day before the invasion, McDonald told key commanders, "Don't worry [about the Grenadian army]. When the army sees we're Americans, they'll give up." Of antiaircraft emplacements around our key targets, his briefers said, "Don't worry. The gunners are poorly trained and don't represent a real threat." Of the Cuban construction workers, LantCom advised, "Don't worry. They're not going to fight."[27]

Seven of LantCom's eight D-day targets were assigned to Scholtes's special operations forces; the only Marine Corps objective at that time was to seize the town of Grenville on the island's northeast coast.[28] JSOC had never conducted an exercise with LantCom, and the command had almost no knowledge of JSOC's capabilities or standard operating procedures. Discord ensued: Lant-Com wanted H-hour to be at first light, 5:00 A.M. Admiral McDonald's staff felt that the 22nd Marine Amphibious Unit "could not operate in the dark." Scholtes stood firm that H-hour had to be 2:00 A.M.[29]

I stayed with McDonald's planners as planners from Military Airlift Command, Tactical Air Command, and even Strategic Air Command were starting to arrive. At this stage, security restrictions had the operation on such "close hold" that other intelligence-gathering agencies had no time to redirect or place assets on the island.[30] General Vessey later called the lack of intelligence "inexcusable."[31] But that was largely a self-inflicted wound caused by his own edicts. It seems inconceivable that the National Security Agency would not have been alerted to the operation; it is the nation's premier source of signals intelligence, probably the richest source of intelligence on islands dependent on international phone calls or radio traffic for timely communication.

Command-and-control arrangements proved troubling as well.

The Caribbean fell under Atlantic Command's area of responsibility, and the command had contingency plans in place for rescue operations in the Caribbean, but under control of headquarters, U.S. Caribbean Forces, in Key West, Florida. All of those plans depended on forces from the Army's XVIII Airborne Corps, principally the 82nd Airborne and 101st Air Assault Divisions.[32] Those plans were officially adopted by the Joint Chiefs of Staff as Operational Plan 2360.[33] In mid-1981, however, LantCom had conducted a large joint exercise in which Marines and Rangers (but no other Army units) landed on a small Caribbean island to practice a rescue of a group of American citizens; that experience strongly influenced McDonald's concept for organizing the Grenada operation.[34]

General Vessey advised McDonald on October 20 to plan on using Marines, special operations forces, and an airborne division—all necessary because of uncertainty about the size and location of enemy forces, the diversity of terrain on the island, and the need to overwhelm enemy forces before they could take Americans hostage, as Iranian militants had done in 1979. McDonald decided to name Vice Admiral Joseph Metcalf III, commander of LantCom's Second Fleet, as commander of Combined Joint Task Force 120.[35] Like Atlantic Command's, Metcalf's staff was principally Navy, but with even less familiarity with special operations work.

Metcalf would control the operations of five subordinate task forces. One was the Marine amphibious task force, to be known as Task Force 124; Metcalf would use the *Guam* as his flagship. Task Group 20-5 would be made up of the *Independence* and its battle group, which Atlantic Command soon ordered to take up station forty miles north of Grenada. It would provide close air support and naval gunfire support. Task Force 123 would be composed of JSOC, the Rangers, and aircrews from the Army's Task Force 160. A fourth group, Task Force 121, would consist of the division ready force of the 82nd Airborne Division, its 2nd Brigade commanded by Colonel Stephen Silvasy; later it would be reinforced by the 3rd Brigade. A fifth task force of eight F-15 fighters and four E-3A airborne surveillance and warning aircraft, Task Force 126, would

operate out of Puerto Rico under the command of Air Force Brigadier General Richard L. Meyer. It would monitor Cuban air activity
and block any attempt to interfere with the invasion.[36]

There was also a sixth task force, the Caribbean Peacekeeping
Force, roughly three hundred strong, to demonstrate regional soli-
darity with the operation.[37] It would not report to Metcalf, but operate "in support" of his combined joint task force. Indeed, on the
Joint Chiefs of Staff organization chart for the invasion, the Caribbean Peacekeeping Force reported to nobody. That would nearly
lead to fatal consequences.

On the night of October 20, General Scholtes was not aware of
any of these command arrangements, even though an official JCS
history of the operation would claim in 1997 that "all the units that
would participate in the invasion had been alerted" that day. It
noted, however, that "strict operational security severely limited those
who were told about the upcoming operation" and complicated pre-
invasion coordination.

Summoned to a planning conference which Admiral Metcalf
called in Norfolk on the twenty-second, the history noted, some
unit representatives "left the conference unsure of their roles" while
still others "were unaware of the conference." The net effect of the
lack of coordination and communication was that the invasion unfolded as if the United States had four or five different offensive
teams on the field simultaneously, none of whom had ever seen the
others' playbooks. Some key players never made it to the huddle as
the operation approached its two-minute warning.

By this time, some of our men had become aware that action
was imminent. "Ranger Rex" Evitts, now a technical sergeant, had
just put in his retirement papers, moved his family, turned in all of
his equipment, and was on terminal leave—living out of his pickup
truck parked outside our trailers by JSOC's main gate. When Master
Sergeant Mike Lampe hinted to Rex that an operation might be unfolding and suggested that he delay his terminal leave, Rex asked
Chief Master Sergeant Kiraly to withdraw his retirement papers.
Evitts scurried to check his gear back out and ended up joining

his buddies in their assault on Point Salines. That evening, at a CINCLANT senior staff meeting, H-hour was established for 0800 hours Zulu time (a universal time formerly called Greenwich Mean Time). The Marines were not pleased by that decision as it would mean assaulting in daylight.[38] The "execute order" to commence operations early on Tuesday, the twenty-fifth, was transmitted from the JCS to LantCom at 10:45 that night, October 22. Much of the planning was still under way.

Prior to that ill-fated planning conference, members of the Barbados Defense Force had penetrated Grenada twice to obtain current intelligence. The information they acquired was passed to U.S. officials, but the specific units tasked to land never received them.

About 9:00 A.M. on the twenty-second, Captain Robert A. Gormly of SEAL Team Six was called and told that he should get to the command center at LantCom. He arrived an hour later with his operations officer and found me huddled with planners from Naval Special Warfare Group Two. I told him of JSOC's mission—go to Grenada and rescue students—and that his mission would be to make sure that my combat control team got to Salines airfield ahead of H-hour to collect pre-assault intelligence and control the Air Force AC-130 Spectre gunships that would support the assault. We had to find out if the airfield was defended, and what with. Was the landing strip clear? Was there enough space on the apron and tarmac to unload transport aircraft? How fast could we clear the field for more inbound aircraft?

LantCom, General Scholtes, and Gormly had decided that the SEALs' role was to insert my team by having us join up with sixteen SEALs and two Boston Whalers (eighteen-foot-long, open patrol boats named after their manufacturer, each with two powerful outboard motors). They would parachute—and their Whalers would be air-dropped—into the Caribbean far from Grenada but near the destroyer USS *Sprague*, with which my men and I and our SEAL detail would rendezvous ahead of time. Why my team couldn't have used the *Sprague*'s smaller Whaler to get to Point Salines was never clear to me, but the insertion was the SEALs' responsibility, not mine, and, to my later regret, I didn't challenge their plan. Lant-Com's planners had decided that the boat drop zone would be forty miles at sea with a nontactical drop in daylight hours from an altitude of twelve hundred feet.

Gormly found out that the *Sprague* was in nearby St. Vincent so its crew could get some liberty ashore. He asked for a covert military aircraft to take his men and my team there to link up with the ship. His request was turned down for reasons of "operational security." LantCom was afraid that word might leak of the pending operation.[39] (That concern was absurd, since Atlantic Command had already been alerted, I learned later, that a joint CIA-Army team was trying to insert a CIA informant by helicopter from Barbados, 150 miles away.[40]) Gormly was told he had to find another aircraft to move six men from his team and four from Det 1 MACOS.

I asked LantCom's planners why we needed a clandestine insertion at all. Why couldn't I fly to Barbados on a commercial plane, take one of the scheduled interisland flights to the neighboring Union Island, just north of Grenada, and take a boat to Grenada, like any other island-hopping tourist? Then I could sashay over to the beach near Point Salines airfield; scope the situation out like any man hoping to find a Victoria's Secret model; and telephone the dope back to somebody in pidgin English (or swim out to a CIA or Navy ship just happening to pass nearby). Admiral McDonald's planners looked at me as if I were some jokester from *Saturday Night Live*.

Soon after Gormly arrived at JSOC headquarters at two o'clock that afternoon, he learned that SEAL Team Six had been given three additional targets. Gormly decided he should lead the assault on one of them, the governor general's mansion, to rescue Scoon and take him to the main radio station, where he would broadcast word to the islanders to cooperate with the forces restoring their democracy. Withdrawing from my mission, Gormly assigned a lieutenant to replace him.

Earlier that morning, on Saturday, October 22, Delta Force had been told that its major target would be Fort Frederick, headquarters for the Cuban military leaders on the island and the spot where key political prisoners were being held. The unit's A Squadron was assigned that target. Delta was given two other targets: the telephone exchange and the downtown radio station. B Squadron, with a Ranger company attached to it, was assigned the latter missions and given a follow-on target, Calivigny Barracks, about eight miles northeast of Point Salines, which was thought to house a small Cuban military contingent. About seven o'clock that morning, the commander of the 1st Ranger Battalion at Hunter Army Airfield near Savannah, Georgia, Lieutenant Colonel Taylor, was ordered back to Fort Bragg. Before leaving, he briefed his executive officer and key staff with what sketchy information he had on the operation, but instructed them that the plan was "close hold" and that the troops were not to be alerted. Lieutenant Colonel Hagler was also ordered back from Fort Lewis, Washington, to Fort Bragg. Neither commander had a map of Grenada, and we had no good photos because cloud cover still obscured the island.

After my reconnaissance, two Ranger battalions in fourteen MC- and C-130s would seize the airfield at Point Salines with one of my combat control teams, preferably by air landing but with parachute assault as a second option. One battalion would secure the area and evacuate the students from St. George's. The other would assist in securing the airfield and then move by foot to Calivigny Barracks. At the same time, the Marines would assault Pearls airport and the town of Grenville. Concurrently, SEAL elements of Task Force 123 would conduct three operations: seize the island's main radio transmitter; secure Governor General Paul Scoon in his residence at Government House until he could be evacuated; and seize the prison at Richmond Hill to protect any political prisoners who might be there.[41] Units from the 82nd Airborne would arrive by dawn and relieve all JSOC forces. Before the day ended (October 22), the plan changed again and now called for the 2nd Ranger Battalion to also seize Pearls airfield, while the Marines would seize Grenville.

Det 1 MACOS had twenty-one men permanently assigned by this time (sixteen combat controllers and five support airmen), but

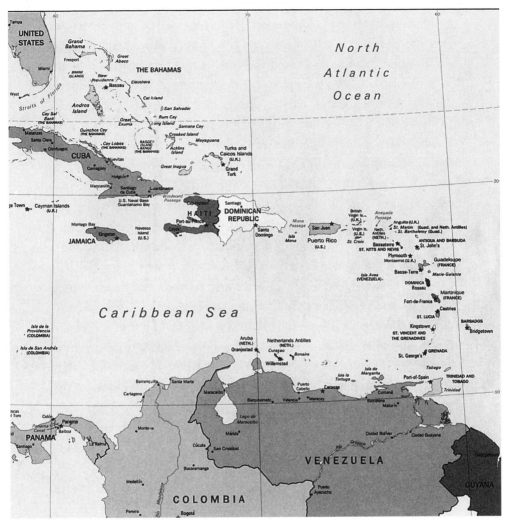

CENTRAL INTELLIGENCE AGENCY

we requested augmentation from the 1st Special Operations Wing's combat control team. Lieutenant Jeff Buckmelter and Sergeants Rex Evitts and Doug Brown would hit Point Salines first with the 1st Ranger Battalion's airfield-clearing team. Sergeant Bob Kelly was attached to Wes Taylor and the 1st Ranger Battalion's Tactical Operations Center. Master Sergeant Mike Lampe, Technical Sergeant Rick Caffee, and Staff Sergeants John Scanlon and Rob Griffin were assigned to the runway-clearing team for the 2nd Ranger Battalion's assault at Pearls airfield. Our senior noncommissioned officer, Chief Master Sergeant Nick Kiraly, and Technical Sergeant Rex Wollmann from the combat control team for Hurlburt's 1st Special Operations Wing were attached to Delta Force's commander, Colonel Sherm Williford, and his deputy commander, Major Lewis H. "Bucky" Burruss, to set up its Tactical Operations Center at Point Salines and support the takedown of Fort Frederick and Delta's follow-on targets. A key job would be to control air support—especially the AC-130 gunship fires. From the partly obscured satellite photos, Delta Force had noticed an antiaircraft gun positioned next to Fort Frederick but was told that "no resistance is anticipated. . . . The positions probably won't be manned."[42]

At dusk on October 22, Admiral McDonald called: He had to brief the Joint Chiefs of Staff in the tank at seven o'clock the next morning, Sunday, and needed General Scholtes's plan refined by then. That left us with a big quandary: Saturday was the day of JSOC's annual birthday ball, due to start at 7:00 P.M. Attending it would eat into badly needed planning time; not going to it would create too much of a stir. Deciding we could not compromise operational security, most JSOC personnel attended the ball. They scooted out as soon as they could do so without attracting attention.

By 11:15 P.M., my men and I were on our way to St. Vincent and the Sprague. I had three NCOs proficient in water operations, Technical Sergeants Johnny Pantages, Dick West, and Jerry Jones. With us were the SEAL lieutenant and five of his men: Mike Naus, Frank Phillips, Mike Purdy, Mark Stephanovich, and Duane

Miller. Our mission as combat controllers was to reconnoiter the target and call in whatever AC-130 gunship and close air support missions might be required during the assault. My men and I took our individual weapons, the absolute minimum amount of ammunition, navigation aids, and our UHF and VHF radios.

The SEAL lieutenant in charge had been given a tourist map of the island for his operational use, but he was well informed compared to the rest of us. The only maps my team got included one that was about an inch square, on a scale of 1:50,000 (one inch on the map equaling fifty thousand inches on the ground— seven-tenths of a nautical mile). It covered only the southwestern tip of Grenada, the area immediately around Salines airfield. We had also purloined a copy of the overhead photo Scholtes had shown us from Reagan's TV speech and a 1938 hydrographic chart that would be of dubious value, given how quickly beaches change and shoals build up in the Caribbean. We arrived in St. Vincent about midmorning on Sunday, October 23, and were driven to the *Sprague* by ground transport the Navy had arranged. The ship left its dock shortly after noon and steamed for the SEALs' drop area.[43]

Meanwhile, JSOC's commanders and planners had returned to "the stockade," as we sometimes referred to the JSOC command center, as soon as they could gracefully leave the Saturday-night ball, and by 1:00 A.M. on Sunday an entirely new round of planning had begun. SEAL Team Six now had four missions: the recon and surveillance mission at Point Salines with me; rescuing the governor general and his wife; and taking down two additional targets on the east end of the island. Another SEAL team from the East Coast would scout out Pearls airfield on the other side of the island.

At six-thirty Sunday morning, Marine Lieutenant Colonel G. W. T. "Digger" O'Dell departed for the helicopter carrier USS *Guam* with a radio team from the Joint Communications Unit. They would serve as the JSOC liaison. It took O'Dell until ten-thirty Sunday night to reach the ship. Once there, he found that no one aboard had ever heard of JSOC. They thought he was from the State Department. But they agreed to put him on the sixth deck, the highest point on the ship, where he could access the right satellite with his SatCom ultra-high-frequency radio.[44]

The *Guam* had sailed from Norfolk on October 17 with two thousand Marines bound for Lebanon. After it received orders to change course for the south, turn off all electronic emitters (radios, radars), and position itself near Grenada, the unit readied itself for a "supporting operation" in what the Marines thought would be a noncombatant evacuation. Contrary to LantCom's earlier insistence that Marines "can't operate at night," its pilots were fully qualified to fly with night-vision goggles; the unit's planners requested an H-hour of 4:00 A.M., well before daylight would begin breaking.

A few hours after midnight on Sunday, October 23, the Joint Chiefs of Staff received word that the Marine barracks at the Beirut airport in Lebanon had been bombed, killing hundreds of Marines. Within hours, news of that tragedy triggered a new concept for operations in Grenada, new missions for everyone, and a new command-and-control structure.

Complicating matters was the fact that there was no one focal point for planning the operation. General Vessey had a previously scheduled speech to make in Chicago on October 21, and he had decided to keep that appointment lest a change in his schedule signal that a military operation might be imminent. Admiral James Watkins, the chief of naval operations, became acting JCS chairman in Vessey's absence, due to the arcane practice of rotating service chiefs in that position whenever the chairman was traveling. After October 23, most of General Vessey's time was taken up with Beirut. Marine Corps Commandant General P. X. Kelley implored him to let Marine forces have a role in the invasion. Most of his colleagues supported Kelley's plea, and, according to the Joint Staff History Office, "Vessey drew a boundary dividing Grenada into northern (Marine) and southern (Army) sectors."[45] For the next few days, most of the chairman's work on Grenada was handled by Vice Admiral Art Moreau, assistant to the chairman (and essentially his alter ego). But Army Lieutenant Generals Jack N. Merritt, the director of the Joint Staff, and Richard L. Prillaman, the director of operations, shared responsibility for directing and coordinating the Joint Staff work to plan the invasion.[46]

The *Guam* was ordered to take the 22nd MAU to the northeast side of the island. But LantCom's liaison officers didn't reach the ship until ten o'clock on Monday night, the twenty-fourth, to brief Task Force 124 on its mission. The Marines learned that they would not be doing a noncombatant evacuation, but would make a heliborne assault to seize Pearls airfield and an amphibious landing to control the town of Grenville on the eastern side of the island. No one told them their mission would be executed simultaneously with several special operations missions or with an Army assault on Point Salines. And the unit's planners still had no maps of the island.

No one, in fact, had any usable maps of Grenada—neither the planners nor the operators. Seven months after President Reagan had twice warned on national TV that the Cuban-sponsored, ten-thousand-foot runway at Point Salines posed a threat to hemispheric security; four days after Prime Minister Bishop had been assassinated; and two days after Reagan had been awakened in the middle of the night, the National Security Council and the Defense Department had yet to ask the Defense Mapping Agency to produce one tactical map of the island. Nor were any satellite photo maps provided.

Strangely, the two official Joint Chiefs of Staff histories of Operation Urgent Fury, both published in 1997, make no mention of the map shortage except for one sentence about Navy A-7 Corsairs attacking what was thought to be a Cuban command post at Fort Frederick: "Lacking military maps or other means of identifying a building next to the fort as a hospital, Corsair pilots bombed the building at 1535."[47] A Navy report admitted that "high-quality maps did not arrive on Grenada until the operation was largely over."[48]

About the same time O'Dell had left for the *Guam* that Sunday morning, Gormly's Blue assault team left on their eight-hour flight to Grenada in two C-130s with two Boston Whalers and sixteen SEALs aboard.

At seven-thirty that morning, the commander of the 1st Ranger Battalion ordered his executive officer to assemble the battalion and prepare it for deployment. Its mission was unchanged: Seize Point Salines and rescue hostage medical students at the True Blue campus. The battalion planned for an air land seizure with parachute assault as its worst-case option. As Gormly and Sherm Williford of Delta Force began discussing their targets, planning on an H-hour of 2:00 A.M., Tuesday, October 25, Gormly ordered his Blue assault team to move to Bragg and go into isolation.

At half past noon that Sunday, October 23, thirty-eight hours before H-hour, General Scholtes left the Pentagon for Fort Bragg, reeling with the latest news: All of JSOC's plans were null and void because the Joint Chiefs had adopted a new CINCLANT plan: a coordinated assault, Marines in the north and JSOC in the south. No joint commander was appointed to coordinate the ground elements. D-day was still set for Tuesday, October 25, with H-hour at 1:30 A.M.

The Ranger missions changed: Now the 2nd Battalion would deploy to the south. Targets for SEAL Team Six and Delta Force changed again. The SEALs would now secure the radio station and a diesel fuel pumping facility. These mission changes changed the entire airflow, all of which had to be resolved in less than forty hours.[49] It was hard to argue about the changes with anybody because the changes were coming so fast and from so many directions.

From my perspective on the *Sprague*, the invasion seemed a long way off, more than forty-eight hours away. Dusk fell as the two C-130s started approaching. Plans called for a daylight drop, but someone had failed to account for a change in time zones. All military planning is usually done on so-called Zulu time, a hypothetical, universal time zone that is not tied to any particular region, but Operation Urgent Fury was planned on local time, eastern daylight time, also called Atlantic standard time, which applies in Grenada.

But as happens every fall, at 2:00 A.M. on October 24, sixteen hours before the scheduled drop, the Atlantic time zone ceased to coincide with eastern daylight saving time, and the drop schedule "fell back" one hour. Thus, the SEALs' daylight drop became a night drop, and given how fast twilight disappears near the equator, it was suddenly pitch black with no moon.[50] Neither aircrew had done a boat drop before, but I didn't think that was any big deal. A drop is a drop. What goes out the aft ramp normally doesn't matter to the pilot.

The planes' instructions were to approach the landing zone over the *Sprague*, marked by a red beacon atop its mast, make a 180-degree turn to the left, and then drop their Whalers between the *Sprague* and one of its Boston Whalers, which would display a white beacon. The trail plane was to drop its boat as soon as it saw the lead aircraft drop its Whaler. Sergeants Pantages and West were in the *Sprague*'s Boston Whaler, anticipating the recovery of the sixteen SEALs parachuting from the C-130s while the planes dropped their Boston Whalers. But squalls and winds had come up just as the planes reached their drop zone. When the lead aircraft dropped its SEALs and its Boston Whaler, the second C-130 was still on its upwind leg but about half a mile from his computed drop point. It had yet to turn into its final approach and its radar spotted the squall ahead, but not in time to warn the lead aircraft. Thus, the first plane dropped the boat anyway—extracted by a drogue chute—and its SEALs jumped, too. The boat disappeared as it struck a wall of water that looked like a tidal wave. Four SEALs disappeared; Machinist's Mate First Class Kenneth Butcher, Quartermaster First Class Kevin Lundberg, Hull Technician First Class Stephen Morris, and Senior Chief Engineman Robert Schamberger were lost. I learned years later that SEAL Team Six had never before dropped its Boston Whalers at night and, in fact, had never done *any* night water parachuting.[51] The second plane dropped its Whaler just as it turned onto its base leg, well before its final approach, and its SEALs jumped as well.[52]

Some of the twelve surviving SEALs swam to the *Sprague*, others clambered into the other Boston Whaler, which West and Jones from my team had recovered, and we all began a long, fruitless, exhausting search in rough seas and total darkness for the missing SEALs. In this instance, concern for their lost comrades overrode the SEALs' focus on the mission. Eventually, the *Sprague* told us it would continue searching. The SEALs who had survived the C-130 drop headed off with me and my team members to reconnoiter Point Salines in the *Sprague's* Whaler, towing our Zodiac. We were about thirty miles away when a Grenadian patrol boat arrived in the area and started panning with its searchlight. It became evident that our recon mission should be postponed. We had trouble finding the *Sprague* but stumbled upon the USS *Caron*, a signals intelligence ship no one had been briefed about. The *Caron*, however, refused to pick us up. We finally found the *Sprague* and were welcomed aboard. The SEAL team immediately radioed Gormly and asked for another Whaler drop so they could make a second attempt to get us to Point Salines.[53] (Standard operating procedure for the SEALs called for using Boston Whalers in pairs; but when the SEALs boarded the *Sprague*, the ship had to tow their Whaler because it had no way of lifting the Whaler aboard, and it capsized in heavy seas. Thus, we were down to one Whaler.)

I radioed General Scholtes to tell him I had been able only to observe that there was a lot of activity in and around the airfield. He commented that he knew that, making it all the more important that we get in there as soon as possible.

Plans for the invasion were still in a state of flux, however. That Sunday night, the twenty-third, Brigadier General Patterson finally got permission to fly to Norfolk with a small staff to join the four 21st Air Force planners already there. He arrived at 10:00 P.M., but found no one to talk to. Everyone had scattered to the four winds to do their individual, frantic planning. A meeting of all flag and general officers was called for seven o'clock the following morning, however. Most arrived on time, but Admirals McDonald and Metcalf didn't show up until around 8:00 A.M. McDonald announced that he had just come from Washington and a meeting with President Reagan. He continued, "President Reagan said it is a 'Go.' Just don't let me down." McDonald's announcement was immediately followed by what Patterson recalls was a "cold feet" discussion: Due to lack of intelligence, JSOC wanted a twenty-four-hour slip in H-hour. That view seemed about to prevail when the State Department representative stood up and expressed concern about the tenuous nature of the coalition of Caribbean nations; he opined that it probably couldn't hold together for another twenty-four hours. "Besides," he asked, "how could the world's strongest military power need any more time against what is probably the world's weakest?"[54] As a compromise, H-hour was slipped to 9:00 A.M., Greenwich Mean Time—6:00 A.M. in Grenada.

Admiral Metcalf had to leave the meeting with his staff to fly to Barbados via C-9 so he could grab a helicopter to the USS *Guam*. Patterson hurriedly introduced him to Colonel Jon Vilensons, the C-141 assistant director of operations at Charleston, and told Metcalf Vilensons would be going with him, working for Patterson as Metcalf's MAC liaison officer.

The same night Patterson had flown to Norfolk, Major General H. Norman Schwarzkopf, commander of the 24th Infantry Division at Fort Stewart, Georgia, was informed that he had been named as an adviser to the Navy's Admiral Metcalf, who commanded the Grenada invasion force—an operation Schwarzkopf had no idea was about to get under way. General Vessey had become concerned that the chain of command for the operation was dominated by naval personnel, so Schwarzkopf was told to be in Norfolk at seven the next morning. There he met Metcalf for the first time, an officer he later described as "wiry, feisty." By then, invasion was only nineteen hours away, but Admiral McDonald told everyone there was "the strong possibility that we won't have to carry it out . . . we are told it is very likely that the rebels will back down." Reminded of the lack of intelligence, McDonald burst out, "All you're going to face is a bunch of Grenadians. They're going to fall apart the minute they see our combat power."[55] Schwarzkopf with a "staff" of two majors and Metcalf left for Barbados immediately after the meeting and arrived there midafternoon on the twenty-fourth. They were greeted at the airport by a large contingent of the press. Word had obviously leaked out that U.S. military action was imminent. By 5:30 P.M., Metcalf and Schwarzkopf were aboard the *Guam* about to eat a turkey dinner when Metcalf's chief of staff announced, "It's a go. We're going. H-hour has been bumped back one hour. It's a go at 0500."[56]

About the time Schwarzkopf was told on Sunday night to head for Norfolk, General Scholtes was notified that he had a 6:00 A.M. meeting in Norfolk. Early Monday morning, Scholtes met again with Admiral McDonald and his staff and for the first time was informed that Admiral Metcalf would be the Joint Task Force commander. That meant that JSOC would be supporting Metcalf. A State Department representative handed Scholtes an hour-by-hour plan, written three and a half weeks earlier, for seizing the island. The plan, cleared and approved by the White House, listed targets and their priorities. It said that Richmond Hill prison must be the primary target because that's where the island's legitimate leaders would likely be held. JSOC had listed the prison as a secondary target and had not focused that much of its intelligence collection requirements on it. The fact that Prime Minister Bishop and his key ministers were now dead did not alter the nearly month-old invasion plan or affect LantCom's view of it. The surprise State Department plan caused all of Delta Force's targets to change instantly. JSOC was handed one other mission: to take three State Department personnel to the governor's mansion to deliver a letter to Governor General Scoon. Scholtes also learned that a three-hundred-man, multinational "peacekeeping force" would land by air at H-hour plus two hours, the first he had ever heard of such an outfit.

As Scholtes reviewed the operation's new targets, SEAL Team Six lost its target in the center of the island but retained the radio station and governor general missions, plus its reconnaissance and surveillance mission with me. The SEALs ended up planning for a total of ten targets, but in fact would execute only three of them, plus the recon and surveillance mission.

During Scholtes's meeting with McDonald, the State Department's liaison officer to JSOC told Gormly that the Cubans on the island would probably stay in their barracks as a result of an "informal agreement."[57] That clearly meant that any hope of surprise was a pipe dream. Unbeknownst to us at the time, moreover, Fidel Castro had already dispatched the former head of the Cuban military mission to Grenada, Colonel Pedro Tortoló Comas, to organize resistance.[58] During that morning's planning session, H-hour was changed from 1:30 A.M. to 5:00 A.M. to accommodate the Marines. Gormly and Williford both protested.[59]

At 2:00 P.M., the Joint Chiefs of Staff briefed Reagan on final details of the impending operation, which they said was scheduled to start at 9:00 A.M., Greenwich Mean Time,[60] or 6:00 A.M. in Grenada.

As if rushing to collect frequent flier miles in two-hundred-mile increments, Scholtes flew back to Fort Bragg, and between 3:00 and 5:30 P.M. the Rangers briefed him on their plan to seize the airfield, hopefully by air landing but with a backup plan for a parachute assault. They were interrupted by a secure phone call for Scholtes. It was Atlantic Command confirming that H-hour had been moved from 1:30 A.M. on the twenty-fifth to 5:00 A.M. Scholtes approved the Ranger battalion commander's request to parachute from five hundred feet of altitude if forced to use the parachute option. The 1st Ranger Battalion was the only participating unit whose mission had not changed from the start of planning for the operation.[61]

After his Norfolk meeting with McDonald and Metcalf, Patterson spent the rest of the day "trying to keep up with the ever-changing assault plans."[62] One thing became crystal clear to him. No one had done any follow-on planning. Once the green light was turned on for an airdrop, what about medical evacuation? Resupply of ammunition and rations? Where would fuel come from? Patterson knew that "Murphy's law would be alive and well" and that the C-130s involved in the assault would be short on fuel, but he was told he could not plan on using Barbados. Puerto Rico was too far from Grenada, so he decided to use Barbados anyway. By late afternoon, Patterson had been designated as commander, airlift forces, for

Urgent Fury. He left Norfolk by a C-21 Learjet for Pope Air Force Base and arrived at Fort Bragg at 7:30 P.M. Sunday. There he met Brigadier General Edsel Field, JSOC's deputy commander, who had previously replaced Patterson as commander of the 317th Tactical Airlift Wing at Pope Air Force Base. Patterson found that the Pope Air Force Base, the JSOC compound, and Fort Bragg were all "in a high state of frenzy." Patterson told Field that they needed to get started with follow-on planning and asked him to cut eight C-130s from the assault force to land at Barbados for Patterson's use as intratheater airlift. The two shook hands on that arrangement.

To illustrate the confusion evident in the changing invasion plans, the arrival times in Barbados of the three giant C-5A transports on which Task Force 160's Blackhawk helicopters were carried were changed like eggs being scrambled by a short-order cook. The plane's crews were first told to arrive at 5:00 A.M., 5:10 A.M., and 5:20 A.M., respectively. A JSOC representative then changed that to "no earlier than 7:00 A.M."[63] Then the helicopter task force commander stated the planes had to be in Barbados by 5:58 A.M. Another JSOC change relayed from General Field told them to arrive at 6:40, 6:50, and 7:00, respectively.

That evening at about 8:00 P.M., Reagan met in the White House family quarters with McFarlane, Weinberger, Shultz, and Vessey to brief five members of the congressional leadership on plans for the rescue mission.[64]

JSOC forces departed Pope Air Force Base (next to Fort Bragg) shortly after 10:00 P.M. Monday, and the Rangers launched for Grenada from Hunter Army Airfield and Fort Lewis, Washington, some in C-141 Starlifters and others in slower MC-130 Combat Talons and C-130s, while aviators from the Army's Task Force 160 flew to Barbados from Fort Campbell, Kentucky, in wide-bodied C-5A Galaxies with their partially disassembled, small, armed MH-6 Little Birds and MH-60 Blackhawk helicopters. The planes took off from Pope Air Force Base, North Carolina; Hunter Army Airfield, Georgia; Fort Campbell, Kentucky; and Fort Lewis, Washington, on flights that took at least seven hours to Barbados, flying circuitous routes in order to nail their proposed arrival times. Throughout that time, the troops were crammed in uncomfortable web seats loaded down with parachutes, weapons, ammunition, and rucksacks. Delta Force planners and aircrews from Task Force 160 planned their assault on Richmond Hill prison in the cargo bays of MC-130s en route to Grenada and C-5As en route to Barbados.

About four-thirty that afternoon, another Boston Whaler had been dropped, this time only fifteen miles from Point Salines. The boat hit the water safely. We waited until well after darkness set in, and about 10:00 P.M. Grenada time, my recon and surveillance team launched from the *Sprague* again in the recovered Whaler towing an inflatable Zodiac and joined up with the newly air-dropped Whaler. The weather was bad, the sea was rough, and problems with motors on our Whaler required the SEAL team leader to ask the *Sprague* for a close tow to within four miles of the island. We made it to within about a mile of the beach running at high speed when a Grenadian patrol boat approached again. When its searchlight panned in our direction, our coxswains cut the boats' powerful engines. As a result of the sudden stop and heavy seas, the wakes behind the boats came over the transoms, flooding the Whalers and our radios and equipment and shutting down their motors. At this point, we had the Zodiac and two inert Boston Whalers. We transferred to the Zodiac. We spent hours working on the motors, drying the spark plugs, and attempting to get back under way. We drifted seaward about four miles from Point Salines. Daylight was about to break, leaving us little time to complete our reconnaissance in the dark.

By then, I realized the SEALs had lost their satellite communications link and we could no longer talk to JSOC. Whatever recon we might accomplish, even if we made it to shore, would come too late. H-hour approached rapidly, and if we were spotted, it could compromise the assault forces. Continuing the mission was fruitless; we had to abort and return to the *Sprague*. We floundered about until dawn was about to break when—thankfully—this time, the *Caron* picked us up.[65]

Even though we never made it ashore, I had seen enough through my binoculars to tell me that the Cubans and Grenadians at Point Salines were expecting us. I could see vehicle lights headed for the airport and scurrying all over the runway. It was clear that a small airport-seizure team would have to precede the Rangers and provide enough protection for the subsequent planes to land; I radioed that information to "Viking" (General Scholtes) from the *Caron*. (Rick Caffee overheard that message and radioed back to me by UHF, "Don't worry about it, Coach: The B-team has a handle on it. Enjoy floating around in your rubber dinghy.")

Aboard the *Caron*, I heard the island radio station urging people to hurry to the airport to repel the invaders. Scholtes suggested the invasion be delayed twenty-four hours to let us develop better intelligence, give everyone time to settle down and regroup, and hone everyone's plan, but he was turned down.[66] The invasion of Grenada had not yet begun, but already everything had gone wrong—and would quickly get worse. Here, for instance, are the final planning times compared to the actual execution times:[67]

EVENT	PLANNED	ACTUAL
Depart Pope Air Force Base	10:08 P.M.	10:17 P.M.
Arrive Barbados	1:48 A.M.	3:15 A.M.
Helicopter buildup	1 hour at most	2 hours
Depart Barbados	3:48 A.M.	5:15 A.M.
Time on target	5:00 A.M.	6:15 A.M.

Airlifting an assault force thousands of miles is a much more complex operation than flying hundreds of people on an American Airlines 747 from Miami International Airport to Mexico City. Here, for instance, is an example from MAC's then-secret, ten-page "Flow Plan" for getting some of the 160th's helicopters, USAF's AC-130 gunships, and the Rangers in their MC-130 Combat Talons to Grenada. The first day of Urgent Fury would entail 95 preplanned sorties (individual takeoffs and landings) and 117 discrete events involving code words like *Amy* (beginning the airhead assault at

Point Salines), *Sadora* (assaulting the governor general's residence), *Lenore* (securing the Fort Frederick complex), and *Clara* (the assault on the telephone exchange and radio relay station). Plans like this had to be reworked time and again as new scenarios for the invasion were conceived, approved, and then discarded or modified. One of Grenada's first casualties must have been the forest that had to be felled to produce all the paperwork these plans consumed.

The commander of Task Force 160, as it turned out, had never been informed of any 9:00 A.M. H-hour, the one decided upon (using Greenwich Mean Time) at Admiral McDonald's conference in Norfolk the morning of October 24. As the C-5s approached Barbados, one of the pilots asked air traffic control what "those lights to our west" were. Air traffic control replied, "Those are Air Force planes doing reconnaissance over Grenada." So much for operational security!

The first C-5 touched down at 6:46 A.M., two minutes late. The last two landed at 6:48 and 6:58, respectively. It took about half an hour to off-load the helicopters, aircrews, and ammunition; the process went smoothly. The one-hour time for off-loading and building up the MH-60s was not met. The C-5s departed for their return trip to Dover Air Force Base, Delaware, by 5:55 A.M., and the Blackhawks lifted off on their missions with Delta Force and Gormly's SEALs twelve minutes later. General Scholtes announced, "It's about time."

General Patterson had been understandably apprehensive about his decision to use Barbados as a staging base for resupply operations after being told he could not do so. He was relieved, however, to see smiles on the faces of the party that greeted his planes, which included the prime minister, the head of the Barbados Defense Force, and Major General George Crist of the Marine Corps. Patterson's contingent was welcomed with open arms and, since a new terminal had just been opened at the airport, was given free use of the old one.

By that time, the final plan called for Delta Force's B Squadron to assault Richmond Hill prison in six UH-60 helicopters from Task Force 160.[68] Part of the squadron would fast-rope down from two

EXECUTION CHECKLIST			FORMAT FOR RADIO CALLS				
NO #	EVENT/SITUATION	RPT	NET	TO	FROM	CODEWORD	TIME
46	UH-60'S DEPART FSB	M	A	J-17	P-41	LAURIE	0648
47	AC-130 #3 AR #2 COMPLETE	M	A	J-17	L-58	HARRIET	0700
48	AC-130 #2 AR #2 COMPLETE	M	A	J-17	L-57	LILLIAN	0700
49	AC-130 #1 AR #2 COMPLETE	M	A	J-17	L-55	MOLLIE	0700
51	AC-130 #3 ON STATION	M	A	J-17	L-57	VIOLA	0800
52	AC-130 #2 ON STATION	M	A	J-17	L-56	ANGELA	0800
53	AC-130 #1 ON STATION	M	A	J-17	L-55	RHODA	0800
	AIRDROP/AIRLAND AIRFIELD SEIZURE OPTION						
54	MC-130 #1 IFLT AIRDROP COMPLETE	M	A	J-17	F-33	NELLIE	0800
55	MC-130 #2 IFLT AIRDROP COMPLETE	M	A	J-17	F-34	KATHRYN	0800.5
56A	AIRFIELD CLEAR	M	A	J-17	D-95	ADRIENNE	
56	MC-130 #3 IFLT AIRLAND COMPLETE	M	A	J-17	F-35	IMOGENE	0830
57	MC-130 #3 IFLT DEPART AIRFIELD	M	A	J-17	F-35	JACQUELINE	0834
58	C-130 #4 IFLT AIRLAND COMPLETE	M	A	J-17	F-36	STELLA	0837
59	C-130 #4 IFLT DEPART AIRFIELD	M	A	J-17	F-36	BERNICE	0840

TYPES OF REPORTS - M-MANDATORY   X-BY EXCEPTION

SECRET

140

helicopters directly into the prison while the other four aircraft would land just outside the prison in preselected landing zones to set up security and a command-and-control party. The six helicopters would then depart for Point Salines. Concurrently with the assault on Richmond Hill prison, A Squadron from Delta Force would land on or parachute onto Point Salines from the MC-130s carrying the Rangers and then be picked up by the six helos for the assault on Fort Rupert. Meanwhile, AH-6 Little Birds would carry part of Delta Force, with some Rangers attached, to the radio station and telephone exchange.[69]

Besides its aborted recon and surveillance mission, SEAL Team Six had two other jobs. One was to rescue the governor general, being held under house arrest, while delivering three State Department representatives to meet with him. The team was to hold the residence until relieved by Rangers forty-four minutes later. The SEALs' second job was to seize and hold the radio station at Beaujolais on the center of the island's west coast so the governor general could be brought there to talk to his countrymen. That SEAL group would be relieved by Rangers four hours after H-hour. Three UH-60 Blackhawks would fly the SEALs to Grenada, two heading to the governor general's mansion and one to the radio station. The aircraft were crowded and uncomfortable, and the flight took an hour and twenty minutes.

The assault scheme for the governor general's mansion was more complex because the State Department representatives couldn't fast-rope, so a landing zone was needed for them. That's why we called them "strap hangers"—baggage we didn't need taking up space we needed for shooters. We never did find out why a SEAL officer couldn't have conveyed to or handed the governor general a written message with whatever the three State Department reps were supposed to tell him. Thus, one helicopter was to hover near the front of the house while SEALs fast-roped down and used a chain saw to clear a landing zone for the second helicopter. The second helicopter would go to the rear of the house, let the SEALs fast-rope down, come around to the front of the house and land, and let the State Department representatives step off.[70]

Simultaneously with this Kabuki dance, the 1st Ranger Battalion was to land or parachute onto Point Salines airfield from MC-130 Combat Talons flown by the 1st Special Operations Wing out of Hurlburt Field, Florida. They would be preceded by one of my combat control teams led by Lt. Jeff Buckmelter, with Doug Brown and Rex Evitts as part of the first "chalk," to help clear the airfield and set up air traffic control. Each of the first two MC-130s would carry a jeep mounting a machine gun. By this time, the mission of the 2nd Ranger Battalion had been changed from seizure of the Pearls airfield to reinforcing the 1st Battalion's assault at Point Salines. Once the 1st Battalion had cleared the airfield, the 2nd Ranger Battalion would air land, pass through 1st Battalion's lines, and proceed to Calivigny Barracks by forced march. As soon as that target was in U.S. hands, conventional forces from the 82nd Airborne Division were to land at Salines and take over. Amid this intricate ballet, the Marines would seize Pearls airfield and the northeastern side of Grenada, where no targets of any strategic significance and few police or Cuban forces were expected to be found.

The special operations plan required that helicopters be off-loaded in Barbados and built up into flyable condition, a task that normally took one hour. The hour-and-twenty-minute flight to Grenada meant that the planes had to be on the ground in Barbados by 2:30 A.M. Because of some inexplicable breakdown in communications the planes weren't cleared to land in Barbados until 5:00 A.M. According to one of the JCS official histories published in 1997, that happened only after General Scholtes personally got on the radio to obtain clearance. The histories claim the planes landed at 3:15 A.M., a forty-five-minute delay (which General Patterson, who was there, disputes). That meant Delta Force could not meet the 5:00 A.M. H-hour that Scholtes had twice protested as being too late. Instead, they would be conducting their assaults in broad daylight—an absolute no-no for all our operations heretofore. Because readying the helicopters for flight had taken longer than expected, they wouldn't hit their targets until 6:15 A.M.[71]

The Barbados miscues were blips on the horizon; little went right after that. Approaching Grenada, the Rangers received word one hour before H-hour that the runway at Point Salines was probably blocked and the airfield was probably defended. It was decided that a jump clearing team would parachute half an hour before H-hour with Buckmelter's combat control team, followed by the rest of the 1st Ranger Battalion in a parachute assault.

The Marines began air operations from the *Guam* at 4:14 A.M. The pilots that LantCom had insisted couldn't operate in the dark were all on night-vision goggles. The Marines began landing near Pearls airport at 5:15 A.M. and took it almost without a fight, but the landing signaled that an invasion was indeed under way. That's when Delta Force and SEAL Team Six departed Barbados in the Blackhawks from Task Force 160. By the time they reached Grenada, they heard Radio Free Grenada announcing that the island was being invaded by U.S. forces.[72] Every gun on the island would be manned, primed, cocked, and ready to fire by the time Delta Force and the Rangers arrived at Salines.

Colonel Taylor decided that his Rangers should jump from five hundred feet to minimize time under canopy in broad daylight and the effects of ground fire. Most of the Rangers had expected to step off the ramp onto the runway at Point Salines and were not wearing their parachutes. They scrambled to don their jump gear and prepared to parachute. Taylor's decision to jump low probably prevented a catastrophe, since there were two quadruple-mounted 14.7-millimeter (.50-caliber) antiaircraft guns on the hills surrounding Point Salines. But they were unable to depress their guns enough to engage the Rangers once they exited the aircraft and were dangling helplessly in their parachutes. Miraculously, not one Ranger was hit and there was only one jump injury. Moreover, the low jump let them land close to one another, assemble faster, and launch their assault swiftly. In addition, an unexpected eighteen-knot crosswind blowing across the runway might have blown many Rangers out to sea had they jumped from a higher altitude.

Half an hour before H-hour, the lead MC-130 carrying Lieutenant Jeff Buckmelter, his combat controllers, and the Ranger runway-clearing team lost its inertial navigation and forward-looking infrared systems, and the plane couldn't see or find Point Salines. The pilots had been told to expect broken cloud cover at five thousand feet and five-mile visibility and were flying on night-vision goggles trying to maintain a thousand-foot separation between aircraft, but seventy-five miles from the island a lightning storm broke. Lieutenant Colonel James Hobson, commander of the 8th Special Operations Squadron, would later relate, "Every time there was a bolt of lightning, you couldn't see shit for five minutes."[73] Told, "Whatever you do, don't drop the Rangers in the water," the initial wave of three aircraft had to pull off eight minutes before the Rangers were to drop. The second wave of three aircraft encountered such heavy fire from the north end of the field that two of its planes had to abort. One of the planes from Pope Air Force Base's 317th Tactical Airlift Wing reported "taking hits" as its troops parachuted onto Salines at 5:52 A.M. Unlike the Army troops, who had been told to expect significant resistance, the aircrews had been told there were only two ZU-23 guns on the island, neither of which was at the airport, and our combat controllers had been advised repeatedly, "The island is lightly defended and we will meet only token resistance." Caffee wrote in his after-action report, "I was scared shitless."[74]

This caused the whole airdrop sequence to come unglued, and Colonel Bruce Fister had to sort it out from an airborne command, control, and communications aircraft. The only plane that dropped Rangers on the first pass, at 5:35 A.M., was the one carrying Lieutenant Colonel Taylor's tactical operations team with Staff Sergeant Bob Kelly. That group was armed with more radios than weapons. The plane with Senior Master Sergeant Mike Lampe, Master Sergeant Rick Caffee, and the 2nd Ranger Battalion's tactical operations team became the second aircraft to jump (after Kelly directed an AC-130 gunship to take out some of the most threatening anti-aircraft weapons).[75] That put even more radios on the target instead of shooters. One plane had a "hung" jumper, a Ranger whose static line had whipped around his parachute pack tray, leaving him dangling from the aircraft and slapping against its aft fuselage. He had to be pulled back into the plane. It took ninety minutes to drop all of the Rangers, while the rest of the MC-130s and C-130s sorted out their formations.[76]

Nevertheless, the combat controllers and Rangers effectively neutralized Cuban opposition at the outset and by 6:30 A.M. had cleared the runway (while under fire from snipers, automatic weapons, mortars, and antiaircraft guns) of obstacles that included twenty-five barbed-wire fences, fifty-five-gallon drums, and heavy equipment such as bulldozers, backhoes, and tarmac rollers. In addition, both sides of the runway had been spiked with concrete-reinforcing rods about three-fourths of an inch in diameter, sticking a foot out of the ground about every two hundred feet.[77] Miraculously, only one broken leg was reported. "Why we didn't impale the whole gang, I'll never know," Caffee later wrote.

Rangers hot-wired the bulldozers to speed the clearing so that C-130s could begin air-landing reinforcements. Rick Caffee was ordered to take over as the primary air traffic controller: "My only problem was that I didn't have a clue as to what was happening with regard to the other aircraft." Mike Lampe had landed in a muddy marsh at the end of the runway, and a Ranger who had landed even closer to the sea probably would have drowned had Mike not helped him out. Mike got out of the muck and joined Caffee "covered from head to toe in gray mud. Great camouflage for a turtle," Caffee recalled. Mike pulled his side arm out of its holster and found it covered with slime, inoperable.

By 7:00 A.M., Company B of the 1st Ranger Battalion started rolling up the flank of the Cuban defensive positions from west to east. The unit's first sergeant led a three-man team to assault a Cuban position, killing two Cubans and capturing twenty-eight others. Ranger snipers took Cuban mortar positions under fire at ranges of six hundred to a thousand meters and killed or wounded eighteen Cubans. A Company of the 1st Battalion assembled on the east end of Point Salines airfield and attacked from east to west. They captured a ZU-23 antiaircraft gun, which they used to take the Cuban positions under fire, and seized a Cuban bulldozer, using it as a tank to assault another Cuban position. Later, the B Company first sergeant sent a Cuban worker into the camp with instructions for the camp to surrender in fifteen minutes "or else." Approximately 175 Cubans surrendered.[78]

As the Blackhawks carrying the SEALs and part of Delta Force were about to depart Barbados, Major Dick Anshus, the ground liaison officer for 21st Air Force, had to stop them on their taxi out because he realized they had left their ammunition behind. Patterson "had a knot in the pit of my stomach" as he watched the Blackhawks lift off, silhouetted by the rising sun. As the Ranger onslaught was getting under way, at 5:45 A.M., Delta Force's six Blackhawks and the three Blackhawks carrying part of SEAL Team Six overflew Pearls airport and saw Marines on the runway,[79] confirming that there would be no surprise in their daylight assaults.

Half an hour later, Delta Force began its assault on Richmond Hill prison with Colonel Williford in command and Major David Grange's B Squadron. Meanwhile, SEAL Team Six began its assault on the governor general's mansion and the station for Radio Free Grenada. It was now 6:15 A.M., full daylight. Delta's helicopters were unable to complete their attempt to force their way into the prison; all six of them were damaged by gunfire, and the attack was a near disaster. The aerial photographs provided to Delta Force proved unreliable: What had appeared to be a close-in landing zone was unusable. Contrary to what they had been told, the prison was on a ridge with walls extending twenty feet up from a steep cliff and surrounded by jungle. Both efforts had to be aborted because of intense ground fire from two ZU-23 antiaircraft machine guns and a company of Grenadian infantry. Sixteen Delta operators and eight men from Task Force 123 were wounded, including Major Jerry

Boykin, the Delta Force operations officer; one man from Task Force 160 was killed. His wounded copilot, a warrant officer, flew the chopper until it lost hydraulic power and crashed on a peninsula. All the men aboard were wounded either by gunfire or during the crash. Two of the helicopters flew to the USS *Moosburger* to unload their wounded. The other three helicopters proceeded to the airfield at Point Salines.[80] (One helicopter had forty-five bullet holes, punctured fuel tanks, holes in the tail and main rotors, and much of its control instrumentation destroyed.[81]) Meanwhile, Lieutenant Colonel Dick Malvesti's A Squadron was to assault Fort George in downtown St. George's.[82]

The SEALs fared as badly at the governor general's mansion. The helicopter carrying Gormly, the State Department representatives, and SEAL Team Six's SatCom system received heavy fire, wounding the pilot. The helicopter was forced to disengage without landing in front of the house and headed for the USS *Guam* with forty-six bullet holes in it, including one round in its gearbox. SEALs in the other UH-60 fast-roped ninety-five feet down in front of the house and moved inside to rescue Governor General Scoon and his wife, but they left their SatCom radio in the helicopter. Moreover, unbeknownst to the SEALs, a staff communicator had changed the frequencies on their radios, for secrecy reasons, just before they boarded their flight to Barbados, and they could not communicate.[83] The mansion was soon approached by armored personnel carriers. Two Marine Corps Cobra attack helicopters diverted to attack them were shot down, in clear view of the combat controllers and Rangers fighting at Point Salines. (The Army personnel noted that the Marine helicopters made easy targets because they were firing from hover, or stationary, positions and because both their pilots and gunners wore white instead of camouflage fabric covers over their helmets, even though the crews had recommended long before that they wear camouflaged covers.)

Gormly had joined the JSOC team at the airfield by hitching a ride on one of the *Guam*'s helicopters. His SEALs were able to hold the mansion, however, until AC-130 gunships became available several hours later to support them. While their radios couldn't communicate with the gunships, they called in fire by talking to Gormly at Point Salines over their MX-360 intrateam radios (while also using a telephone in the mansion to reach the air terminal at Point Salines), and Gormly used his VHF radio to relay information to the gunship. Gormly's other SEALs were inserted successfully at Radio Free Grenada and destroyed the transmitter, but a successful counterattack later forced them to abandon that target because that team also had no communications. Eventually they hid in heavy foliage on some cliffs near the water until night, when they moved to the water and swam out to sea. The *Sprague* picked them up about seven o'clock Tuesday night.[84]

It took the Rangers from 7:00 A.M. until 9:30 A.M. to finish their drop and until noon to fully secure Point Salines airfield. By 9:00 A.M., part of the 1st Battalion had reached the nearby True Blue medical campus. They rescued the 138 medical students there, only to learn there were 224 more of them in a beachfront hotel behind fortified enemy positions near Grand Anse, another campus about three kilometers to the northwest. This was the first anyone in the invading force had heard of a second campus. A Ranger officer had the foresight to dial the Grand Anse campus to see if the students he was asked to rescue were still there. Those students would not be rescued until the next day, when his Rangers launched an airmobile assault that lasted only twenty-six minutes. When mechanical problems grounded one of their helicopters, twelve Rangers remained behind enemy lines to make seats available for the students. The Rangers conducted escape and evasion operations, captured a boat, and headed to sea under cover of darkness.[85]

During that rescue, however, American troops learned that there was yet a third campus with 202 students at Lance aux Epines, a peninsula near St. George's. Amazingly, the president of St. George's Medical College had been visiting the United States just before D-day and had been interrogated about the layout of the True Blue campus, but neither CIA nor military intelligence officials had questioned him, nor had he volunteered any information about students at Grand Anse or Lance aux Epines.[86]

Still another surprise confounded the JSOC forces that had landed at Point Salines: the arrival of the Caribbean Peacekeeping Force at 10:45 A.M., soon after the first contingent of 82nd Airborne troopers air landed there. Neither group had been told anything about a Caribbean Peacekeeping Force, which they initially thought might be enemy forces.[87] Admiral Metcalf had decided to send the Caribbean Peacekeeping Force to Point Salines instead of Pearls, as originally planned. Accompanied by General Crist, their arrival at Point Salines was a complete surprise to General Scholtes and to the 82nd's General Ed Trobaugh, who used them to guard Cuban prisoners while the Rangers and airborne troops moved northwest toward St. George's.[88]

The Marines launched a second heliborne assault on Grenville at 6:30 A.M., and took it by 7:30 without a fight, but from the bridge of the *Guam*, about five miles away, Schwarzkopf and Metcalf had seen tracers arching up over the Rangers as they parachuted at Salines and observed the intense antiaircraft fire the special operations helicopters were running into at Fort Rupert and Fort Frederick. Some crashed into the sea; others set down on the ship's flight deck shot full of holes and leaking hydraulic fluid as Metcalf received an urgent message from the office of the Navy controller in Washington, who told him he was not to refuel the Army helicopters because funds-transfer arrangements with the Army had not yet been worked out. Metcalf handed the "bullshit" message back to his chief of staff and said, "Give them fuel." Metcalf and Schwarzkopf decided they had to bomb Fort Frederick, which their intelligence people monitoring radio traffic had identified as the rebel headquarters.[89]

Chief Master Sergeant Nick Kiraly and Technical Sergeant Rex Wollmann provided targets to the AC-130 gunships and Navy attack aircraft for the assaults on Fort Rupert and Fort Frederick. But the Navy's A-7 Corsairs and the Marine Cobras that showed up overhead did not have their radio frequencies, nor did the combat controllers have the planes' frequencies. The two combat controllers began broadcasting on the emergency UHF 243.0 and VHF 121.5 frequencies while Delta Force provided them target coordinates from the ground forces' inadequate maps. But the Navy and Marine Corps pilots reported that *their* maps showed those target coordinates to be out at sea. Fortunately, a JSOC intelligence liaison assigned to Delta had other maps, and new target coordinates allowed the Marine Cobras to begin strafing runs on the targets while taking heavy fire. A-7 Corsairs from the *Independence* began bombing Fort Frederick and Fort Rupert in midafternoon. Lacking military maps or other means of identifying a building next to Fort Frederick as a hospital, the Corsairs bombed the building at 3:35 P.M. Grenadian troops had occupied the building before the attack, emplaced several gun positions, and evacuated all able-bodied staff and inmates to Fort Frederick. They had locked up the hospital's mental patients in one wing of the building, and seventeen or eighteen of them were killed during the air attack,[90] but the gun positions were eliminated.

By 2:05 P.M. on Tuesday, October 25, a battalion of the 82nd Airborne Division began landing at Point Salines to reinforce the Rangers and JSOC forces. By that time, Metcalf and Schwarzkopf had decided to open a "second front" at Grand Mal, north of St. George's and to the rear of Cuban and Grenadian forces, using a 250-man Marine amphibious force they had sent to Pearls and Grenville but that had been unable to land there because of unfavorable hydrographic conditions. After a SEAL team reconnoitered the Grand Mal beach, the Marines landed at 7:00 P.M. in thirteen amphibious vehicles and moved south and east toward the governor general's mansion with five tanks.[91] They reached the residence at seven-twelve the next morning, October 26, rescued the governor general, and relieved twenty-two embattled SEALs. The Marines then moved a few miles east to Fort Frederick in St. George's southern suburbs and ten hours later subdued the defenders there and captured the fort.[92]

That morning, a second battalion from the 82nd Airborne landed at Point Salines. General Trobaugh's Task Force 121, now combined with JSOCs, moved toward Lance aux Epines in search of more medical students. His troopers ran into stiff resistance at Frequente, a Cuban stronghold one mile north of True Blue, and Trobaugh asked Metcalf for aid. Metcalf ordered the Marine attack helicopters to assist the Army, but there was no exchange of liaison officers or radio frequencies for the Army or Air Force gunships, and the Marine pilots could raise no one on their radios. Eventually, the helicopters stumbled on the right frequencies and established contact with the engaged ground force. Then the problem of not having common maps arose again. Having lost two of its four AH-1T gunships, the two remaining Marine Corps Cobra aircrews were nevertheless able to provide effective supporting fire.

The students at Lance aux Epines still awaited rescue, and Schwarzkopf recommended an air assault, but there were no Army helicopters available, so he asked the Marines to take the Rangers there. According to Schwarzkopf, the Marine colonel in charge of the entire battalion landing team objected, "I'm not going to do that. We don't fly Army soldiers in Marine helicopters. . . . If we do it, I want to use my Marines. They'll rescue the hostages." He told Schwarzkopf that would take "at least twenty-four hours." Schwarzkopf exploded, gave the colonel a direct order, and told him he'd be court-martialed if he disobeyed it. The Marine acceded. That afternoon at four-fifteen, the 224 students were rescued; only two Rangers were slightly injured. The unusually light casualties were due in part to a resourceful student who had telephoned the makeshift Army command post in the partially completed air terminal at Point Salines and helped coordinate the rescue. Also helpful was the fact that the Marine helicopter squadron commander and the Ranger battalion commander had been Virginia Military Institute classmates and sat down to quickly agree upon their plan.

At the same time, the 82nd's Second Brigade attacked to the east and seized the Calliste Village complex, killing sixteen Cuban soldiers and capturing eighty-six others.

That night, Metcalf named Schwarzkopf as his second-in-command of Joint Task Force 120.[93] That resolved many of the problems that had ensued because General Vessey had simply drawn an arbitrary boundary across the island to divide Marines and Army forces and because Admiral McDonald had not named a joint ground force commander or assigned liaison officers to any of the units.

By noon on Wednesday, October 26, Delta Force reassembled at Point Salines, ready to head back to Pope Air Force Base. They had been engaged twenty-four hours longer than expected and almost thirty-six hours longer than normal. Part of SEAL Team Six was still with me aboard the USS *Caron*.

The next day, October 27, a third battalion from the 82nd landed at Point Salines. The paratroopers advanced methodically eastward across southern Grenada, leaving no pockets of resistance. Growing impatient, the Joint Staff told Metcalf's staff that General Vessey wanted his forces to seize Calivigny Barracks, thought to be the main base of the People's Revolutionary Army, by nightfall. Schwarzkopf challenged the JCS intervention in the tactical command of ground force operations. Nevertheless, Metcalf was ordered to take the barracks before dark. Without the 82nd Airborne's own helicopter gunships, Trobaugh decided to use the Rangers, but his men depended for fire support on naval aircraft and naval gunfire, and their radios could not communicate with ships of the *Independence* battle group. It was decided that the 82nd Division Artillery would lay down a thirty-minute artillery barrage, but five hundred rounds fell harmlessly short of the target. The cannoneers had left their aiming circles behind. There were still no maps, and there was no way to communicate between the batteries and the assault force to adjust fire. That left naval gunfire and close air support, but the lack of maps and lack of interoperable radios made both propositions dicey. Three helicopters crashed during the landing, killing several Rangers. Since there were no Cuban or Grenadian troops at Calivigny Barracks, one must assume the Rangers died from friendly fire. (The official JCS after-action reports steadfastly dodge the issue.)

Throughout the preceding two days, I had watched Urgent Fury from the decks of the USS *Caron* and would have been unable to help anyone but for the initiative of one of my noncommissioned officers. Thankfully, on our second night aboard the *Sprague*, Master Sergeant Johnny Pantages had extended the grid lines on my 1:50,000 map of Point Salines so that we had coordinates for a much larger part of the island, all the way to Fort Rupert and Fort Frederick. I made that map available to the *Caron*, which, to my surprise, also had no map of the island. We changed the batteries in our radios, ones the Navy didn't own but that could communicate with ground forces. Our improvised map covered Radio Free Grenada, where the SEALs were surrounded and pinned down, and that let us give the *Sprague* its map coordinates to relay to other ships. We ended up coordinating naval gunfire support for the SEALs and other troops during the first and worst days of fighting.[94]

The Rangers seized control of Calivigny Barracks by nine o'clock that evening, but only after three helicopters had collided in a crowded landing zone, killing or wounding almost two dozen Rangers. Ironically, there were few enemy troops there; Schwarzkopf claimed, "No enemy troops were there at all—we'd been chasing ghosts."[95]

The next day, October 28, three more battalions from the 82nd arrived. Six battalions of paratroopers, plus the division artillery, were now on the island, totaling more than five thousand troops. American forces had taken close to six hundred Cuban soldiers and construction workers prisoner.[96] However, Navy Corsair attack aircraft accidentally wounded or killed seventeen U.S. troops while strafing sniper positions firing on an airborne battalion attacking near Frequente. Thus, at least forty Rangers and paratroopers were hit by friendly fire in addition to seventeen innocent mental patients.[97] Eighteen U.S. service members died; apparently no records exist detailing how many of them, if any, were killed or wounded because of fratricide. The Naval Gunfire Liaison Company didn't have the necessary communications instructions to clear the target with the unit's fire support element. It is conceivable that more than a third of all American casualties on Grenada may have resulted from friendly fire.[98]

The next day, my men and I were ordered to transfer to an LST (landing ship tank) that came alongside the *Caron*. It took us to Point Salines, where I checked on the work and welfare of my men who had taken part in the action with the Rangers, other SEALs, and 82nd Airborne troopers. That night, my team and I climbed aboard a C-141 and were flown home to Pope Air Force Base.

For two years, we had worked out of two trailers parked just outside of the main gate of the JSOC compound, but just before the Grenada invasion, we had finally moved into a new building. We were on the first floor; an intelligence cell occupied the basement; a Delta Force element was on the second floor. But I returned to our new quarters depressed and aware that we—the team that was supposed to lead the invasion—had failed in our mission.

CHAPTER TEN

GRENADA IN A REARVIEW MIRROR AND "SHOOT-OUT" IN A NUCLEAR POWER PLANT

Looking back, it's easy to spot many things we did wrong on Grenada—and very few that went right. This was true through every level of the chain of command. The incompetence unveiled by the planning behind Urgent Fury and the lives unnecessarily lost had a profound impact on me, and I decided to quit the Air Force and retire early. To this day, I cannot honestly explain why. Perhaps it was because I had been so personally involved in two seriously failed missions or I had lost confidence in myself. Perhaps I was just worn out emotionally.

Two days after returning from Grenada, I told General Scholtes that I had decided to put in my retirement papers—but first I told him why the operation was a textbook case of how *not* to employ special operations forces. I didn't need to tell him, of course; Scholtes already knew. The screwups weren't his fault; Urgent Fury turned his gut as much as it did mine. But the American public, indeed the world, was told this was a classic example of American joint operations. They were told how brave American soldiers had saved six hundred medical students from peril and how swift intervention had saved Grenada from becoming another bastion of communist influence, spreading mischief throughout Central America and the Caribbean. President Reagan later called the operation a "textbook success" and Defense Secretary Weinberger labeled it "a complete success," as if both men were equating success with perfection. But that is *not* how most of its participants would describe Urgent Fury: We did succeed in rescuing the students and restoring Grenada to democratic rule, but not with the precision we had been trained to expect.

What were the lessons of Grenada?

My own mission, for one, was grossly ill conceived. I never understood why the SEALs' boat drop was initially laid on forty miles away from the island.[1] There isn't a place on earth where the radar horizon extends more than twenty-four miles. I never understood why the SEALs jumped from the C-130s loaded down with combat gear when they could have stowed most of their equipment in the Boston Whalers and retrieved it once the boats were on their way to the island. Some SEALs were not even wearing lifesaving vests (LPUs, or life preserver units); others never got to inflate theirs. They were so weighted down by web harnesses, weapons, and ammunition one can only assume that they were unable to hit the quick-release mechanisms on their parachute harnesses. Thus, they were towed underwater when their parachutes collapsed in the gusty winds and sank as the parachutes' wet nylon acted as huge anchors.

We learned other costly lessons. We needed special waterproofing for our communications gear, especially the MX-360s and PRC-68s. We needed better ship-to-shore radios so we wouldn't have to rely on hard-to-come-by satellite communications systems. We needed more dependable engines for our boats, and more dependable boats as well. The "splashproofing" we had used for our commo equipment—wrapping it in plastic and tape or using zipper-lock bags—didn't work underwater. We had lost comm when we needed it most.

Farther up the chain of command, the concept of operations had changed constantly, as did the final assault plan. The former commander in chief of U.S. Special Operations Command, Army General Peter J. Schoomaker (who had been a JSOC operations officer during Grenada), would note in an interview just before his retirement late in November 2000:

> Plans changed. Targets changed. Responsibility shifted. Different people were using different maps, charts, and grids. The Marines were brought in at the last minute.

> The time of the invasion was changed to daylight. We suffered a lot of casualties in Grenada we shouldn't have suffered. We hit targets, as a result of shifting plans and delays, in daylight that we should have never hit in daylight.[2]

Our communications planning was terrible; even JSOC had problems. We had virtually no intelligence. The CIA, the Defense Intelligence Agency, the National Security Agency, and the State Department provided nothing.

No one had a clue about the size and disposition of Grenadian and Cuban forces—even though the State Department had a White House–approved plan for seizing the island. The SEALs, for instance, went to a radio relay station, not the radio station, because that's where signals intelligence said the radio station was. Had the JCS not kept NSA out of the loop, it could easily have pinpointed the station's location. There was virtually no human intelligence available.

A Marine Cobra armed helicopter pilot aboard the *Guam*, Lieutenant John Peyton DeHart, narrated a contemporaneous record of the entire operation and noted that the pilots, once they heard the *Guam* was headed toward Grenada, scoured the ship for maps and finally found an atlas in the library. In it, they found a map labeled "Grenada," but it was of Guiana, the region on the north coast of South America that comprises Guyana, Suriname, and French Guiana. When they turned to the page indexed for Guiana, there was another map of Guiana. Grenada appeared on another map— about the size of a pinhead.

Not one pilot saw a map or photo map of the island until about one hour before midnight, about four hours before Marine helicopters took off from the *Guam* to launch the invasion. They were ordered to their cockpits that morning just as a driving rain squall broke over the ship's deck. As the men hunkered down and dashed to their cockpits,[3] their satellite photo maps of the island, with key gun positions circled and labeled in felt-tip marking pens, deteriorated into a sticky, gooey mess. The gag order that prevented the Defense Mapping Agency from printing maps of the island until October 25, after the invasion was under way, would prove to be a "killer oversight."

It is virtually inconceivable for special operations to undertake any mission without some kind of rehearsal. For Grenada, there was no such rehearsal. This lapse greatly compounded our problems coordinating with conventional forces, already bad enough because we had never worked with the Marines. Our missions were simply not the kind of special operations we had practiced. We trained one way but fought another. Units were kept in the dark about the presence and missions of adjacent forces.

Only luck saved one SEAL unit from incurring additional casualties because of a failure to share vital information. Lieutenant DeHart wrote after the operation, "We mere helicopter pilots on the other side of the house did not know that the Army would be making a landing at Pt. Salines." DeHart said that after the operation he met a Navy SEAL lieutenant whose call sign was "Iron Mike" in the wardroom of the *Guam*. Iron Mike asked if DeHart had seen him waving from the base of a hill that DeHart had attacked overlooking Pearls airfield. DeHart replied, "See you? No. And I wasn't even looking for you because I hadn't been told anyone was going in before us." The SEAL told DeHart, "Oh, well, I broke cover to stand up and point to the top of the hill where the gun was. Since you rolled in on it, I figured you saw me." DeHart was convinced that the officer had broken cover for no good reason. He wondered if he would have assumed the SEAL was one of the bad guys if he had seen him.[4]

Grenada would have gone much more smoothly had it been handled either by JSOC on its own, by XVIII Airborne Corps, or by LantCom forces on their own. Our mistakes took a heavy toll because we employed night tactics in a daylight engagement and had no contingency plan for a daylight assault. We failed to anticipate problems at Barbados. There were crucial breakdowns in relations among the services, and among the CIA, the Pentagon, and the State Department.

The worst problem of all was that JSOC and CINCLANT never learned to talk on the same wavelength. Atlantic Command failed to pass on so much essential information that we were flying blind most of the time. Perhaps that shouldn't have surprised us: The last time Norfolk had mounted an invasion was when American troops landed at North Africa in 1942, and that had not gone well either. There, too, the U.S. high command significantly underestimated the enemy. Vichy French troops with antiquated weapons, who were expected to welcome American forces, fought hard against the Allied landings, especially in Algeria, and an anticipated rapid advance to Tunis failed because the Germans arrived in Tunisia first.

All of this had a telling effect on the operators in every JSOC unit. Every planner and commander involved in the operation had been extremely rushed during the preceding thirty-six hours. Individuals were reacting to situations instead of developing plans. It was impossible to find one good focal point for information because inputs were coming from so many directions and so rapidly that our communications operators were tasked beyond any reasonable level.[5] Individual team members obtained varied and unique levels of information, and not everyone knew everything he was supposed to know. The resolve of the command was not thoroughly understood; General Scholtes was getting direction from too many sources. And we had failed to consider at what point the mission should be postponed or canceled.

At the White House, contingency planning began well before October 19 to evacuate roughly six hundred American medical students studying on the island and up to four hundred other Americans, but the Joint Staff had little interest in such an operation. According to Robert M. Gates, the CIA's deputy director for intelligence at the time, Vice Admiral Art Moreau, the assistant to the chairman of the Joint Chiefs of Staff, who stood in for General Vessey at a number of White House meetings, refused even to discuss the subject at one meeting chaired by the National Security Council (NSC).[6] Despite the coup on October 12 and repeated State Department warnings October 13–17 that an evacuation might be necessary, a JCS warning order for the operation wasn't issued until late on October 19, twelve hours after Bishop was assassinated.[7]

There was one problem with Reagan's final order on October 22 to launch the operation in forty-eight hours: The Joint Chiefs of Staff apparently failed to tell Weinberger, and CIA Director William Casey must have failed to tell Reagan, that the United States had virtually no intelligence regarding the island and no maps of it. No one knew how many American students were there, or their locations. No one knew how many armed Cubans were on Grenada or what they might be armed with. No one knew how many armed Grenadians were likely to oppose the U.S. intervention. Satellite photos proved almost useless because the area was partly obscured by clouds, and the weather got worse as the operation progressed. Worse still, the Central Intelligence Agency had no human assets on the island to help provide information.[8] Only months after the president had twice told the nation that developments on Grenada threatened our hemisphere's security, America found itself dismally unprepared to act.

Urgent Fury was so FUBAR'd[9] that almost any story told about it seemed plausible, and virtually every version of every story made print. The operation blatantly contradicted every one of the six principles of special operations—simplicity, security, repetition, surprise, speed, and purpose.[10] The plan changed too often and too dramatically to be simple. Security was lost four days before the invasion with news reports that Navy ships were steaming for Grenada and reports the evening before it that Air Force transport aircraft were leaving Fort Bragg in droves. There was no "repetition"—no one got to rehearse anything.

Surprise was lost executing daylight assaults and because of news reports of an impending invasion. Speed did not characterize any unit's work, a result of unexpected levels of resistance and the absence of intelligence and maps (plus the entirely different maps provided to the Navy and Marine pilots). Our purpose floundered: The command that planned Urgent Fury had no concept of our capabilities or limitations. Our missions changed too fast for us to focus on executing anything right.

Launching Urgent Fury, America's military hierarchy lost sight of the single most important principle of war—the objective. The Joint Chiefs of Staff, the Atlantic Command, and the commander, Second Fleet, let events be dictated by the mistaken belief that Marines can't fly at night. A quick phone call to Marine Corps headquarters or to Camp Lejeune, where the 22nd MAU trained and was home-based, would have dispelled that myth. Yet on the basis of it, the Marines were assigned secondary targets. The airport at Pearls and the town of Grenville had no strategic significance; they certainly did not represent the enemy's center of gravity. And there was no compelling reason why Point Salines and Pearls had to be attacked simultaneously. Thus, it made no sense to postpone the special operations assaults until 5:00 A.M. or later in order to synchronize them with the Marines' attacks. Rather than make everyone attack in broad daylight, it would have made far more sense to postpone the operation by one day, thereby letting it unfold in an orderly sequence, hitting our primary targets at night and the secondary targets after sunup.

Military leaders do not brag about their errors or failures any more than other professionals do. The Joint Staff would say of the operation: ". . . the plan which evolved made the best use of the forces allocated, and their capabilities, training, and readiness." General Vessey summarized it this way on *Meet the Press* two weeks after Grenada was over: ". . . the operation went reasonably well. . . . Things did go wrong, but generally the operation was a success."

General Schwarzkopf was more candid in his 1992 memoir:

> . . . We had lost more lives than we needed to, and the brief war had revealed a lot of shortcomings—an abysmal lack of accurate intelligence, major deficiencies in communications, flare-ups of interservice rivalry, interference by higher headquarters in battlefield decisions . . . and more. Yet I was heartened that these deficiencies had come to light in our *own* after-action reports.

The general must have been referring to the military's classified after-action reports, which no one in the public had seen by the time his book came out. Except for the Navy's 1988 "Lessons Learned" report, which acknowledged only the failure to ask the Defense Mapping Agency to produce maps of the island for the ground forces until after the invasion had begun, no unclassified after-action report was made public until 1997, five years after Schwarzkopf's memoir was published. General Colin Powell, Defense Secretary Caspar Weinberger's senior military assistant during Urgent Fury, would later acknowledge that the operation "was hardly a model of service cooperation." Powell called it a "sloppy success" and "messy." Defense Secretary Weinberger, however, put matters in a more favorable light in his memoir, *Fighting for Peace: Seven Critical Years at the Pentagon*, stating:

> If the measure of success is attaining our political objectives at minimum cost, in the shortest possible time, then the Grenada operation has to be judged to have been a complete success.[11]

Weinberger did, however, acknowledge that the operation could have run smoother. President Reagan delighted in telling and re-telling one story about Grenada's "textbook success"[12] that came to him by way of one of this book's authors. He used it in formal speeches after the invasion, from January through October of 1984, some in Washington and some as far away as Korea. At a January 20 forum for three-thousand-plus presidential appointees, Reagan in-terrupted his prepared remarks to say,

> I wasn't going to tell you this, but you're so nice. [Laugh-ter] I wasn't going to do it because I've told so many people here on this stage, and they've had to listen to it several times. But if you don't know, recently one of our young lieutenants—a Marine lieutenant flying a Cobra—was off Grenada and then went on to Beirut. And from there he wrote back to the *Armed Forces Journal* something that he had been doing. He said that he noticed every news story about the Grenada rescue mission contained a line that ap-peared in *every* story—that Grenada produces more nutmeg than any other place in the world. And he decided that was a code, and he was going to break the code. [Laughter] And he did.

> He wrote back and said, "Number One: Grenada produces more nutmeg than any place in the world. Number Two: The Soviets and Cubans are trying to take Grenada. Num-ber Three: You can't make good eggnog without nutmeg. And Number Four: You can't have Christmas without egg-nog. [Laughter] Number Five: The Soviets and Cubans are trying to steal Christmas. [Laughter] And Number Six: We stopped them." [Laughter][13]

Remember General Schwarzkopf's beef about "interference by higher headquarters in battlefield decisions"? The Joint Staff would claim that "mission type orders were given where the upper levels of command decided the 'what' of the mission and the lower elements decided the 'how.' " Admiral Metcalf would claim, "[We] had no mucking around from on high." But interference became so prevalent that, recalling "previous experiences in Vietnam where a considerable portion of his time was consumed in appeasing the upper elements of his chain of command," Metcalf put a Navy captain in charge of four members of his staff whose full-time job was

> working the up side of the chain of command to the National Command Authority. In addition, his operations officer manned a secure phone connection to CINCLANT during all active combat operations. Not less than two situations reports were submitted each hour. . . . This saturated up-channel reporting . . . [and] not only kept his seniors fully informed, but kept their staffs busy and allowed him the time and created conditions such that he could retain control over military action at the local level.[14]

General Shy Meyer, the Army chief of staff at the time, couched the problem differently in a draft transcript of his postretirement Oral History debriefing: "The last thing you want is a bunch of dipshits in the Pentagon running something. And I am serious. Including the JCS—they are not organized to run something."[15]

While I was awaiting retirement from the Air Force, we deployed to California to rehearse an airfield takedown in a high-altitude, high-opening parachute jump. Rick Caffee was the jumpmaster, leading me, Mike Lampe, and Mac McReynolds out the ramp from twelve thousand feet onto a target located at about five thousand feet altitude in the mountains. Rick's parachute didn't open properly: He had a "horseshoe" malfunction as the parachute's shroud lines wrapped around his legs. Rick cut the lines away and pulled his reserve chute, but just as it elongated and before the canopy could blossom, he hit the ground, shattering his leg. We called in a medevac helicopter, but found that it had no stretcher aboard! I tore into the crew with some brutal language and sent them back to get the right equipment while Mike and Mac worked to sedate Rick and relieve his agony. Rick spent nine days in the hospital and walked around for a year with his leg held together by a metal plate, reminding us once again that we were in a dangerous business.

But we also had fun. One week later in 1983, after he had been promoted to major general to become MAC's director of operations, General Cassidy was preparing to leave for a third-star post as the Air Force deputy chief of staff for personnel; Cassidy's aide told me the boss was putting together a foursome for golf early on Saturday morning, and gave me their names. I rounded up two other combat controllers on the MAC staff plus Captain Craig Brotchie, had us all put on full diving and scuba gear with Chief Master Sergeant Nick Kiraly, who "just happened" to be at Scott on temporary duty that week. An hour before sunup we headed out to the fifteenth hole. It was a par five with a small, shallow, slightly brackish pond next to the putting green, covered by water lilies. Cassidy was known to play a fast round of golf; teeing off promptly at 7:00 A.M., by 9:15 his foursome had reached the fifteenth. We peeked through the lily pads just enough to gauge their progress down the fairway. Once all four players were on the green, we stood up and—dripping wet and covered by water lily vines—marched in step to the edge of the green, saluted, and presented each of the players with a Det 1 MACOS coin—"First In, Last Out"—engraved with his initials. "Sir," I reported to Cassidy, "we thought you all might need ball markers. Special tactics congratulates you on your promotion and wants you to know, 'If you're ever up the creek, we'll be around to help.' "

Cassidy was speechless, then burst out in a spontaneous laugh that relieved me no end. He asked me jokingly, "Just what do you think you're *doing*, Lieutenant Colonel Carney?" I was going to tell him, "Trying to prove that we got your message, sir," but Captain Brotchie preempted me: "Just routine training, sir: getting ready for some more water jumps off Key Largo next week."

"SHOOT-OUT" IN A NUCLEAR POWER PLANT

The Wackenhut Corporation offered me an unusually lucrative job as training manager for its security force at the Savannah River nuclear power plant. I was pleased to learn that my noncommissioned officer-in-charge, Nick Kiraly, would accept a job there along with other former members of special tactics, Delta Force, and the Rangers. I was looking forward to developing a premier security force.

I soon learned that this would not be the case as I got my first taste of bureaucracy outside the military. As training manager, I would report to the director of operations and training, who worked for the site manager. On top of that layering was oversight from a ten-to-fifteen-man group of Department of Energy personnel, who were to monitor my progress on a daily basis. I found it ludicrous that the government had more checkers than I had trainers. The only bright spot was that Wackenhut had hired Colonel Bud Sydnor, the retired ground force leader of the 1970 Son Tay POW raid. Bud was a consultant, and he was developing training lesson plans. During the plant's annual antiterrorist readiness test, we showed how security could be improved. When a "terrorist" group from the FBI tried to take down the plant, we waxed their butts: Alerted by my nighttime team on perimeter security, the men from Delta Force used rappelling rope made into Swiss seats to strap themselves to the ceilings inside the facility where they could shoot straight down on the intruders.

Our measures to tighten security were deemed extreme and upset the FBI, Department of Energy, DuPont (which managed the facility for DOE), and Wackenhut's hierarchy. When I shortly thereafter told the program manager that I was resigning, Mr. Wackenhut called to convince me to stay on, and mentioned that he would name me director of training. However, the die was cast.

I had often wondered why Bud Sydnor had not been hired to become the training director instead of me. What I learned was that

Bud was smarter than the average bear. He was not about to be caught up in the Wackenhut/DOE/FBI/DuPont country line dance. When I later decided to return to the Air Force, I asked Bud his opinion. Without a flinch, he said, "Get back in the military. You can always do this. You need to finish your work in special ops." Once again I was blessed by the counsel of a great American, a great soldier, a gentleman, and a friend.

CHAPTER ELEVEN

TWA 847 AND *ACHILLE LAURO*

The two years after my retirement turned out to be the busiest ones for my old unit. It trained harder than ever after Grenada under the command of Lieutenant Colonel Charles Tappero, a balding, affable officer built like a wrestler. In two short years, it deployed on eight contingency operations while logging the equivalent of eight around-the-world trips.

During a quarterly exercise in the western Pacific early in 1985, the unit almost lost Mike Lampe. He and Rick Caffee were leading a Ranger team for an airfield takedown when the helicopter they were in slowed to a near hover and started to land on a pitch-black night. While the aircraft was still forty or fifty feet in the air, however, a Ranger preparing to exit the bird lost his balance and inadvertently whacked Mike on the back, the usual signal to "Exit *now!*" Mike leaped or fell out of the helicopter onto the coral taxiway below—*into* it, actually. Sensing instantly that something was amiss and clutching his weapon with his right hand, Mike had reached out with his left arm to cushion his fall, and his arm penetrated the coral like a pickax, his forearm embedded almost up to his elbow.

Grenada had made it apparent we needed pararescuemen to

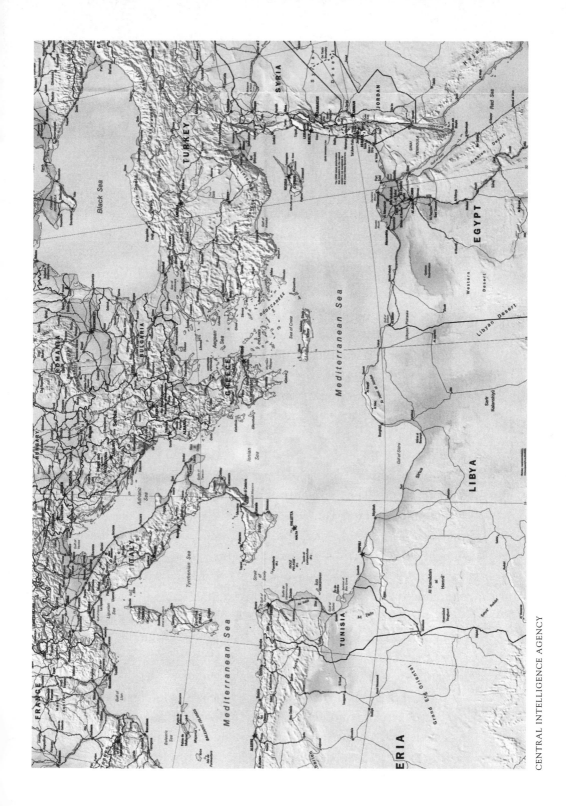

work with our combat control team. Master Sergeant John Pighini, a pararescueman who joined the unit in 1984, worked with another paramedic to pull Mike's arm out of the taxiway. With his wrist bent ninety degrees, Mike was in too much shock to feel any pain. They nevertheless gave him double doses of morphine, but it took an hour to get a medevac plane in to fly him to the nearest military hospital because Ranger casualties from a related aircraft mishap took priority. (One of them had a crushed pelvis; another had a badly broken leg and crushed testicle.)

Mike's arm turned out to have multiple compound fractures, and some pieces of the bones were barely more than dust. His X rays made his wrist look like an eggshell that someone had hit with a mallet. Mike was finally evacuated to Tripler Army hospital in Hawaii, one of the world's premier medical facilities, but there his problems were compounded by a huge, gruff, haughty, Samoan nurse who kept calling him "Mr. Lumpken" and insisted he take huge doses of Mr. Lumpken's medicine, which was really for a patient in an adjacent room.

By the time his team returned to Fort Bragg, Mike was on the phone to Lieutenant Colonel Tappero, begging to get him home. He would plead, "The nurse keeps calling me 'Lumpken' and insists on giving me Mr. Lumpken's medicine." Mike was not about to let Tripler "fix" his arm. In fact, the first hospital said it might have to amputate it, but Mike persuaded doctors not to. We finally diverted an Air Force flight surgeon to fly home by way of Hawaii with orders to bring Lampe back, kidnapping him if necessary. That's exactly what happened as they wheeled Mike out of the hospital in a wheelchair, ignoring frantic, loud protests from the hospital's staff, and lifted him into a waiting airplane. It was one of our best snatches ever.

At Fort Bragg, Mike underwent three separate, painful operations over the next eight months, dutifully following the excruciating physical therapy needed to restore some muscle strength. Miraculously, Mike's arm healed. Nine months to the day from that accident, he deployed on what became known as the TWA 847 and *Achille Lauro* operations.

The latter operation, while I was still retired in 1985, almost ended up in a slaughterhouse from friendly fire. It was one of eight real-world missions that my former team—by then renamed Det 4 NAFCOS (Detachment 4, Numbered Air Force Combat Operations Staff)—would undertake in 1984 and 1985,[1] a period during which Joint Special Operations Command was headed by Major General Carl W. Stiner.[2] He deployed the unit on one emergency after another, including the TWA 847, *Achille Lauro*, and Pan Am 83 hijackings.

On June 14, 1985, TWA Flight 847 from Athens to Rome was hijacked by Lebanese Shiite Muslim extremists, triggering a seventeen-day drama that was covered extensively on international television. The plane was diverted to Beirut, then to Algiers, and back to Lebanon. There Navy diver Robert Stethem was murdered and his body dumped on the tarmac. The plane then flew back to Algeria, where terrorists released a letter signed by twenty-nine passengers calling on President Reagan to refrain from launching a military rescue. The plane returned to Lebanon, where the hijackers released three Greek-American passengers while Amal leader Nabih Berri said the hostages had been scattered to thwart a possible rescue. The next day people watched in horror when the TWA pilot leaned out his cockpit window at one point to answer a TV reporter's questions while a grinning terrorist held a gun to his temple. The next day five hostages were paraded before a chaotic press conference in Beirut and pleaded with Reagan not to launch a rescue attempt.

The incident represented one of the first times SEAL Team Six could have been used to rescue hostages from a hijacked airliner. Indeed, members of the unit deployed quickly to Sigonella, Italy, cocked and locked for a takedown in Algeria that would essentially mirror the Israeli Entebbe rescue, with the SEALs landing on taxiways for the takedown of the hijacked plane, followed by a C-141 to evacuate precious cargo. That option, however, was turned down by the American ambassador, and the rescue force headed for an air-base run by one of our NATO allies on Cyprus in the eastern Mediterranean to await another window of opportunity. The SEALs, led by Captain Robert Gormly, with five special tactics men led by Lieutenant Colonel Tappero and Captain Jeffrey Buckmelter, hunkered down there with Major General Stiner and his operations section. While Tappero was sent to the U.S. embassy in Beirut with a small team to gather on-the-spot intelligence and coordinate a possible rescue with local authorities, Stiner's force was confined to the base's hangars throughout the daylight hours to avoid being spotted by unfriendly reconnaissance satellites. His men spent more than two weeks there, using their time to plan and gear up for one rescue scenario after another while Stiner gave them periodic lessons on the Middle East and let them relax with indoor volleyball games. Only at night could they enjoy the fresh air and exercise.

Early on, Mike Lampe had a run-in with Military Airlift Command headquarters when Stiner asked for the two C-5s carrying his helicopters to bring them from Sigonella to the island and off-load them so his men could practice various takedowns at night. MAC objected, claiming the runways and taxiways weren't big enough. Lampe had noticed in the base operations office a photo of a C-5 on the ramp there and realized there was some sort of disconnect. He came to realize that the taxiways did not meet peacetime operating standards, but they did meet wartime operating standards, and Mike argued that their mission was essentially a wartime one. He and JSOC's operations officer arranged with the base's tenants to reposition their own aircraft to make more room for the C-5s to off-load their helicopters on the crowded ramps, which were finally delivered.

The TWA 847 rescue never developed because the hijackers kept flitting from one destination to another, occasionally releasing a few hostages. Eventually, the crisis petered out on the last day of

June after Muslim leaders called for U.S. and Israeli guarantees that there would be no reprisals, and the last thirty-nine hostages were released.

One of the unsung heroes of that crisis was Richard Halloran, the *New York Times* military affairs correspondent at the Pentagon. As usually happens when a hijacking is reported, journalists clamored for TWA to release a list of the plane's passengers, and TWA complied. Journalists at the Pentagon quickly asked which of the passengers were military personnel, and the Defense Department's public affairs office honored the question, releasing a list showing not only their names, but their hometowns or duty stations as well.

When Halloran noticed that Stethem's duty station was shown as Dam Neck, Virginia, he thought the "diver" just might be a member of SEAL Team Six. (The terrorists may have thought so as well, which may be what cost Stethem his life.) Halloran rushed into the office of the director for Defense Information and politely but firmly suggested that the Pentagon withdraw the list, pointing out that identifying passengers as military personnel and their home stations could jeopardize their lives and the safety of their families, too. Unbelievably, Halloran had to argue his point, but he finally won. Luckily, other journalists agreed with him, declining to print the names and duty stations already in their possession.

ACHILLE LAURO

That October, a near tragedy in our attempt to nab hijackers of the *Achille Lauro* cruise ship proved how badly we needed more medics on our combat control teams.

The terrorists had shot and murdered a sixty-nine-year-old disabled American citizen, Leon Klinghoffer, throwing his body overboard into Mediterranean waters as the ship sailed from Egypt's Port Said for a scheduled stop in Ashdod, Israel.[3]

Six years later, Oliver North would note in his memoir,[4] "A lot of people gave me credit for the *Achille Lauro* success." Some "success": It almost got Gormly's SEAL Team Six annihilated, along with several men from my former Special Tactics Squadron and some very senior officers from the Joint Special Operations Command, including its commander, Major General Stiner—all of whom came within a whisker of being gunned down by our allies, the Italians. It also fractured our relations with the Egyptians for a while.

North wrote that working with Vice Admiral Art Moreau, assistant to the JCS chairman,[5] he learned from communications intercepts soon after our spy satellites failed to find the ship that Abul Abbas, head of the Palestinian Liberation Front and a member of the PLO excecutive committee, had been granted diplomatic clearance into Egypt and had begun to play the role of a neutral peacemaker, dispatched by Yassir Arafat to "resolve" the hijacking. The *Achille Lauro* headed for the port of Alexandria, where Abbas started "negotiating" with the terrorists. (They greeted his messages with the words, "Commander, we are happy to hear your voice.") Apparently a deal had been struck with the Egyptian government. Abbas radioed the terrorists aboard the ship that if they surrendered to the Egyptians, they would be granted safe passage out of the country.

As soon as word arrived at the Joint Special Operations Command that terrorists had seized the cruise ship, Delta Force and SEAL Team Six were ordered into action. Despite a standing agreement that Military Airlift Command would have air transport for them ready to take off from Pope Air Force Base and Norfolk within four hours, more than twelve hours passed before the right planes became available and an armada of five aircraft headed for Larnaca in the Greek area of Cyprus. Two C-141s carried SEAL Team Six, two giant C-5s their helicopters, and a Gulfstream C-20 executive jet carried the commander of Joint Special Operations Command and his battle staff. With Stiner was Delta Force's deputy commander, Lieutenant Colonel "Bucky" Burruss, a small

Delta Force explosive ordnance detachment, and nine men from the 24th Special Tactics Squadron, headed again by Lieutenant Colonel Tappero. During their ten-to-twelve-hour flights, Klinghoffer was murdered.

The delay in getting our special operations units into the air was inexcusable: The Air Force had hundreds of transport planes, but had long refused to leave even two of them ready on an alert pad at Pope Air Force Base for just such contingencies, and the time lapse caused the *Achille Lauro* rescue to turn into a debacle.[6] By the time our special operations teams landed in Cyprus, weather had deteriorated badly in the eastern Mediterranean, and our reconnaissance satellites and Navy surveillance aircraft from the carrier *Saratoga* lost track of the ship. By then, the terrorists realized that its captain had been routinely radioing his exact position to the ship's home office in Genoa, Italy, and they took over the radio room, ending such transmissions while demanding safe haven in the Syrian port of Tartus. The *Achille Lauro* headed there, but President Assad denied them access after the United States protested in the strongest possible diplomatic language.

Somehow, the Israelis located the ship's exact position, and our satellites were able to begin tracking it again. An assault party from SEAL Team Six, with all nine of the special tactics men attached, came within fifteen minutes of taking down the *Achille Lauro* as it turned toward Alexandria. The team was speeding up to the *Achille Lauro*'s stern in a helicopter skimming the waves—ready to fast-rope down onto the aft deck and blow obstructions to let a larger boarding party land there—when the ship disappeared again from our instantaneous satellite readout system. We had no choice but to abort the mission. There was no doubt in anyone's mind the takedown would have succeeded. Once again, it proved there was no room for error—ours, or a billion-dollar spy satellite's.

Diplomatic negotiations ensued as the Egyptian government equivocated on what it planned to do with the four terrorists aboard—or allowed off—the *Achille Lauro*. Once again, according to North, the Israelis came to our rescue: They learned that the

Egyptians were planning to fly them out of the country that night, when the crisis was entering its fourth day, and let them continue on to Palestine Liberation Front headquarters in Tunisia. The Israelis even obtained the identity, tail number, and takeoff time of the commercial EgyptAir 737 that would fly them out of Al Maza air base, outside of Cairo. They learned, too, that Abul Abbas himself would be aboard the flight.

North wrote that he and Moreau came up with a plan to have Navy F-14 fighters from the *Saratoga* intercept the plane over international waters and force it to land at Sigonella, a joint Italian/NATO air base in Sicily where U.S. cruise missiles were deployed. North would later claim they obtained the president's permission for the operation over Defense Secretary Caspar Weinberger's vehement objections that it would harm U.S. relations with Egypt.[7] At eleven-fifteen that night, EgyptAir 2843 (its tail number, since it was not a scheduled flight) took off and headed for Tunis, which quickly denied landing rights, as did Athens, Greece. Four F-14s intercepted the plane south of Crete and directed the pilot to head for Sigonella. The pilot radioed Cairo for instructions, but his transmissions were jammed by Navy E-2C Hawkeyes. The only communications EgyptAir 2843 had left were with the F-14s; it turned toward Sigonella.

Thwarted in their earlier, aborted rescue, Gormly's SEALs were loading their gear at Sigonella to return to the United States, and Stiner's command section was doing the same at the base in the eastern Mediterranean. Mike Lampe was policing up the base's control tower when he got a call from Colonel Dick Malvesti, JSOC's new J-3, that he and Stiner's team were to load up and head immediately for Sigonella, not the United States. Malvesti told him of the plan for Navy aircraft to intercept the EypyptAir plane and force it down there. As soon as the terrorists landed, Stiner's SEALs were to seize them, hustle them aboard their own aircraft, and take off for the United States.

Soon at least ten U.S. planes were converging on Sigonella—the four F-14s, Stiner's special operations armada, and the E-2C. It was time to get permission from Italian Prime Minister Craxi for the planes to land there, but Italian authorities and the U.S. embassy in Rome said they did not know where he was and couldn't contact him. North would claim that he and Moreau had one of their staffers, Michael Ledeen, an old friend of Craxi's, track him down at a favorite hotel where he once had lived. Craxi wanted to know, "Why Sicily?" According to North, Ledeen joked with him that "no other place in the world offers such a combination of beautiful weather, history, tradition, and magnificent cuisine." Craxi relented, but phone connections between Rome and Sicily were less than dependable and his order to let the planes land was late getting through. Sigonella's air traffic controllers refused permission to let the American planes land until the Navy aircraft declared an airborne emergency.

The EgyptAir 737 landed, with Stiner's command team in a C-141 right behind it. His SEALs quickly surrounded the airliner while armed AH-6 Little Birds hovered overhead, ready to provide fire support. Stiner, a tall, lanky, no-nonsense leader whom author Tom Clancy would later describe as "a real old-fashioned Southern gentleman—who kills people,"[8] told Lampe to radio the EgyptAir pilot and instruct him to lower the plane's built-in door stairs and have the terrorists walk off. But the Italian air traffic controllers were having "shit fits," as Lampe later described their transmissions, yelling contrary instructions to the Egyptian pilot and telling the Americans to stand fast. Stiner and Lampe realized that the Sigonella control tower couldn't match special tactics' capability to readily switch between HF and UHF frequencies, and Stiner had Lampe contact the EgyptAir pilot and tell him to switch to a new frequency. He complied. With clear communications, Stiner took Lampe's microphone and told the pilot, in effect, "This is the American general commanding a task force that has your plane surrounded. Off-load your passengers now or we'll have to storm the aircraft." A short debate followed while the terrorists pulled down all the plane's window shades. Finally, the pilot descended the plane's stairs and walked up to Burruss and Malvesti, complaining that he was cold. They got him a jacket while Stiner repeated his instructions. He and Stiner talked.

Thirty minutes passed, then an hour, when suddenly Stiner's men saw dim blue lights flashing at the far end of the runway. The lights grew bigger and bigger until all Stiner's men could see were bright blue lights atop Italian carabinieri vehicles converging on their perimeter. "Things got tense," Lampe would recall later in a typical understatement. The Italian officer-in-charge made it through the perimeter to Stiner while his men got out of their cars and surrounded Gormly's SEALs. Gormly told his SEALs over their intrateam radios, "Chill out. Don't pull the trigger. Let's not let this Mexican standoff turn into a massacre." Both groups lowered their weapons—very carefully.

Stiner and the Italian officer left their position and repaired to base operations with Gormly and the EgyptAir pilot. For what seemed like an hour or two, Stiner conferred by a satellite communications radio telephone with the chairman of the Joint Chiefs of Staff and the American ambassador in Rome. Throughout that time both the SEALs and the carabinieri remained locked and loaded, all of them tense. It was a hair-trigger situation.

Stiner finally returned and told his men the Italians had the upper hand. They watched the plane's crew and five terrorists walk off the aircraft and disappear with the carabinieri. Stiner's men repaired to a hangar to relieve themselves and then climbed into their C-141s to grab some shut-eye. Early the next morning, they noticed a lot of activity around the EgyptAir plane. It was being refueled, and soon a van appeared from which eight or ten people boarded the aircraft. Stiner told his sergeant major to have the Navy ready a T-39 Sabreliner executive jet for takeoff and track the EgyptAir plane and make sure it flew to Rome, not to North Africa or elsewhere.

In the meantime, the carabinieri surrounded Stiner's men again, weapons ready. As soon as the EgyptAir pilot started taxiing, two Navy junior-grade lieutenants took off in the T-39 on the parallel taxiway (with the carabinieri scrambling to get out of the way) with

Delta Force's Lieutenant Colonel Bucky Burruss aboard plus Stiner's Lieutenant Colonel Malvesti and his operations NCO, along with a satellite communications radio and antenna. The Navy pilots immediately flew their plane right up under the 737's tail, lights off on a pitch-black night, to create a single radar image. A short time later, two Italian Air Force fighters pulled up on the port wing of the 737 but did not see the T-39. Suddenly one of the Italian pilots decided to reposition to the starboard wing by flying just under and behind the T-39 and nearly collided with it. Someone yelled "Look out!" just in time, and the quick-acting Navy pilot hit the air brakes and dived just below the Italian fighter. It still failed to spot the T-39, however, which quickly tucked back under the Egypt-Air's tail.

Not until the Italian fighters broke off on the short final approach to a military air base outside Rome did the T-39 separate enough from the 737 for the Italian ground control approach radar to pick it up. A surprised tower operator asked the plane what it was and what was its intent. The pilot replied that he was flying a U.S. Navy aircraft with orders to follow the 737, but the tower denied him permission to land. "Then I'm declaring an emergency," the pilot replied, and when the tower operator asked the nature of his emergency, he answered, "Uh . . . I'm out of fuel." Given permission to land, he taxied the T-39 near the 737, while Burruss's team popped open an overwing escape hatch to set their SatCom antenna on the wing. They watched Italian officials board the 737, remove its crew and passengers, and close up the aircraft. They reported all this to Stiner, who resignedly told them to return to Sigonella.[9]

No blood was shed, but Stiner's crack teams flew home empty-handed. *Achille Lauro* hardly proved a "success."

Within days, the Italian government allowed Abul Abbas to escape to Yugoslavia dressed in a pilot's uniform. He then fled to Iraq under diplomatic immunity from Belgrade, which had relations with the PLO. An Italian court convicted eleven of the fifteen men charged with involvement in the hijacking. All four of the men who carried out the hijacking, whom North would describe as "just two-bit trigger men," got off with sentences of fifteen to thirty years in prison, even though the prosecutor had asked for life sentences. One of them, Magied Yussef al-Molqi, had even admitted to killing Leon Klinghoffer. In 1991, Abul Abbas and two of his associates were tried in absentia and found guilty of organizing the hijacking and sentenced to life terms in prison, but Iraq would not extradite them.

Aerial photo of the Desert One crash site showing the remains of the C-130 transport, with an abandoned RH-53 helicopter in the background and a destroyed RH-53 at the far right.

Ground level view of the C-130 transport showing Iranian soldiers sorting through the wreckage.

Colonel John T. Carney Jr., USAF, shown here in 1997 receiving the annual U.S. Special Operations Command Medal from its commander in chief, General Hugh M. Shelton (who later became chairman of the Joint Chiefs of Staff), with former Army Chief of Staff General Edward C. "Shy" Meyer in the background. Better known simply as "Coach" to his men, Carney formed America's first Special Tactics team in 1977, a highly secret, six-man "pick-up" unit of combat controllers known for years only as Brand X. After missions in Iran and Grenada, Carney's Special Tactics teams grew to include USAF pararescuemen for operations in Panama, Somalia, Kuwait, and Iraq as part of the 1720th Special Tactics Group, with Carney as its commander (and a promotion to full colonel, unprecedented for an officer who early in his career had twice failed selection for promotion to major). Today that unit (now known as the 720th Special Tactics Group) comprises seven squadrons deployed worldwide as part of U.S. Air Force Special Operations Command. Fully 70 percent of its stateside personnel have been deployed in Afghanistan since late 2001 as part of Operation Enduring Freedom. (U.S. Special Operations Command)

Chief Master Sergeant Mike Lampe, USAF, became the second noncommissioned officer-in-charge of Brand X and rose to become the senior enlisted advisor to the commander in chief of U.S. Special Operations Command from 1991 to 1997. (U.S. Air Force)

Nine of the first members of Brand X at Wadi Kena, Egypt, before leaving for Oman and Desert One on the 1980 Iranian rescue mission. From left to right: M.Sgt. Mitch Bryan, T.Sgt. John "J.K." Koren, T.Sgt. Mike Lampe, S.Sgt. Bud Gonzalez, S.Sgt. Dick West, the author with one of the trail bikes, M.Sgt. Bill Sink, Sgt. Rex Wollmann, and Sgt. Doug Cohee. (Sink and Cohee almost never forgave me because they had to remain behind to provide security.) (U.S. Air Force)

The Ranger air drop over Point Salines Airfield. (U.S. Air Force)

The author with four Special Tactics team members after the initial assault on Grenada. From left to right: Technical Sergeant Rex Evitts, Lieutenant Jeff Buckmelter, author, Chief Master Sergeant Mike Lampe, and Staff Sergeant Rob Griffin. (U.S. Air Force)

U.S. soldiers storm the Commandancia, headquarters of Manuel Noriega's Panamanian Defense Forces, during Delta Force's rescue of CIA agent Kurt F. Muse from nearby Modelo prison. (U.S. Army)

The 1724th Special Tactics Squadron (formerly Brand X) as it readies for the 1989 invasion of Panama, Operation Just Cause. (U.S. Air Force)

Sergeant K. "Lucky" Cook, Special Tactics member, accompanying Manuel Noriega on a Special Operations MC-130 Combat Talon II en route to Homestead AFB, outside Miami, Florida, after the conclusion of Operation Just Cause in Panama.

This painting, entitled *We Are Here to Get You Out,* was done by Bill Jackson. It depicts members of Delta Force riding on the skids of an MH-6 helicopter en route to the Modelo prison in Panama to free imprisoned CIA agent Kurt F. Muse.

Technical Sergeant Thomas W. Beddard, a Special Tactics pararescueman, rushes out to protect Lieutenant Devon Jones, a Navy F-14 pilot shot down on the second day of the 1991 Gulf air war deep in Iraqi territory. (U.S. Air Force)

Left: Colonel Charles A. "Charging Charlie" Beckwith, Delta Force's founder and first commander. (U.S. Army) Right: General Duane H. Cassidy, Commander in Chief, Military Airlift Command and U.S. Transportation Command. (U.S. Air Force)

Above: Colonel John Carney (left) and General Duane H. Cassidy, Commander in Chief, Military Airlift Command and U.S. Transportation Command. (U.S. Air Force)

Right: "Dial 911; get Fort Bragg." Defense Secretary Donald Rumsfeld speaks to Air Force combat controllers during a visit to Pope Air Force Base and Fort Bragg near Fayetteville, North Carolina, on November 21, 2001. Rumsfeld told the men, "The world knows why, when the president dials 911, it rings right here in Fayetteville." (U.S. Army photo by Specialist Jon Creese.)

Master Sergeant Bart Decker of the 23rd Special Tactics Squadron enjoys a Macanodo cigar during a lull at his observation post overlooking Afghanistan's Balkh Valley. (U.S. Air Force Special Operations Command)

A U.S. Navy SEAL sniper on a special reconnaissance mission in Afghanistan in late January 2002. (U.S. Navy photo by Photographer's Mate First Class Tim Turner)

The first cavalry charge of the twenty-first century: Master Sergeant Bart Decker of the 23rd Special Tactics Squadron leads anti-Taliban forces from the Northern Alliance on a horseback charge in the Balkh Valley as he moves from his infiltration site near Mazir-i-Sharif in mid-November 2001, during one of the first offensives of Operation Enduring Freedom. Two U.S. Special Forces members follow him, just beyond the gully. (U.S. Department of Defense)

The War Boss: The commander in chief of U.S. Central Command, Army General Tommy R. Franks, whose area of operations covers twenty-five countries in the Persian Gulf and Central Asia, briefs reporters near his headquarters in Tampa, Florida, on military operations in Afghanistan on November 27, 2001. (Defense Department photo by R. D. Ward)

Second Lieutenant Billy White (left) and Technical Sergeant William "Calvin" Markham of Hurlburt Field's 23rd Special Tactics Squadron stand beside a Russian HIND helicopter destroyed at Kabul Airport. (U.S. Air Force)

A Special Tactics team mans an observation post in Afghanistan's Tora Bora mountain region. Their laser target designator is on the right. (U.S. Air Force)

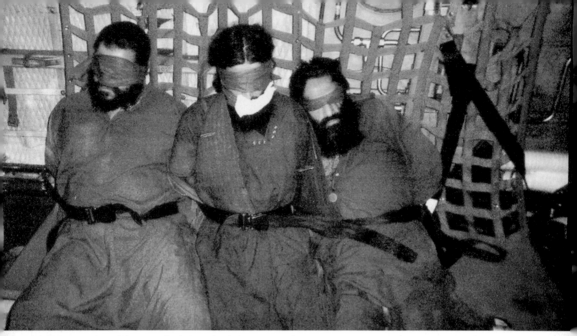

Captured Taliban and al-Qaeda fighters on their way to Guantanamo Bay, Cuba. (U.S. Air Force Special Operations Command)

Hamid Karzai (fifth from left, standing) is surrounded by Northern Alliance fighters and the U.S. Special Tactics and Special Forces men who called in air strikes to save him and his forces from being overrun by Taliban/al-Qaeda fighters during one of the fiercest early battles of Operation Enduring Freedom. Nine months later, on June 14, he was elected interim president of Afghanistan by the loya jirga, or traditional grand council of 1,575 delegates from every Afghan ethnic group and region, the country's first such broadly representative election in more than twenty years. (U.S. Special Operations Command)

One Special Tactics and two Special Forces team members direct air strikes while Northern Alliance fighters look on. The Special Tactics man (ninth figure from right in black watch cap) has a SatCom handset to his right ear.

The logos of U.S. Special Operations Command and its four component commands (clockwise from upper left): Army Special Operations Command, Naval Special Warfare Command, Joint Special Operations Command, and Air Force Special Operations Command.

Performing a diversified job in adverse environments requires a broad range of equipment. (U.S. Air Force Special Operations Command)

CHAPTER TWELVE

GROWING PAINS

My retirement proved short lived when then Lieutenant General Duane Cassidy, the Air Force's deputy chief of staff for personnel and soon-to-be-new commander in chief of Military Airlift Command, talked me into putting my uniform back on.

My first task would be to establish and command the first combat control squadron ever, the 1723rd CCS at Hurlburt Field, Florida, home of the 1st Special Operations Wing. The squadron had important detachments at Rhein-Main Air Base in Germany, Clark Air Base in the Philippines, Eglin Air Force Base in Florida, Kirtland Air Force Base in New Mexico, and a smaller one—known as Operating Location Alpha—at the Royal Force Air Force Base near Woodbridge in the United Kingdom. In 1986, the detachment in Germany had been battling with the wing staff over whose training was more important. I stood my ground about our training standards. In only eighteen months, the unit went from being unable to pass its Operational Readiness Inspection to the highest rating that MAC's inspector general could give it.[1]

Within a year, Cassidy had me assigned to the staff of MAC headquarters as director of combat control and pararescue operations. My new task would be to reorganize and triple the size of combat control throughout MAC and, later, turn them into "special tactics" units with the addition of pararescuemen. At this point in time, morale problems persisted because of halfhearted support from elsewhere in the Air Force and competition for our missions from the other military services. By the time of our next major operation, Operation Just Cause in Panama, six years after Grenada, we had one hundred and twenty-five men in special tactics units (compared with a total of twenty-four during Grenada, although we were supposed to have had fifty then). Still, we were woefully understrength compared to our authorized billets.

A few months later, Cassidy became MAC commander in chief (CinCMAC) and earned his fourth star when General Thomas E. Ryan retired. I decided to give General Ryan a special farewell salute and arranged for four men from the 24th to fly from Pope to Scott Air Force Base and make a high-altitude, low-opening parachute jump over the base's golf course while Cassidy and Ryan were enjoying Ryan's last active duty round of golf, taking time out from Cassidy's official visit for a pre-change-of-command orientation. Led by Rick Caffee, the team timed its jump perfectly and landed silently out of nowhere on the putting green at the infamous fifteenth hole just as Ryan was lining up a twenty-foot putt trying to win the hole. Rick and his men saluted smartly and presented Ryan with a silver-plated, general officer's .45 Colt automatic. They urged him a happy retirement and told him to "never make a putt you don't need." Ryan holed his putt and ended the round with five dollars of Cassidy's money.

Word of the stunt spread quickly around MAC, and not just at Scott Air Force Base. Special tactics had finally made a big impression on our own command—and especially on our new commander in chief. Cassidy, however, was not pleased. He took command the next day and summoned me to his office. "John," he told me, "that was a great gesture. But *don't* ever do it again! Can you imagine the newspaper headlines had word gotten out about your frivolous antics burning that much gas to fly guys one thousand two hundred miles to western Illinois just so they could parachute a new pistol to a retiring four-star general?" I was embarrassed that I had not foreseen the possible repercussions, and I was determined to find a way to let Cassidy know I understood the message.

Cassidy and I had first met under awkward circumstances about four years earlier at Norton Air Force Base, where he was the wing commander. I had flown there almost "undercover" in dungarees and a T-shirt from Fort Bragg, and the plane stopped to refuel before heading to Hawaii for a counterterrorist exercise. I was the only passenger in the back of that huge cargo plane. Apparently curious about this waste of a valuable airlift asset, Cassidy came out to the ramp, introduced himself, and asked who I was, what outfit I was from, and what I was doing. I saluted smartly and told him my name, but had to insist that I could not identify my unit or mission. The wing commander was not pleased, but he was polite and wished me a good trip.

After the Ryan caper, Cassidy had me work with the MAC staff and the air staff in Washington to find the manpower spaces to create special tactics units that would comprise both pararescuemen and combat controllers. Major General Bill Mall was commander of 23rd Air Force (then headquartered at Scott) and was instrumental in pushing for me to have additional oversight of the pararescue career field, which had no champion at the top and offered little chance for progression beyond the rank of chief master sergeant. (There were no pararescue officers, and the prevailing thought was that they needed some officer leadership—although the men did not want any.)

Special operations units began to be revitalized within all the services. Demand for combat control and pararescue support grew far beyond our means. My old unit, Det 1 MACOS (Detachment One, Military Airlift Command Operating Staff) at Pope Air Force Base and Fort Bragg, had become Det 4 NAFCOS when Military Airlift Command created 23rd Air Force in early 1983 and put all its special operations units under that umbrella. No one could figure out what Det 4 NAFCOS stood for either—Detachment 4, Numbered Air Force Combat Operations Staff. Recruiting personnel became increasingly difficult for a secret unit whose existence we could not acknowledge.

By 1985, so many "special mission" units needed our support that, once again, everyone wanted their own form of a special tactics unit—the SEALs, Rangers, Task Force 160. We were suddenly competing not just within the Air Force, but with our sister services and even with the CIA for volunteers *and* for our mission. Virtually every special operations unit wanted some form of an organic special tactics team, even the CIA's Special Activities Division, sometimes known as its "field operating group." General Cassidy brought those initiatives to a screeching halt by insisting that if the units were going to use Military Airlift Command aircraft in environments as dangerous as the ones they were about to enter, they would be guided to their targets and exfiltrated by MAC combat controllers.[2] Two-thirds of the three-step dance that Lieutenant General Sam Wilson had used to describe special operations in 1982—"Get there, get it done, and get back"—was MAC's job, after all, and Cassidy wanted the men reconnoitering and marking the landing zones and drop zones or pickup points all trained to the same standards and for those units to be centralized and virtually interchangeable.

We created a new squadron, the 1724th Combat Control Squadron at Pope Air Force Base and Fort Bragg out of Det 4 NAF-COS, but it remained a unit we couldn't talk about.[3] We were also still woefully short of people for the missions given us, but Military Airlift Command headquarters, and Air Force headquarters, turned deaf ears on our plea for more personnel spaces.

That began to change dramatically in 1986 after Congress was driven to distraction by the continued wrangling among the secretary of defense, Joint Chiefs of Staff, and military services over the proper organization of and support for all special operations units. In time, the grim lessons of Grenada finally emerged and would prove to mark a profound and fortuitous turning point for all of America's special operations forces.

After three years of acrimonious public debate and fierce opposition by almost every member of the Joint Chiefs of Staff, plus bullheaded opposition from Weinberger himself, the U.S. Congress decided to totally reorganize and revitalize special operations. Led by four visionary members—Sam Nunn, the highly respected Democratic senior senator from Georgia, and William S. Cohen, the independent-minded Republican senior senator from Maine, as well as Congressmen Earl Hutto of Florida and Dan Daniel of Virginia—Congress voted in October 1986 to create a new unified four-star command, the U.S. Special Operations Command. It was an unprecedented congressional initiative. It even gave the command full responsibility for its own budget rather than having to piggyback on halfhearted support from skeptical military and civilian leaders throughout the military departments.

The so-called Nunn-Cohen Amendment first passed on August 9, 1986, in the closing late-night hours of Senate debate on the fiscal year 1987 National Defense Authorization Act. This was just four days after JCS Chairman Admiral William Crowe and Richard Armitage, then the principal deputy assistant secretary of defense for international security affairs, had testified before the Senate Armed Services Subcommittee on Sea Power and Force Projection, chaired by Cohen, that the Joint Chiefs and the civilian leadership of the Defense Department were going to "fix" SOF's problems by creating a new Special Operations Force Command, SOFC, to be headed by a three-star general. Cohen sarcastically expressed skepticism about Crowe's and Armitage's enthusiastic support for special operations and remedying its problems. Cohen and Nunn, who co-chaired the subcommittee, had been prepared to believe them, however, and said they were going to enter only a "sense-of-the-Senate" resolution the next day favoring a new four-star Special Operations Command. Cohen then called upon Major General Richard A. Scholtes to testify, but he sensed that Scholtes had a lot more to vent than he was willing to say in an open, unclassified session. Cohen ordered the hearing room cleared of everyone but the senators and their staff members, and in a closed-door, classified hearing, Scholtes unloaded about special operations' grim Urgent Fury experiences. That testimony made Nunn and Cohen realize that Crowe's "fix" represented a halfhearted measure at best, and they decided to reject the Crowe-Armitage protestations.[4] They agreed to withhold their sense-of-the-Senate resolution and to personally draft a draconian special operations overhaul instead.[5] Nunn and Cohen then collared Scholtes and asked him to recount his experiences again before a hastily called meeting of the "full" Armed Services Committee, attended by Senators J. James Exon, a Democrat of Nebraska, and John W. Warner, a Republican from Virginia. They then led Scholtes around the Capitol complex to brief other senators privately and told them of the more forceful legislation they planned to introduce the following day. Senator Warren Rudman of New Hampshire, a highly respected Republican member of the Senate Defense Appropriations Subcommittee, volunteered to append the Nunn-Cohen Amendment to that committee's fiscal year 1987 defense appropriations bill *and* to make it an amendment to the continuing budget resolution it was also drafting—just in case, as so often happened, Congress did not get around to passing a new appropriations bill before the new fiscal year began on October 1. Thus, the Nunn-Cohen legislation quickly became an amendment to *three* bills pending before Congress.

Admiral Crowe was apoplectic when he heard that Scholtes's testimony in closed session about the miscues on Grenada had persuaded the Senate to pass a far more sweeping overhaul of special operations forces only days after he thought he had won support for his strawman Special Operations Forces Command.

The bill that Cohen and Nunn tabled on the Senate floor late on the night of August 6 paralleled a proposal that Cohen had surfaced in *Armed Forces Journal International* the previous winter, calling for a new unified, four-star command.[6] However, the Nunn-Cohen Amendment was drafted in such a hurry by them and their staff members that legislation passed inadvertently providing for a four-star officer, instead of a brigadier general, to command a Special Operations Command subordinate to both the U.S. European Command and the U.S. Pacific Command, plus a brigadier general in charge of a special operations component command in every other theater.[7] In effect, there would be *three* four-star officers leading special operations, more than half as many men as sat on the Joint Chiefs of Staff. Cohen realized the error—but the bill had passed the Senate, and the Senate would soon adjourn for the chamber's traditional, monthlong August recess. It took some frantic, unusual, and possibly even illegal parliamentary maneuvering for Cohen, Nunn, and their staffs—notably Ken Johnson, Chris Mellon, and James R. Locher III—to get the Senate's unanimous consent to correct the legislation before it later went to a Senate-House conference committee that met to resolve other issues outstanding between the invariably conflicting versions of an authorization bill.

Roughly similar but far less sweeping legislation had been proposed in the House by Representative Earl Hutto, a Democrat from Florida heading a new Special Operations Panel of the House Armed Services Committee, and later by Representative Dan Daniel, a Democrat from Virginia who headed the committee's Readiness Subcommittee.[8] Both proposals had been drafted by a former special forces officer, Ted Lunger, who had served as Hutto's senior staff member and who was an outspoken, persistent proponent of special operations. Daniel's final version of the special operations amendment, its language now as forceful as Cohen's, passed the House and Senate on October 15 and was signed into law by President Reagan on November 14, 1986.[9] It provided for a one-star general or flag officer to head a new special operations component within each of the nation's five combatant or regional war-fighting commands.

Despite its unanimous passage, the Pentagon proceeded to enact the Nunn-Cohen legislation with what would later be described as "malicious implementation," a phrase used in a scathing letter sent on March 11, 1987, to Secretary Weinberger by Daniel, Hutto, and Representative John Kasich, a Republican from Ohio who served with them on the House Special Operations Panel. Five months passed before the new Special Operations Command was formally activated on April 16, 1987, but the ceremony opening its headquarters at MacDill Air Force Base near Tampa, Florida, was not held until seven months after Reagan had signed the Nunn-Cohen Amendment. Weinberger did not attend the ceremony but sent his deputy, William Howard Taft III, to represent the Defense Department. The bill had also provided for a new assistant secretary of defense for special operations and low-intensity conflict. But no one was named to fill that post for six months; even then the candidate nominated by Defense Secretary Weinberger and the administration was rejected. He was a former Justice Department lawyer with no special operations experience and a former assistant secretary of the Army for readiness who had openly opposed the reorganization legislation. Senators Cohen and Ted Kennedy, a Democrat from Massachusetts, sent Weinberger a letter in May 1987 telling him that the Senate Armed Services Committee had "decided to put a hold on *all* statuatory nominations before the Committee" until a suitable nominee had been approved. Six more months passed with no nomination tabled, and Congress finally directed that Army Secretary John O. Marsh Jr. (whose son happened to be the doctor for Delta Force) be named to fill the post as an additional duty on an interim basis (as "acting" assistant secretary).

In the summer of 1988, a full year and a half after Nunn-Cohen had been made law, another candidate, Ambassador Charles Whitehouse, was named and finally passed confirmation. He had no special operations background but extensive diplomatic experience on low-intensity conflict issues, especially in the political and economic arenas. Equally important, he was a neighbor and close friend of former Deputy Defense Secretary Frank Carlucci, then serving as President Reagan's national security adviser, and thus seemed able to get *some*one's attention. Nunn-Cohen had also provided that U.S. Special Operations Command should have its own budget, but its first submissions were so watered down by the military services, the Joint Staff, and the office of the secretary of defense that Cohen finally proposed another amendment to his own legislation requiring an entirely new and separate budget submission for SOCOM, one the services would not be allowed to diddle with and whose funds could not be diverted to conventional forces.[10]

The "malicious implementation" that so worried members of Congress reflected years of distrust, jealousy, and neglect of special operations forces within all of the services by their fellow service members and most of their military hierarchy. The divisions were acrimonious and often bitter. They were so deep that in early 1984, a three-star general serving in one of the Air Force's most important and sensitive posts, as USAF's deputy chief of staff for operations, had left congressmen aghast after he testified in a secret session before Congressman Earl Hutto's Special Operations Panel about members of Delta Force and other "special mission" units. He characterized them as "trained assassins," "trigger happy," "out-of-control cowboys on loose reins" who might "freelance a coup d'état" in a nation friendly to the United States.[11] His testimony was never made public, even in a "redacted" or unclassified version, and is still locked up in a vault somewhere within the House of Representatives. But word of it spread behind the scenes and persuaded a lot of members of both the House and Senate that all was not well in special operations. (The officer was promoted to four stars within a year and given command of all of America's strategic nuclear forces.)

Despite the landmark and unprecedented Nunn-Cohen initiative, special tactics units continued to suffer severe manpower problems. They were resolved almost by accident, after Military Airlift Command conducted an in-depth manpower survey brought about by a query Defense Secretary Dick Cheney sent to the Air Force in 1989 asking, "What is the 1724th Special Tactics Squadron? What is combat control? Who owns them?" The manpower study identified the need for 220 personnel slots, including both operators and support personnel, to accomplish the missions we were performing with only about 50 people assigned (although we were "authorized" about 80 slots at the time).

But the issues that had triggered Cheney's query gave me a revealing view from the trenches of how high-level bureaucracy works.

Early in 1986, at a senior-level forum on special operations and low-intensity conflict held at Washington's National Defense University, General Cassidy and my coauthor, Ben Schemmer (then editor of the independent monthly magazine *Armed Forces Journal International*), had a slight but strained confrontation over the readiness of Air Force special operations units. Cassidy had noted with pride during a question-and-answer session that MAC's special operations units were in splendid shape. Schemmer rose to ask, if Air Force special operations was in such good shape and getting so much high-level support, why MAC's 1st Special Operations Wing (SOW) had just failed its Operational Readiness Inspection, in large part due to a shortage of critical spare parts. Cassidy was told by the four-star moderator, retired Army General Paul Gorman, that he didn't need to answer the impolitic question, but to his credit he insisted on doing so. Cassidy essentially ignored the reference to the 1st SOW's ORI and charged that Schemmer's question had disparaged the men in that unit (when Schemmer was really disparaging the lip service given by most other Air Force leaders to special operations in general).

Cassidy and Schemmer had never really met before, and Schemmer introduced himself during the next coffee break. He noticed Cassidy's jump wings and asked how he had earned them. Cassidy told him about the water jumps with special tactics. Schemmer said that he, too, was jump qualified but had never made a water jump, and asked if *he* could jump with our men as well. At a dinner that evening addressed by Secretary of State George Shultz, Schemmer repeated his request in front of Air Force Vice Chief of Staff General Pete Piatrowski, noting that he had most recently jumped with the head of the Airborne Department at Fort Benning. Piatrowski approved the proposal, and Cassidy scheduled the jump within a week or so.

Notwithstanding jocular entreaties from Cassidy and Air Force Chief of Staff General Charles A. Gabriel that we feed Schemmer to the sharks, Schemmer survived three water jumps in one day. We were jumping somewhat above the maximum allowable winds and had told Schemmer to work the risers on his parachute so that he was facing into the wind as he neared the water; also, instead of hitting the quick-release mechanism to get rid of his parachute, he should lean back and let the wind still inflating his canopy propel him along the water until Mike Lampe and I could race up in a Zodiac and collapse his chute for him. With Mike handling the engine as the Zodiac approached Schemmer, I stood up in the prow and made a perfect swan dive to "rescue" him—but a sudden wind gust sent him scooting away from me, and I landed in the water about three yards short. Mike ignored me thrashing about in the water, raced ahead, cut his engine, and dived to collapse Ben's chute while Rick Caffee rushed up in another Zodiac to rescue me floundering in the water.[12]

Thus began a long friendship between my men and the outspoken editor, long a vocal proponent of special operations, noted for his book about the 1970 raid to free American POWs from Son Tay prison, only twenty-three miles from downtown Hanoi.[13]

After endless briefings and papers back and forth between MAC and USAF headquarters, and no doubt motivated by the momentum behind the Nunn-Cohen legislation, the chief of staff of the Air Force decided in October 1987 to reorganize all combat control and pararescue teams under one group, the 1720th Special Tactics Group, led by a combat controller and reporting to the commander of 23rd Air Force. General Cassidy named me to head the group, writing me a note stating, "As our country's premier combat controller, you are going to the perfect assignment for you—'command.'" I was soon promoted to full colonel—from "below the zone," ahead of those lieutenant colonels who were normally eligible for consideration. The promotion was unheard of for an officer who had been passed over twice for major, and it was the first time a combat controller had made full colonel.

My refusal to accept the fliers' point of view that combat control should be assigned to flying units and used only in a support role as a training aid for the aircrews finally prevailed. Years later, my men gave me a plaque that was inscribed:

To every man, there comes in his life that special moment when he is tapped on the shoulder and offered the chance to do a very special thing, unique and fitted to his talents. What a tragedy, if that moment finds him unprepared and unqualified for the work that would be his finest hour.

I knew then, however, when Cassidy's note arrived, that such a moment was upon me. It had taken almost twenty years, but now the units could develop common standards, procedures, organization, equipment, and training to get ready for war. I didn't mind if my men occasionally failed while training. I told them, "Do not be discouraged by failure. Learn from every setback you encounter; take ownership of the failure and overcome it."

To stand up the group, I persuaded MAC to give me about thirty of the manpower slots that MAC had validated, as part of Cheney's manpower study, for the 1724th Combat Control Squadron. Initially the group comprised only the 1724th Special Tactics Squadron from Fort Bragg and the 1723th Combat Control Squadron from Hurlburt Field (which soon became the 1723rd Special Tactics Squadron). Eventually, the group tripled in size and became a group of seven squadrons deployed worldwide.[14]

A year or two after I took command of the group, unbeknownst to me, men of what by then had become the 24th Special Tactics Squadron invited Schemmer to observe a source selection field exercise in the mountains of northern Georgia, culling new candidates. No journalist had witnessed that process before. Schemmer was sworn not to print or mouth a word, but he returned home impressed by the heavy workload imposed on so few men and by how understrength the unit was compared to its authorized billets and the missions assigned to it. (At that time, in the spring of 1989, special tactics teams were not only maintaining their own vehicles, motorcycles, and Zodiacs and rigging all their equipment for paradrops, but packing their own parachutes as well. There was too little time for realistic training because that time had to be sacrificed for other chores.)

Soon after Dick Cheney became secretary of defense in late March 1989, Congressman Les Aspin, chairman of the House Armed Services Committee, held a small brunch in his honor at the Potomac Yacht Club in Alexandria, Virginia. Aspin invited Schemmer, who, as it turned out, had just published a scathing editorial castigating Cheney for publicly reprimanding an Air Force four-star general for testifying "off message"—too candidly—before Congress; Schemmer charged that Cheney's reprimand was a shallow ploy simply to show the Pentagon who was in charge. Cheney turned to Schemmer at the brunch and disarmed him by asking, "So what can I do that's *constructive?*"

Torn between concern for the effectiveness of special tactics and his promise not to divulge his presence at our source selection work, Schemmer decided to appeal for Cheney's support of the unit. "Mr. Secretary," he responded, "you have a classified unit that is really the tip of America's spear. They lead Delta Force and SEAL Team Six into harm's way and care for 'precious cargo' as well; they're 'the first in and last out' when you get into deep grease. But they are woefully understrength and need your help. I just spent part of last week with them, and they are in circuit overload." By then Congressman David McCurdy, a highly respected member of the House Select Committee on Intelligence, had joined them. Cheney asked Schemmer what the unit was; with McCurdy present, Schemmer hesitated until both men pointed out that McCurdy was on the Intelligence Committee and the House Armed Services Committee and that Schemmer could thus speak openly.

He told Cheney the unit's designation. Cheney immediately reached into his coat pocket, took out a piece of notepaper and pen, jotted down the squadron's number, stuck the paper in his breast pocket, and promised he would look into it. McCurdy quickly chimed in with high praise for the unit: "Oh, I know them. In fact, I made some water jumps with them." Schemmer said he had, too (as Cheney raised his eyebrows), and the conversation ended. Within minutes, Admiral William J. Crowe, the Joint Chiefs of Staff chairman, approached Schemmer and asked him what Cheney had been making notes about. Schemmer respectfully declined to say on grounds the subject really shouldn't be discussed in the midst of so many people circulating casually over brunch.

Appalled that he had broken his oath to my men, but relieved that the Secretary of Defense himself might intervene on their behalf, Schemmer called Mike Lampe the next morning and told him of the incident. Lampe told the squadron commander, then Colonel John Buck. I had no knowledge of this until General Cassidy called to ask me what the hell was going on and asked me whom I had been talking to (as if he thought *I* had had the conversation with Cheney).

Instead of directing the Air Force to give us the manpower we needed, it seemed that Dick Cheney had gone ballistic over a perceived security breach about our unit—a unit about which, apparently, he had been told nothing and had to learn of from a journalist. Nothing happened for half a year to improve the unit's readiness—no new personnel slots, no more men assigned, nada, zip. But Cheney had quietly ordered the Air Force to conduct a detailed manpower study of our special tactics units, a task assigned to MAC, while I got some immediate, new high-level direction from the upper ranks of the Air Force. I was ordered to reassign Colonel Buck (who had been in command for two years and was ready for transfer in any event) and arranged for him to fill my former slot on the MAC staff overseeing all combat control and rescue operations, where he was in perfect position to guide Cheney's manpower study. Then I had to discipline Chief Master Sergeant Lampe, who later claimed he had to spend the next several weeks ignominiously coaching basketball practice at the Pope Air Force Base gymnasium.

The Cheney manpower study took months to complete but eventually proved a major turning point for us. It validated the need for 220 manpower billets in Colonel Buck's squadron, including support personnel. MAC endorsed that requirement; so did the newly formed U.S. Special Operations Command. By that time Lieutenant Colonel Craig F. Brotchie had taken command of the fifty-man unit (whose personnel authorizations had grown significantly, but whose

operator strength lagged behind because of severe manning shortages). The squadron's strength, however, would finally grow in the
coming years to 190 men.

During this period, we had been working hard to integrate
pararescue teams into our operations to care for "precious cargo"—
rescued hostages and wounded operators. Our motto became "First
There—That Others May Live." But the long-overdue transition of
pararescuemen into special tactics represented the culmination of a
drawn-out, bitter battle between the Military Airlift Command, Air
Force headquarters in the Pentagon, and the newly formed U.S.
Special Operations Command.

The biggest change was that we finally succeeded in getting
approval to merge part of the Air Force's minuscule but seasoned
cadre of pararescuemen—parajumpers or PJs—into Special Tactics.
We won 104 of them, although it took several years to get the manpower authorization for them and then to meld all of them into our
teams.

That transfer involved an epic struggle between General
James J. Lindsay, the first commander in chief of the new U.S. Special Operations Command created by the Nunn-Cohen Amendment, and General Duane Cassidy's successor at MAC, General
Hansford T. Johnson. Lindsay wanted to keep the PJs in existence
as part of his special operations forces, but Johnson wanted to
eliminate the career field entirely. Lindsay agreed to fund the PJ career field within his budget. Johnson agreed to "cross-walk the
money, but not the people."[15] He wanted the people authorizations
for MAC's conventional air rescue forces. By law (Cohen's amendment to the Nunn-Cohen Amendment, mandating that SOCOM
have its own budget, known as "Major Force Program 11," prepared
independently of the Army, Navy, and Air Force budgets), MAC
had to provide Lindsay the organization needed to accomplish
SOCOM's mission. But Johnson, who "did not see special operations in the same light" that Cassidy had, reminded 23rd Air Force,
the precursor to Air Force Special Operations Command, "You are
Air Force first!" The standoff resulted in "what's mine is mine" games

between the two four-star generals, and Major General Thomas E. Eggers, commander of the 23rd, was caught in the middle.[16]

Lindsay finally forced the issue with the Air Force chief of staff in March 1990 by insisting that 23rd Air Force be designated a "major command" and provided with the appropriate manpower. After weeks of wrangling (some of it over what heraldic emblem would be appropriate, finally resolved by chosing the F-5 dagger issued to British commandos in World War II and also used then by a number of Air Force units), Welch agreed late in April to stand up SOCOM's Air Force component as a major USAF command. But when time came in May for the air staff's first meeting of the organization's transition team, no one from Special Operations Command was invited because "General Welch saw no need for a unified commander in chief to be involved in the stand-up" of an Air Force major command.[17]

On May 22, 23rd Air Force was officially redesignated Air Force Special Operations Command (AFSOC), a component command of U.S. Special Operations Command (USSOCOM), and General Lindsay told its members during an activation ceremony at its Hurlburt Field headquarters, "You are truly the tip of the USSOCOM spear." That same day, General Johnson graciously granted "MAC approval for AFSOC personnel to travel aboard its aircraft."[18]

Although the elevation of Air Force Special Operations Command to major command status institutionalized the special operations warfare specialty in the Air Force, the whole megillah also illustrated a recurring problem: the halfhearted support that special tactics continued to enjoy from its parent service at a time when special operations was enjoying a phenomenon of budget growth while the rest of the Air Force was decreasing in size. We were still undermanned and hurting for personnel slots.

Shorthanded as we had been, we had sent seven or eight of our men, including Sergeant Rick Caffee, for pararescue medical training at Shepard Air Force Base or to the Pararescue School at Albuquerque; the slots were arranged for us by a true pararescueman at Aerospace Rescue and Recovery Service headquarters, Senior

Master Sergeant John Pighini, the medic who had helped pull Mike Lampe's arm out of the coral taxiway in 1985. The need for paramedics in special tactics units had become painfully evident in Grenada, where Delta Force and the Rangers took so many casualties (including many from errant friendly fire) and was only reinforced during the exercise in which Mike Lampe had almost lost his left arm.

By March 1990, we had 125 combat controllers and had adopted 88 men from MAC's pararescue teams while 179 of them stayed in MAC's more conventional units under the Air Rescue Service or served with Tactical Air Command. Later that year, we gained sixteen more PJs.

As group commander, my job was no longer to lead missions, but rather to plan for the future, improve our mission performance standards (and not just for execution, but planning for them as well), sharpen our training, and raise the bar even higher as we screened new candidates. In a sense, I was working with men who excelled at pickup games, but I insisted that they become master planners as well, and I decided that my job was to be the best master planner of them all.

That began with deciding new criteria for source selection, and we constantly honed them. Rather than compromise on personnel standards, even though still understrength, we tightened our selection criteria, decided to merge combat controllers and pararescue teams, and formalized the rigid screening process that had begun right after Grenada, when Mike Lampe and Rick Caffee got into a long discussion aboard their C-141 riding home about how we should select their replacements. Only two out of twenty-seven carefully selected candidates from almost 160 volunteers passed our first formal, semiannual field tests near the Ranger mountain camp in north Georgia, a site picked by John Pighini because he had been through the Ranger course.

Part of our source selection challenge was that the PJs and combat controllers had represented two distinct career fields, each with its professional jealousies. The PJs had a formal selection process;

combat control did not. Thus we decided that part of the selection process would not only involve "meat and potatoes"—skills and endurance tests—but also entail detailed psychological screening and provide a bonding period in which we could test men from two competitive career fields and meld them into a team.

By 1989, we had refined the process to the point that we had a cadre of truly quiet professionals. There was no room for Rambo tactics or behavior; we rehearsed everything we could anticipate and then planned for the unexpected.

That year, Mike Lampe had become our noncommissioned officer-in-charge, and he set the standard when he was selected as one of the twelve Outstanding Airmen of the Year at the annual Air Force Association meeting in Washington, the first person from special tactics ever to be so honored. (Since that signal honor, nine other men from special tactics have been chosen for the distinction.)

By then the average noncommissioned officer in special tactics (if one dared call any of them "average") was a thirty-year-old E-5 (staff sergeant) who had served nine years in the combat control career field and who had completed at least a twelfth-grade education. (I made sure that commanders arranged training schedules to give every man who wanted more schooling time to pursue some form of a college degree, whether by correspondence school, evening courses, or enough annual leave and compensatory time off for "complete immersion studies.") His military training included basic airborne training, the static line jumpmaster course, a land and sea survival course, Air Traffic Control School, the combat control basic course, the naval gunfire course, the enlisted "terminal attack" course, high-risk escape, evasion, search and rescue training, and the Marine Corps artillery spotting course. I had also insisted that volunteers for our units take the military freefall or HALO (high-altitude, low-opening parachute mission) course and go to combat diver scuba school. These NCOs were highly trained, thorough, quiet professionals.

Even more stringent standards applied to our noncommissioned officer pararescuemen, who averaged thirty-eight years of age with

fourteenth-grade educations and carried the rank of a master sergeant. (These PJs wear maroon berets, distinguishing them from combat controllers, who wear red berets.) In addition to the military training noted above (except only for the combat control basic course and Air Traffic Control School), each PJ had earned national board certification as an emergency medical technician with annual intermediate training in advanced combat life support, death-threatening life support, and the pararescue advanced casualty care course, plus upgrade training in paramedic, wilderness, and tactical medical care. We also required that each PJ pass the dive supervisor's course. Each man averaged fourteen years in the pararescue career field.[19] They were all consummate pros.

Some of the men, moreover, were cross-trained as combat controllers and pararescuemen, some were HALO jumpmasters, and many had previous combat experience. There was simply no room for amateur night in special tactics. Once they had passed our source selection process and qualified in unit proficiencies, we knew they were ready for real-world emergency deployments.

But a new problem arose. Some staff weenies had decided to split the special operations or special tactics teams out from conventional combat control teams, and within a year combat control as a whole was back to the shell of readiness that had characterized it in the early 1980s. The teams floundered about between 1990 and 1996 because the Air Force had reorganized so many times and combat control units had changed flags so often they simply quit putting up new unit crests. At one time the teams at Pope Air Force Base had proposed four unit crests for approval—one for Air Mobility Command, one for MAC (its successor), one for Air Combat Command (the successor to Tactical Air Command and SAC), and one for Air Force Special Operations Command. Not one of them was approved.[20]

CHAPTER THIRTEEN

PANAMA—"JUST CAUSE"

A t last, after eleven years in special operations at the head of special tactics and after three flawed or failed rescue attempts, our most complex operation ever succeeded in swift fashion. Shortly after midnight on December 20, 1989, special mission units, working with two brigades from the 82nd Airborne Division and one brigade from the 7th Infantry Division, began taking down the four-hundred-mile isthmus of Panama.

American forces seized the fifty-four-mile-long Panama Canal in a week, and captured Manuel Noriega, sustaining twenty-three fatalities; almost half were from special operations forces. The operation was a major success. But things got off to an inauspicious start for the 24th Special Tactics Squadron. It was commanded then by Lieutenant Colonel Craig Brotchie, who previously had commanded the 23rd Special Tactics Squadron at Hurlburt Field, Florida. I had served with him for many years, first in 1981 when he formed the first official, permanent special tactics unit at Fort Bragg, and later in follow-on assignments when he commanded the unit in the Philippines that came under me as commander of Hurlburt Field's 1723rd Special Tactics Squadron, and then when I became commander of the

1720th Special Tactics Group. I always knew Craig was the right guy for the 24th, and the only thing standing in his way was a promotion to lieutenant colonel. In the summer of 1989, Major General Bob Patterson helped me get him selected for promotion to that rank from below the zone, and we sent him to command the 24th that October.

By then the unit had been rehearsing the Panama takedown for months. Manuel Noriega had become a bad actor; our former CIA operative had become a linchpin for the South American drug trade, and it was clear he had to go. But in every rehearsal, as in almost every operation the 24th had ever mounted, it needed augmentation from the squadron at Hurlburt Field or one of the other combat control units. That created problems, however: First, operators at Hurlburt (white, sandy beaches, beautiful women, and no Army people) knew they would get the call for real-world missions without transfer to Fort Bragg (no beaches and lots of Army troops); second, augmentation requests from the 24th always highlighted the need for operators—shooters, foot soldiers—but rarely noncommissioned officers and never officers. The result was that the Hurlburt troops were getting great training but never deployed as a unit, and hard feelings developed between the two squadrons.

My discussions with Brotchie made clear that he intended to break this paradigm. Craig wanted to experiment with assigning the 1723rd JSOC missions so both units could practice fighting the way they were organized and trained. I endorsed his concept, knowing it was going to be controversial with the 24th and contentious with JSOC. Men from the 24th knew that the Hurlburt guys were good, but felt that if they were *that* good and dedicated to the mission, they should have volunteered for Fort Bragg. JSOC, for its part, "owned" the 24th and didn't like including outsiders in its operations. The fact that the 24th needed augmentation was like one of those dirty secrets everyone knew about but no one wanted to admit. But I knew Craig was right, and what we set in motion for Panama would ultimately prove the value and ability of *all* our squadrons and show naysayers the need to have a group headquarters to sort out the rifs, have a deployable staff, and stand up more special tactics squadrons.

The first night's missions in Panama were going to be a complex game of three-dimensional chess, hitting twenty-seven targets simultaneously, and no one was under any illusion it would be a cakewalk.

The 24th's noncommissioned officer-in-charge was Mike Lampe, by then promoted to chief master sergeant. Because of widespread news coverage that Manuel Noriega, who had invalidated the free elections of a new government and assaulted his opposition candidates in May 1989, had proclaimed himself supreme leader of Panama and declared a state of war with the United States on December 15, Mike's three young sons perceived that military action was impending in Panama for their father's unit. Lampe was at home on December 16, 1989, having just returned from his seventh dress rehearsal for Operation Just Cause, when a special TV bulletin noted that an American Navy lieutenant had been shot in Panama by Manuel Noriega's thuglike "Dignity Battalions" while his wife was detained and assaulted.

Mike's ever-present beeper went off, signaling him to return posthaste to our alert quarters. His children tried to prevent him from leaving. He lied to them, saying it was just another "no-notice" exercise and that he'd be home in time to drive the whole family to spend Christmas with relatives in New Hampshire.

Lampe went into quarantine with the rest of our unit and several days later flew to Fort Benning to marry up with the 3rd Ranger Battalion and then flew eight hours to Panama in a C-130 that was so cold its toilets froze over. Fortunately, he had taken along a large box of quart-sized zipper-lock bags; thus, his men and the Rangers were able to make it to Panama without any bladders bursting.

In an unusual switch of roles, wary JSOC planners had assigned Mike as its "eyes and ears," to parachute with nine other combat controllers and several pararescuemen from Hurlburt's 23rd Special Tactics Squadron—led by Captain Michael Longoria and Senior

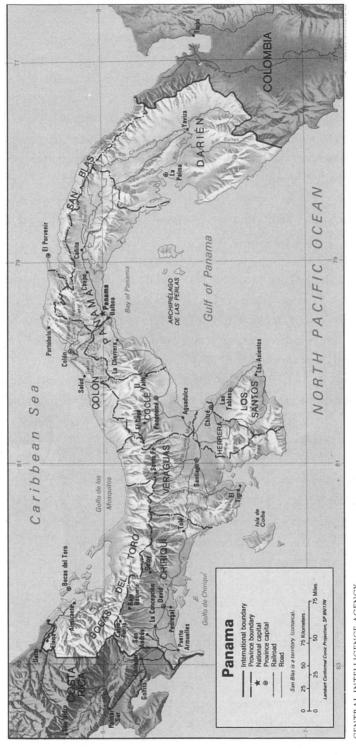

Panama

International boundary
Province boundary
★ National capital
◉ Province capital
Railroad
Road

San Blas is a territory (comarca).

0 25 50 75 Kilometers
0 25 50 75 Miles

Lambert Conformal Conic Projection, SP 9N/17N

CENTRAL INTELLIGENCE AGENCY

Master Sergeant Wayne Norrad, plus three pararescuemen from the 24th (since the 23rd had no PJs assigned yet and immediate medical care would be critical)—when the 3rd Ranger Battalion dropped on the airfield at Rio Hato, sixty-five miles from Panama City. They jumped from only five hundred feet of altitude under intense ground fire. Enemy opposition continued off and on for hours after the drop even while backup transports were air-landing other troops, including seven more combat controllers from the 23rd Special Tactics Squadron plus additional pararescuemen from Eglin Air Force Base's 1730th ParaRescue Squadron.

Mike's first job was to help coordinate the terminal guidance effort for the Ranger battalion's tactical operations center. As the sun started to rise on the airfield, he moved to the Panamanian Noncommissioned Officers Club, where one of the buildings was turned into a makeshift operating room, and he started coordinating the medical evacuation of wounded Rangers.

The day after the airfield was seized, he accompanied a Ranger platoon to Noriega's hideaway beach house not far from Rio Hato, one of the target's primary misions. There, one of the Rangers providing security at Noriega's office gave Mike an oversized fourteen-karat-gold paper clip from a drawer in Noriega's desk half filled with them—perhaps a thousand paper clips in all. Having missed the Panamanian drug lord by only fifteen minutes, the Rangers had rifled the desk looking for clues to the dictator's next whereabouts when they stumbled across the gilded office supplies that befitted Noriega's massive ego.

The Rangers and Mike Lampe didn't return home until January 7. He gave his wife, Teresa, one of Noriega's gold paper clips for a Christmas present. She presented him with a beautifully wrapped shoe box—filled with "Help Wanted" ads for civilian employment.

Typical of the struggles that special tactics had long experienced to become accepted as part of special operations' first-string team, Brotchie had to fight his way through three skeptical, recalcitrant full colonels—including the Ranger regimental commander—and appeal to JSOC's commander, Major General Wayne A. Downing, to have his own men reconnoiter Torrijos/Tucumen airfield and install special all-weather navigational beacons before the 1st Ranger Battalion, led by Lieutenant Colonel Robert Wagner, would assault it shortly after midnight on December 20. The target was not only Panama's main international airport but also the home of the Panamian Air Force. But, Brotchie argued, what if the aircrews couldn't see the field? What if it was fogged in, as so often happened at night in Panama's climate? Not even JSOC's air component commander would lead the effort to get Downing's approval. Brotchie thought he would be beating his head against a brick wall when he went to see the general, but Downing listened to how Brotchie's men had planned and rehearsed the caper, accepted Brotchie's invitation to come watch another rehearsal, got briefed on a weather forecast, and approved the plan.[1]

Brotchie's team, twenty-five combat controllers and pararescuemen led by Captain J.K. Koren, was supposed to be picked up in a C-130 at Pope Air Force Base and fly to Hunter Army Airfield near Savannah to link up with the Rangers for the primary assault on Torrijos/Tucumen International Airport, the most critical part of the initial assaults, the only field that could handle the armada of jumbo aircraft scheduled to bring in most of the follow-on forces. Failure to take down that target was the only showstopper that could cause the entire invasion to fail.

At the Pope loading ramp, however, Koren watched the C-130 take off without his men—and inexplicably empty! Because all the other airplanes had full manifests and other flight plans, J.K. and his men had to "drive" to the war. They unrigged their gear from its palletized airdrop configuration, loaded it back aboard a five-ton truck, drove four or five hours down Interstate 95 to Savannah through one of the Southeast's worst ice storms in years, unloaded their equipment, rerigged it for a parachute assault, and flew four and a half hours to Panama in two special operations, low-level C-141s. While they were en route, two MH-6 Little Birds from the Army's 160th Special Operations Aviation Regiment landed four of Koren's men—led by Technical Sergeant Bob Kinder with Staff

Sergeant Bob Martens, Sergeant Bard Baxter, and a pararescueman who had infiltrated Panama earlier—to set up two zone marker beacons at midfield on the edge of the airport as navigational aids for the Ranger assault. The remainder of Koren's team made a combat jump with the Rangers while slightly exhausted.

Although some Rangers landed in ten- to twelve-foot-tall cunna grass and took two hours to join the rest of the airfield clearing and combat control team, they were able to seize control of the airfield in about forty-five minutes. The special tactics controller, Master Sergeant Tim Brown, radioed the planes bringing in a brigade of the 82nd Airborne Division, scheduled to land as the first follow-on forces, that instead of making a planned parachute assault, they could air-land instead.

How the 82nd troopers would drop right on top of the Rangers and then through JSOC lines had been one of the planners' biggest worries. But special tactics and the Rangers had practiced and done airfield assaults so often that Brotchie was confident, as was I, that Koren's team and the Rangers would have the threat neutralized and the airfield cleared long before the 82nd Airborne men arrived. Brotchie's leaders and men had warned him that the most dangerous part of the first night's operation would be to drop the 82nd on a combat jump in the dark on top of the Rangers on a secure airfield, with the potential for a lot of friendly-fire incidents and with aircrews not nearly as well seasoned or rehearsed as those who regularly supported special tactics, the Rangers, and JSOC. And so it was to be.

The 82nd's paratroopers would not listen to proposals for an air landing. The planes approaching Torrijos/Tucumen right after daybreak (delayed by icy weather at Pope Air Force Base) were in a combat spread and, by God, the paratroopers were going to make their combat jump, no matter what. Major General James H. Johnson, the commanding general of the 82nd, happened to be on the first of eight C-141 troop-carrying airplanes headed for the airfield behind a series of twenty-eight such planes dropping heavy equipment.[2] Koren told the planes' formation commander that if he insisted on making a parachute assault, at least he should do so in trail formation, one plane behind the other, because there would be no opposition from the ground and because dense swamps surrounded what would be a very narrow drop zone on an airfield six kilometers long but less than two kilometers wide.

Undeterred, the planes continued in a combat spread (which lets all paratroopers jump at once, minimizes overall exposure time to ground fire, and hastens assembly time on the ground). Rank hath its privileges, and rank let the 82nd parachute the way it wanted to; but roughly a third of the brigade's vehicles, howitzers, and ammunition pallets landed in deep mud well to the east of the runway, hidden by nearly impenetrable, twelve-foot-high swamp grass.

A swarm of Army helicopter pilots were quickly dispatched to retrieve the errant equipment. An Army officer would later admit, in response to a press query from Bob Ropelewski, senior editor of *Armed Forces Journal International*, only that one fifteen-ton Sheridan light tank had landed in a swamp; he failed to mention that it had become so mired in the muck that soldiers who were trying to retrieve it and its ammunition blew it up instead.[3] A Military Airlift Command spokesman told Ropelewski that everything was "right on the zone." When Ropelewski pointed out that helicopter pilots told him they had spent many hours using captured Panamanian Defense Force (PDF) helicopters to airlift pallets from the swamp to drier ground at the airport, MAC public affairs officer Major Steve Harden responded: "That's because the marsh is right on the edge of the drop zone."

Later, a two-month-long, formal Air Force investigation of the unusual drop was launched; its report made no mention that the combat jump had been "totally unnecessary,"[4] onto an airfield already in friendly hands. In fact, the Rangers had almost captured Manuel Noriega: Before the 2,176 paratroopers from the 82nd Airborne had begun their drawn-out assault, a Ranger roadblock team encountered a two-car convoy trying to escape the airfield. The

Rangers stopped the first car but missed the second one. Later the Ranger regimental commander found out that Manuel Noriega had been in the second vehicle.[5]

The whole Panama operation, handled by Joint Task Force South, was conceived, planned, and executed by XVIII Airborne Corps under the command of then–Lieutenant General Carl Stiner, to whom the commander in chief of U.S. Southern Command, General Maxwell Thurman, had delegated complete operational control. Stiner turned Operation Just Cause into what might be called "the world's first special operations invasion." SOF forces, led by General Downing, included Delta Force, SEAL Team Six, the 23rd and 24th Special Tactics Squadron, the 75th Ranger Regiment, the Army's 160th Special Operations Aviation Regiment, hundreds of troops from the 3rd Battalion, 7th Special Forces Group (Airborne), and myriad USAF special operations units. Together, they made up the Joint Special Operations Task Force. They played pivotal roles in combat that soon involved 24,500 American soldiers and thousands more airmen. However, the official XVIII Airborne Corps' history of Just Cause makes no mention of any Delta Force, SEAL Team Six, or any special tactics unit participation. None of those units even appears in the history's two "Lists of Participating Units" (179 units, all battalion or squadron size or larger, appear on one list, and 169 of them on the other). In all, forty combat controllers and pararescuemen from three special tactics squadrons in the 1720th Special Tactics Group took part in Just Cause. Four of these men earned their second combat jump star—Mike Lampe, Rick Caffee, Tim Brown, and John Scanlon—along with four Rangers who had also jumped into Grenada six years before.

Launched on December 20, Panama was the largest nighttime assault since the Normandy invasion of World War II. As should have happened in Grenada, the night operations minimized casualties and battle damage on both sides while causing maximum confusion among defending Panamanian forces. Twenty-seven targets were struck almost simultaneously by hundreds of U.S. Army helicopters operating unlighted at low altitude, around numerous natural and man-made obstacles, into confined landing zones under hostile fire. Dozens of unlighted Air Force helicopters and fixed-wing special operations aircraft operated close to the Army aircraft, without any ground-based radar controllers to ensure separation of the aircraft. Yet there were no accidents, not even a near miss. That was due in large part to the work of our combat controllers, who guided air operations from the ground.

More than twenty-one hundred paratroopers from the 82nd Airborne and seven thousand troops from Fort Ord's 7th Infantry Division joined in the assault, linking up with thirteen thousand American troops already stationed in Panama.[6] The U.S.-based ground troops deployed from four bases (one more than thirty-five hundred miles from the objective); all were on the ground within fifty-three hours of President George H. W. Bush's decision on December 17 to intervene and wrest power from Panamanian dictator Manuel Noriega.

Weather complicated the invasion. Fog in northern California near Travis Air Force Base was so bad, according to one Military Airlift Command message, that "it hampered 7th Infantry Division soldiers from Ft. Ord in *finding* the base" (emphasis added), from which they flew more than nine hours before air landing in Panama.[7] Fort Ord is 150 miles from Travis, one reason the Army eventually moved the division to Fort Lewis, Washington, which has an adjacent airhead, McChord Air Force Base.

At Pope Air Force Base next to Fort Bragg, a steady, freezing rain with twenty-eight-degree temperatures coupled with a shortage of de-icing equipment delayed the takeoff of most 82nd Airborne units, which then flew 1,425 miles to jump six hours later at Tocumen/Torrijos and Rio Hato, near Madden Dam, where the ground temperature was a balmy eighty-six degrees. The parachute drops were made from two C-5As, sixty-three C-141s, and nineteen C-130s, while twenty-seven other missions air-landed the rest of the stateside-based forced-entry units.

Because radio intercepts made it clear that the Panamanians knew an invasion was imminent (especially after American TV broadcasts announced that an armada of transports was taking off from Pope Air Force Base), General Stiner moved up H-hour by fifteen minutes to forty-five minutes after midnight, Panama time. Still the special tactics teams and Rangers jumping at Tocumen/ Torrijos encountered sporadic ground fire and those jumping at Rio Hato, significant enemy fire, as did forces simultaneously attacking PDF headquarters at the Comandancia.

Fourteen of the MAC aircraft sustained minor battle damage from ground fire during the invasion, but all were back in operational service within two weeks. Forty-five of the approximately 170 Army helicopters involved took hits; four of them were lost.

Compared to the hundreds of aircraft and thousands of troops involved, casualties were small: 22 men killed in action and 324 wounded. Army commanders believed that there would have been even fewer casualties and far less battle damage to their aircraft had weather not delayed the arrival of many 82nd Airborne units until after daylight. They were to have arrived an hour and a half after the initial assault at 1:00 A.M., but they arrived five hours later and then had to be airlifted by Army helicopters to their designated objectives in broad daylight, when most of the helicopters were hit. The late arrival of the airborne units represented the biggest bobble in the whole invasion plan.

About fifty special operations helicopters from the 160th Special Operations Aviation Regiment engaged in the assault and took most of the hits, forty-five of them during the first day or two of the operation. Three of the four lost helicopters were from that unit, likely because their targets included many of the most heavily defended Panamanian strongholds. All but one of the other helicopters hit were returned to service within twenty-four hours.

The absence of midair collisions and near misses was striking, given that up to 150 fixed-wing aircraft and about as many helicopters were often operating simultaneously in a small, twenty- by twenty-mile block of airspace. (That is roughly the area contained within the I-95 Beltway surrounding the District of Columbia.) Apart from consummately skilled piloting and precision combat control work, the successful completion of so many missions by so many different aircraft stemmed largely from the fact that pre-planned air routes, altitudes, and operating areas had been assigned to all aircraft and their missions well in advance of the invasion—and the complex-choreography assault was then rehearsed repeatedly in stateside exercises. In addition, over the several months preceding the invasion, U.S. forces conducted almost weekly exercises in Panama (called "Sand Fleas" and "Purple Storms") that "desensitized" the Panamanians, rehearsing "going on right under the nose of the PDF for three of the air assaults," according to Colonel Douglas Terrell, commander of the 7th Infantry Division's Aviation Brigade from Fort Ord. Terrell commanded Task Force Aviation, the composite team of Army helicopters from various U.S. and Panamanian bases. Terrell told Ropelewski, "The PDF thought we were doing it to strengthen security or to protect our forces. We operated with different size forces at different times of the day and night. It really did desensitize them."

Even the Army aircrews were "sensitized": For the week before the assault, they were not allowed to drink alcoholic beverages (without being told the real reasons); they had to carry their personal weapons and protective vests whenever they flew; and they had to keep their protective masks in their aircraft. Terrell, a Vietnam veteran, talked with them candidly about what it was like to be shot at. Lieutenant Colonel Benton H. Borum, one of Terrell's subordinate commanders, later said that the coaching may have resulted in more restrained reactions than might have otherwise been expected when the aircrews encountered enemy fire during the first assaults.

Many of the special operations helicopters used in the operation were covertly brought to Panama well in advance of the invasion. Late in November, for instance, six AH-64 Apache attack helicopters were put into a hangar at Howard Air Force Base and kept there until the invasion began, although they flew every night observing some of the sites they would later attack. A few days before the initial assaults, twenty MH-6/AH-6 special operations scout/attack helicopters from the 160th Special Operations Aviation Regiment at Fort Campbell, Kentucky, were flown to Panama by C-5As, off-loaded during the night, and hidden in two hangars until the December 20 initial assaults. Some Air Force MH-53J Pave Low and MH-60 combat search-and-rescue helicopters flew in under their own power and were also kept hidden in hangars. So, too, were four Air Force AC-130 gunships flown to Panama well before the operation. The clandestine pre-positioning of all those aircraft contributed greatly to the surprise evident in the initial assaults.

During the operation itself, helicopters were confined to altitudes below twelve hundred feet, keeping them out of the way of faster-moving fixed-wing aircraft. Three forward-area refueling points were established near Howard Air Force Base, one several miles north of Panama City, and one at Fort Sherman on Panama's northern coast; this let the helicopters stay out of the way of fixed-wing traffic operating at Howard. Only preplanned aircraft on preplanned routes were allowed into Panamanian airspace during the initial assaults. This helped eliminate clutter on tactical radio frequencies during what were perhaps the most critical stages of the operation. No radar was available to track all of the air operations. Although pilots were too busy to talk to air controllers during the first assaults, combat controllers had to intervene frequently to clear airspace for side-firing AC-130 gunships orbiting at about three thousand feet and directing their fires onto critical targets. Seven AC-130s from USAF's 1st Special Operations Wing, Florida, flew a total of seventy-four such sorties or missions, many of them to knock out antiaircraft weapons at Tocumen/Torrijos airport and Rio Hato before the Rangers air-dropped there. Colonel George A. Gray III, the wing commander, said later that his gunships, which opened fire at forty-five minutes after midnight, fifteen minutes before H-hour, "had only about ten minutes to prepare" other targets at the Comandancia before ground forces attacked the PDF headquarters building.

Overall, Panama proved a unique challenge integrating conventional and special operations. This was especially true with respect to aviation elements, where SOF and conventional Army aviation units provided their own command and control, although the Air Force handled overall airspace coordination. Air traffic and combat controllers from all three elements manned the Air Operations Center to resolve potential conflicts.[8]

As things would turn out, the closest conflict that actually arose between special operations and conventional aviation units unfolded near Fort Amador on Panama City's southern waterfront. There, helicopters from the 228th Aviation Brigade airlifted assault troops to a small peninsula where the Panama Canal runs into the Pacific Ocean; there was U.S. military family housing on its eastern side and Panamanian Defense Force barracks on its west side, the two separated by a golf course. A few hundred yards to the northeast, Delta Force was attacking a prison (the Carcel Modelo, or Modelo prison, one block away from the PDF's Comandancia) to free imprisoned CIA agent Kurt F. Muse, a forty-year-old clandestine radio operator who had been arrested the previous April for "crimes against the security of the Panamanian state" and "promoting subversion." Muse had smuggled out a letter to President Bush in the spine of a book, urging American action. Noriega had announced repeatedly that Muse would be executed if the United States attacked Panama. Delta's rescue team had reached the prison in an M-113 armored personnel carrier from the 5th Infantry Division (Mechanized) and raced to Muse's cell, killing five or six guards on the way (including the one who was supposed to shoot him if the Americans invaded). The commandos rushed Muse to the prison's roof for extraction by an overloaded MH-6 Little Bird. With a member of Delta Force on each side to protect him in the rear passenger compartment and three Delta Force members on each skid on the sides of the helicopter, the aircraft lifted off and was struck repeatedly by sniper fire. Its controls went almost dead. The chopper literally slid down the side of the prison, wobbled about twenty feet in the air through an intersection, barely made a left turn, and crashed on its side in an alley parking lot north of the prison. Three members of Delta Force were injured and one was hit in the leg by a round that lodged in his chest. Muse escaped injury.

The alley was the wrong place to be at the wrong time because an AC-130 was pounding the Comandancia, but the men kept their wits about them and evaded both friendly and enemy fire. Signaling with an infrared strobe light visible to a Blackhawk pilot with night-vision goggles, a Delta member called in another M-113 held in reserve for the mission, and it picked up the rescue team from a nearby courtyard. The operation had lasted only six minutes. In time, all four Delta Force members recovered from their injuries,[9] in part because of immediate medical care from our PJs.

Almost simultaneously, a conventional OH-58 scout helicopter was shot down while supporting the landing at Fort Amador. It was the only conventional forces helicopter shot down during the first night's fighting.

The situation was especially perilous because all this was happening in the dark of night. Every crew member on all the aircraft involved in the initial assaults wore night-vision goggles, including crew chiefs and door gunners. Most used ANVIS-6 systems unique to aircrew use, the latest equipment then available.[10] More sensitive than earlier night-vision systems, they let aircraft operate safely in very tight landing zones and avoid transmission power lines and telephone poles and wires, and distinguish friendly from enemy forces on the ground. U.S. troops wore armbands and reflective tape patches that were readily visible through the night-vision goggles, enabling helicopter and AC-130 gunship crews to provide accurate and effective suppressive fire once special tactics combat controllers on the ground cleared airspace for them to engage.

Complicating the air traffic control problem somewhat was that two aircraft saw combat for the first time in Panama, eleven of the Army's AH-64 attack helicopters (first deployed in 1985) and two Air Force F-117 stealth fighters (operational since 1983). Three of the Apaches, all from the 82nd Airborne Division's Aviation Brigade (along with four of its smaller AH-1 Cobras), sustained battle damage, taking a total of forty-six hits from enemy fire in such vital components as engines, gearboxes, tail rotor drive shafts, rotor blades, and flight control components. None of the aircraft was forced down, however, and all returned safely after their missions. Colonel Gene Cole, the brigade's commander, told Ropelewski that the AH-64's forward-looking infrared systems and other night-vision devices allowed the aircraft to look at the objectives from long range and identify their targets before making their firing runs. Of the 250 hours the aircraft flew in Just Cause, about 140 hours were on night missions. Only two missions had to abort because of equipment failures, but Panama's high humidity blurred some of the video imagery generated by the helicopters' optical and infrared sensors. Ropelewski reported that resourceful maintenance crews solved the problem by removing those avionics and baking them in an oven for short periods.[11]

The F-117s flew more than twenty-six hundred miles from the 37th Fighter Wing at Tonopah Test Range Airfield in Nevada, each dropping a two-thousand-pound bomb near an infantry barracks at Rio Hato to stun and disorient Panamanian troops there fifteen minutes before Rangers from Fort Lewis's 2nd and Fort Benning's 3rd Battalion of the 75th Rangers parachuted onto the adjoining airfield from five hundred feet under heavy fire. It took them only twelve seconds to hit the ground.

General Stiner himself had made the decision to use the F-117 (approved by Defense Secretary Dick Cheney) for the first time because it was so ideally suited for night operations, and its night attack capabilities and precise weapon delivery system would likely minimize both friendly and hostile casualties, stunning instead of killing hundreds of Panamanian troops. But the Panamanians weren't the only ones *almost* surprised by the F-117 attacks: the Rangers at Fort Benning were told of them (by mistake it turned out) in their initial planning meeting; and the special tactics men accompanying them learned of the strikes from the Rangers, not the Air Force, whose senior leaders had seldom been in tune with its special operations units.[12] The *New York Times*'s Michael Gordon found—more than three months after Defense Secretary Dick Cheney himself had raved about the F-117's precise debut performance, claiming it had delivered its bombs with "pinpoint accuracy"—that one of the planes had to veer off from its planned aim point at the last minute and "missed its target by more than 300 yards."[13] Still, the attacks achieved their purpose: Paratroopers found the completely disoriented Panamanian soldiers running around in their underwear asking, "What the hell was that?"

But some of those who jumped at Rio Hato questioned the use of the 2,000 lb. bombs. "Why wake up the enemy fifteen minutes before our airborne assault? It was 1:00 A.M." Chief Master Sergeant Wayne Norrad noted later, "I believe we would have had fewer casualties had those bombs not been dropped. It seemed like a way to get Tactical Air Command some role in the invasion so Military Airlift Command wouldn't get all the credit."[14]

Notwithstanding the embarrassing F-117 hiccup, the overall precision of supporting fire from the AC-130s, AH-6 Little Birds, AH-1s, and AH-64s was a key factor in the success of Just Cause. Many of the assaults had to be conducted in heavily populated areas within Panama City, but there was surprisingly little collateral damage evident except in the slums adjacent to the well-defended Comandancia. (The United States steadfastly refused, however, ever to release any estimate of overall civilian casualties.) All of the gunship crews, both fixed wing and helicopter, were prebriefed time and again about the need to minimize Panamanian casualties, both military and civilian, and the rules of engagement that would be followed to prevent them. Terrell of the 160th told Ropelewski that his helicopters were fired upon repeatedly by Panamanian defenders scattered among the general population of Panama City and other residential areas, from houses as well as crowds, mostly from people who then disappeared back into the houses and crowds. Often his aircrews refused to fire back just to avoid hitting civilians and damaging houses.

In addition to a total of eight F-117 sorties, Air Force A-7 Corsair fighter-bombers flew seventy-six attack sorties, their scope limited by the lack of night attack capability and the proximity of so much of the fighting to civilian population centers. "Tactical air support wasn't needed," according to Terrell, "because the threat didn't warrant it. . . . No artillery was fired for the same reason—to avoid collateral damage."[15]

After-action reports filed by combat controllers and pararescue-men illustrate the complexity and intensity of the whole operation and the myriad, overlapping, and often simultaneous tasks that combat controllers were called upon to perform. Operators from Howard Air Force Base's combat controllers were embedded into every team from the 7th Special Forces Group, assigned to Southern Command's Special Operations Command under Colonel Jake Jacobelly. Those men earned their pay as they directed AC-130 gunship fires against many H-hour targets and subsequent ones, yet were never mentioned in any unit histories of events in Panama.

There were scores of unsung heros in the combat controllers and PJs in Just Cause. Staff Sergeant Frank D. Medeiros Jr., from Eglin Air Force Base's 1730th Pararescue Squadron, for instance, was on the first aircraft to air-land at Rio Hato, about one hour and forty minutes after Mike Lampe and the Rangers parachuted onto that objective. The field was still under fire when he stepped off the plane loaded down with two radios, a Heckler & Koch submachine pistol, two nine-millimeter pistols, a flare gun, rucksack, inflatable mast pants to hold fractures in place, and Gentex helmet with ANPVS-7 night-vision goggles. Within minutes of helping to clear the runway and taxiways of several arriving aircraft, Medeiros was called on his intrateam radio to look after two injured U.S. soldiers on the northeast side of the runway. There he found a Ranger jumper with a compound tibia/fibula fracture, his leg broken in two places, and one with a fractured femur of the right leg who had lost a lot of blood. He began treatment on the second patient and called for transport. He then discovered a civilian car south of the Pan American Highway shot full of holes with a female in the backseat; she had a fatal head wound. Called upon to clear the runway north of the highway, he proceeded there under enemy fire with another paramedic on a big motorbike and found five civilian casualties with multiple bullet wounds, called for transport, and immediately loaded the wounded onto a plane on the airfield's north cross taxiway.

Medeiros got a call alerting him to help a doctor treat an Army soldier with a sucking chest wound. He injected saline solution to hydrate the patient and helped the doctor prepare a chest tube procedure. The doctor had run out of morphine, so Medeiros administered twenty milligrams from his own medical kit until the soldier was sedated. But they came under fire from the active runway across the highway. Two MH-60 helicopters engaged the target with Hellfire missiles and mini-gun fire, but Medeiros was soon told there were casualties there. He and three other PJs found four seriously wounded Rangers, one needing cardiopulmonary resuscitation, one with multiple shrapnel wounds, one with two amputated arms, plus an unconscious Ranger with massive lower-leg injuries. They began treating the Rangers and were loading some on litters when they took enemy fire and a firefight broke out. They moved the casualties to the opposite side of an all-terrain recovery vehicle with six litters and loaded it with all four Rangers; within five minutes, another firefight broke out. But there was no cover and a Ranger there was killed. Medeiros began marshaling helicopters into a landing site near the joint casualty collection point (JCCP), and his team loaded two litter patients and two ambulatory ones on an MH-60 while other critical casualties were put into a waiting C-130 and quickly flown out of Rio Hato.

By then his men were exhausted and had to hydrate themselves with intravenous saline solution to regain some energy. An hour later, word came from the 2nd Ranger Battalion's combat command post, to their south, of a new critical Army casualty with a sucking chest wound. Medeiros headed there on his motorcycle while three other PJs followed on another rescue all-terrain vehicle (RAT-V). The doctor there insisted the casualty not be moved to the JCCP for evacuation, so Medeiros called for a medevac MH-53 to land in a small parade ground right beside the Ranger command post. But high-velocity downwash from the aircraft's huge rotor blades ripped shingles off the building and sent them flying in all directions, and the helicopter had to abort. Medeiros and his buddies loaded the Ranger on the RAT-V, drove him and other casualties to the JCCP, and saw that they were flown out of Rio Hato along with one civilian killed in the action.

"Things slowed down after that," Medeiros would report, "and we got some rest." He and his fellow pararescuemen had been handling one emergency after another for more than ten hours, often while under enemy fire. From then until three o'clock that afternoon, they were able to work in shifts.[16]

In those early hours of Just Cause, Medeiros had personally treated twelve badly wounded U.S. soldiers and eight civilians, put three killed civilians into body bags, helped marshal aircraft on Rio Hato airfield and clear it of planes, trucks, parachutes, and stray or discarded equipment and ammunition that would have made the airstrip inoperable. As among all special tactics personnel, Medeiros's work was complicated by several factors: 1. All air traffic control operations—managing an estimated 356 sorties into and out of Rio Hato within about three days—had to cease while AC-130 suppressive fire was called in; 2. While close air support missions responded to sporadic enemy mortar attacks; 3. While intermittent but sometimes intense small-arms and heavy machine-gun fire hit the airfield; 4. When landing or departure directions were hastily changed throughout the night due to enemy contact at various parts of the airfield; and 5. Because several aircraft missed their approaches prior to landing since all operations were conducted without runway lights (using only infrared T-box beacons) and the planes' landing lights weren't turned on until within only one mile of touchdown.

Compounding their work, the men found that their Gentex ballistic helmets needed dual-communication callers and would not let them hear sounds from the surrounding environment—bullets whizzing near them, for instance, as well as warnings or challenges and replies from nearby friendly troops. (Mike Lampe was almost shot "for failing to respond to a challenge," First Lieutenant Jeff

Schuldheiss of the 23rd Special Tactics Squadron would note in his after-action report.)

Although Medeiros's motorcycle didn't have a working odometer, he probably rode a hundred miles up and down the runways and taxiways on his overloaded, oversized military bike. He was awarded the Bronze Star Medal for Valor.

It is hard to convey how expertly our pararescuemen were trained and how professionally they handled severe trauma cases, but one example from the after-action report of Staff Sergeant Chet Ebeling will help. (Ebeling parachuted with the 3rd Ranger Battalion onto Rio Hato, landed totally lost in tall grass with his radio broken, out of contact as he listened to bullets whizzing around him for the first two hours of the operations, and readily admitted he was so tense and scared that "I threw up!")

Once Ebeling was able to join up with his teammates, he was called to help evacuate a badly wounded Ranger from a house by the beach in Rio Hato. He had been shot in the head and chest twelve or thirteen hours earlier during the initial assault and had an open head wound two inches long extending to the skull aft of the coronal suture; also, there was no apparent exit wound from where he had been shot in the upper right chest, puncturing his right lung. Army doctors there were trying to place a tube in the Ranger's chest to relieve heavy bleeding into his lung.

The patient was "in nowhere near a stable status," Ebeling found. "Evacuation . . . was tenuous at best," but Ebeling's team had inserted an IV and the Ranger was moved to the Rio Hato airfield for evacuation. Master Sergeants Don Shelton and John Smith monitored the Ranger's airway, respiration, chest tube, pulse, and IV, and changed the IV as their patient was loaded aboard an MH-53. Five minutes after takeoff from Rio Hato, their patient developed severe respiratory stress; the airway was becoming difficult to monitor and maintain. His pulse was high but weak, and constant care had to be taken to keep his chest tube and Heimlich valve functioning. The paramedics were losing their patient from uncompensated shock and respiratory stress. They made a collective decision to place the Ranger in a "reverse Trendelenburg position," which elevates the feet to induce blood flow into the upper body, but the Ranger vomited blood and bodily fluids. Master Sergeant Shelton was able to clear and reestablish the airway, and their patient began breathing again. Respirations slowed, his pulse dropped, and he soon opened his eyes for the first time since the PJs had seen him. They changed his IV, cleaned his face of dried blood and vomit, and moistened his lips with a damp surgical sponge. For the first time, the PJs felt they had stabilized the patient and were reasonably confident he would survive air evacuation to the casualty collection point.

After the forty-five-minute flight from Rio Hato to the JCCP, the three PJs took the Ranger directly into surgery, bypassing the triage area, and personally debriefed the doctors in the operating room. The Ranger survived initial surgery and was air-evacuated to the United States. Our PJs had saved his life.

The work performed by pararescuemen like Medeiros and his teammates validated our insistence on integrating pararescue with combat control work and to cross-train our special tactics teams to the maximum extent possible. One Sergeant would note in his after-action report, "Our PJs/CCT worked so well together that it should have been that way a long time ago."

In one instance, the *absence* of a combat controller may have contributed significantly to friendly casualties. That was when sixty-two men from SEAL Team Six assaulted Punta Patilla Airfield to prevent Manuel Noriega's private Learjet from taking off. For reasons never made clear, the mission commander (the same officer who had led the ill-fated SEAL mission that was supposed to insert me and my special tactics team onto Point Salines airfield in Grenada) decided not to let the combat controller assigned to him, Staff Sergeant Pat Rogers, accompany his team. The SEALs made up Task Force Papa, comprising three SEAL platoons that were inserted from Howard Air Force Base, eight miles away, in fifteen combat rubber raiding craft and in two patrol boats from Rodman Naval Station on the west side of the Panama Canal. However, the force ran into much heavier enemy opposition than expected and was unable to call in AC-130 gunship fire because of radio problems. Rogers, left behind on the perimeter of the airfield, could hear the SEALs calling for help, but the AC-130 crew couldn't hear the SEALs' transmissions. More than three hours elapsed before a different AC-130, which the SEALs were able to contact, came on station. Four SEALs died in that action, which involved four separate firefights, and eight were wounded in a planned five-hour mission that lasted thirty-seven hours.[17]

It seemed like an eternity before Manuel Noriega was finally located, fleeing into the Papal Nunciatura at four-thirty on Christmas Eve afternoon, only four days after our initial assaults on Panama. He surrendered to General Downing on January 3, was hustled aboard an MC-130 Combat Talon, and was whisked by Drug Enforcement Administration agents, with Sergeant K. "Lucky" Cook and one other Special Tactics man as guards, to Homestead Air Force Base near Miami.

Convicted of drug running and money laundering in 1992, he is still in federal prison serving a thirty-year sentence and is not eligible for parole until 2006. In 1999, Panama's high court asked the United States to extradite him so Panama could jail him for conspiracy to commit murder and the torture and firing-squad executions of nine Panamanian army officers who had attempted to overthrow his regime in October 1989. He could also face twenty years in jail after being condemned in absentia in the 1985 torture and death of Hugo Spandafora, a doctor and journalist who had been one of his most vocal critics. Noriega and his wife (whom he had married while hiding in the Papal Nunciatura) also face charges of money laundering in France.[18]

Panama proved the first major success for American special operations forces—at least the first one the public heard about. SOF had finally "grown up," although there were some senior people in the Defense Department and military hierarchies who were obviously uncomfortable that we were as good as we were.

For me, the mission was particularly gratifying, even though it was the first time I had been sitting on the sidelines—more a general manager than a coach or a quarterback. The 23rd had performed an important mission on its own and had given notice that it was a unit to be reckoned with. The 24th had matured to the next level as well. I was proud, but more important, I knew we would become even more relevant in the future.

CHAPTER FOURTEEN

"DESERT SHIELD," "DESERT STORM," AND "PROVIDE COMFORT"

When Iraq invaded Kuwait on August 2, 1990, the Pentagon was more than a bit embarrassed—not simply because it was caught by surprise, but because it had virtually written off the prospect of any such war. When Defense Secretary Dick Cheney appeared before the Senate Armed Services Committee for his confirmation hearing in 1989, the subject of Iraq never came up. Faced with deploying a quarter million, and then a half million troops to Saudi Arabia, the Pentagon discovered that it had quit producing desert camouflage netting two months before Saddam Hussein moved into Kuwait City. Yet it was still producing green/brown camouflage for the forests and fields of Europe, two years after the Berlin Wall came down. Our allies weren't much more prescient: The British had sold Iraq its desert camouflage uniforms, sure they would no longer be needed. Worse, the Senate Defense Appropriations Subcommittee noted that the Defense Mapping Agency had submitted a budget request that year for 5,459 maps for U.S. European Command and U.S. Atlantic Command, but that the Pentagon's maps of Saudi Arabia were, on average, four to five years old—in a region where sand dunes may shift two kilometers a year and wadis half to three-quarters of a kilometer a year. And this was

Iraq

International boundary
Province (muḥāfaẓah) boundary
★ National capital
⊛ Province (muḥāfaẓah) capital
Expressway
Road
Railroad

0   50   100 Kilometers
0   50   100 Miles
Lambert Conformal Conic Projection, SP 12°N/38°N

Boundary representation is
not necessarily authoritative.

CENTRAL INTELLIGENCE AGENCY

225

only seven years after the Joint Chiefs of Staff had failed to order any maps for the invasion of Grenada until the operation was almost over.

America is not very good at prognosticating its future. In 1989 and early 1990, President George Bush's National Security Council staff had been too busy to prepare a National Security Strategy, so they contracted it out. Released in March 1990, six months before Saddam Hussein invaded Kuwait, the document came out too late to affect the defense budget that the Bush administration sent to Congress on January 6. But Iraq wasn't mentioned once; nor was oil; "energy supplies" were mentioned once, but all it said was that "the free world's reliance on energy supplies from this pivotal region and our strong ties with many of the region's countries continue to constitute important interests for the United States"— "important," not "vital." In military lexicons, "important" interests are ones you protect; "vital" interests are ones you go to war over.

Why did we deploy 240,000 troops to Saudi Arabia within months? Why did nineteen nations amass there, as of October 1, 1991, along with seventy-nine naval ships, seventy air squadrons, and ninety-three ground force battalions? Because it suddenly became evident that Saddam Hussein, who already owned 10.1 percent of the world's proven oil reserves, had just captured 9.6 percent more of them and was threatening to take over another .25.7 percent. Half the world's oil is an interest "vital" to all America, regardless of what the National Security Strategy had or had not said in March 1990.

Similarly, the 1988 bipartisan Commission on Long Term Strategy mentioned "oil" only once in its sixty-nine-page report, "Discriminate Deterrence." Iraq did not even make the dispatches; the biggest threat postulated in the Persian Gulf region was from a Soviet incursion there.

Special tactics units played significant roles in the 1991 Persian Gulf War. More than 160 men deployed under my command of the 1720th Special Tactics Group for that operation from thirteen different units, taking 125 tons of equipment with them from regular, reserve, and Air Force National Guard bases.

During the buildup of allied forces in Saudi Arabia, special tactics men led by Captain Tony Tino and Chief Master Sergeant Wayne Norred handled all of the traffic at King Fahd airfield, which became the busiest airport in world history. Some days they controlled as many as eighteen hundred takeoffs and landings.

The air war opened at 2:38 A.M. on January 17 when four USAF MH-53 helicopters guided eight Army Apache attack helicopters to destroy two Iraqi early-warning radar sites guarding the southwestern approaches to Baghdad. Our pararescuemen were part of that initial strike. Within hours, special tactics teams had installed radar beacons all along the Saudi-Iraqi border to direct allied aircraft through other gaps in the enemy early-warning system.

Four days after the air war began, an Air Force special operations helicopter with Sergeant Thomas Beddard, a special tactics pararescueman, aboard rescued the first downed airman, Lieutenant Devon Jones, a Navy F-14 pilot shot down sixty miles northwest of Baghdad. When the MH-53J took off for that mission 130 miles into Iraq, the fog was so thick that even when flying a hundred feet off the ground, the crew could not see it. They were unable to locate the pilot because the map coordinates given them were fifty miles off. They had to return to their Saudi base to refuel and launched again, this time with a better fix on the pilot's location. Just as they reached him, an Iraqi truck descended on them and the copilot had to direct two Air Force A-10 "Wart Hogs" flying overhead to "smoke the truck." During that six-and-a-half-hour mission, the helicopter crew showed their professionalism by hiding in the desert from an Iraqi fighter searching for them. It was the deepest rescue of the war, for which the aircrew received the coveted MacKay Trophy.

Another successful combat search and rescue occurred on February 17 when an Air Force F-16 went down in southern Iraq thirty-six miles from the Kuwaiti border. Slightly injured, the pilot parachuted into a heavy concentration of Iraqi troops but established contact with rescue forces. Two MH-60s from the Army's 160th Special Operations Aviation Regiment landed two of our special tactics pararescuemen to pluck him from the desert and return him to King Khalid Military City, where a waiting flight surgeon sewed him up. Also awaiting him was his wingman, who had flown there as soon as he completed his mission to greet his buddy.

There were other successful rescues, but most of the aircrews downed in the Gulf War were not rescued, for a variety of reasons. They needed better survival radios (and we required a voice transmission before we could attempt a snatch); there were few sightings of open parachutes (required before a rescue mission could be launched); many pilots landed in areas occupied by heavy concentrations of Iraqi troops and, as often as not, the Iraqis beat our rescue teams to the downed airmen.

A nine-man special tactics team organized a successful underwater search and recovery operation for the airmen aboard an AC-130H Spectre gunship, *Spirit 03*, shot down while supporting U.S. Marines defending the town of Khafji on January 31, killing all fourteen crew members. It was the greatest single combat loss for coalition air forces during the war.

One twenty-man British Special Boat Service (SBS) mission included three U.S. special forces men and a combat controller, Master Sergeant Steve Jones, who was handling close air support. They were inserted by two helicopters on the night of January 25 to within thirty kilometers southwest of Baghdad to cut a buried fiber-optic cable supposedly used for Scud command and control and as a link to the Republican Guard. They found no fiber-optic cable, but crammed eight hundred pounds of explosives into the hole they dug and blew up the conventional cables. After one and a half hours on the ground, the team returned safely by helicopter. The special tactics member of that team was accused of a serious security breach for having left his calling card at the target. I happened to be present when a Special Forces colonel from U.S. Central Command showed up at King Fahd airfield, just south of the Iraqi-Saudi border, to investigate the allegation. He insisted on talking to the non-commissioned officer in question, but I couldn't let him because the man was secreted in a secure briefing room with some British special operations troops planning their next (and time-sensitive) mission. The officer even claimed the Brits wanted the NCO amputated from their work because he had compromised security. I was finally able to persuade the officer that none of my men ever carried "calling cards" and that no one from special tactics would have left one in denied territory under any circumstances. As it turned out, it was one of the colonel's own men, a special forces member, who had left a calling card, and his men were axed from further SBS missions. SBS then asked that we provide four special tactics combat controllers for any further such forays.

Once again, special tactics commanders had to argue their way onto the main playing field. Even after ten years of "First In, Last Out" work with America's special mission units, special tactics was not accepted as part of the first team by Delta Force, SEAL Team Six, or even by our own service.

What was particularly strange during the buildup of forces for Desert Shield and preparations for the Gulf War was the absence of JSOC forces. The key forces that the previous December had been the spearhead for the invasion of Panama were nowhere to be found in the plans for liberating Kuwait and defeating Iraq. "Conventional" special operations units like the 5th Special Forces Group, the 1st Special Operations Wing, and regular Navy SEALs were deployed, but clearly they weren't being given a starting role. Almost immediately, General Carl Stiner, by then the four-star commander in chief of U.S. Special Operations Command, opened a dialogue with Central Command's CinC, General H. Norman Schwarzkopf, on how he could leverage SOF forces, to include JSOC. He was willing to send a senior special operations general officer to take over for Schwarzkopf's day-to-day SOF commander, Colonel Jesse Johnson. Stiner even flew to Saudi Arabia to see Schwarzkopf, but was rebuffed. After that it fell to Major General Wayne Downing of JSOC to convince Schwarzkopf that his units had much to offer in prosecuting the war. After several tries, it became apparent to everybody that Schwarzkopf was going to run the war *his* way, and that meant tanks—*lots* of tanks. It's as though Schwarzkopf had sworn to relegate George Patton to a minor footnote in military history. This was going to be *his* war, and the stars of Panama were not welcome.

That sent shock waves through JSOC's special mission units. While the wave of terrorism that was lurking somewhere to sweep over the world was supposed to be more than enough to keep JSOC busy, the truth was that we just weren't wanted in Central Command's area of operations. By October 1991, Fort Bragg had become a ghost town: All of the XVIII Airborne Corps units were deployed, including the 24th Infantry (Mechanized) Division, the 82nd Airborne, and the 101st Airborne (Air Assault) Division. Special forces units were moving out, too, but JSOC was just sitting on the sidelines. That had a big impact on our special tactics teams. I had always tried to keep the 24th Special Tactics Squadron manned with our most seasoned men, but now we were busy deploying almost everyone *not* assigned to the 24th. The 23rd Special Tactics Squadron from Hurlburt Field and combat controllers and PJs from all the other stateside units were deployed early to plan for combat and to support troop movements and supply shipments in preparation for war.

JSOC units continued to train hard and search for a way to help win the war. Finally it happened: The terror in Israel caused by sporadic but deadly Scud missile attacks threatened to undermine the tenuous coalition of forces arrayed against Iraq. The only way to keep Israel from a preemptive attack against Iraq, fracturing the coalition, was to promise to stop the Scud launches. Israel, never ready to back down from a fight, could only be appeased by the political decision to commit JSOC to that task. I don't know how Schwarzkopf reacted to orders from Defense Secretary Cheney and JCS Chairman Colin Powell to commit JSOC's units to that mission, but there was a collective sigh of relief throughout U.S. Special Operations Command. As if to get even for being made to use forces he had kept out of his turf, Schwarzkopf imposed a stringent manpower cap on how many JSOC men General Downing could deploy.

In November, before JSOC even had a mission there, Downing had discreetly deployed a very small team of unit representatives to scout the theater for some bed-down locations. Colonel Craig Brotchie, still commanding the 24th, grabbed Major Mike Longoria, operations officer of the 23rd, and the two took off on a thousand-kilometer road trip looking at airfields. They found a small commercial airfield at ArAr in northwestern Saudi Arabia that could serve as JSOC's primary option. In January, after Schwarzkopf had been ordered to get JSOC involved, its units deployed there.

JSOC had worked hard on options to neutralize the Scuds. Intelligence was sparse, and we were impressed by Iraq's ability to hide and camouflage its Scud infrastructure. What emerged was a two-pronged strategy. First, small mounted patrols would be inserted by helicopter deep into Iraq to search for and destroy the missiles. Second would be flights by Army aviation teams flying predetermined routes using the Defensive Armed Penetrator, a modified MH-60 helicopter from the "Night Stalkers" of the 160th Special Operations Aviation Regiment with an array of firepower—.50-caliber machine guns; a 7.62-caliber mini gun (its version of the Gatling gun); 2.75-inch rockets, each spewing about eight hundred arrow-like flechettes that could wipe out an area the size of a football field; Hellfire fire-and-forget missiles; and gun-camera systems that would let us review what, if anything, they had destroyed.

Lieutenant Colonel Eldon Bargewell, the Delta squadron commander in charge of JSOC's Scud hunt, told Brotchie he didn't need men from the 24th Special Tactics Squadron on the missions just to control aircraft if the need for AC-130 gunship fire, close air support, or heavier air strikes should arise. Each patrol would have only ten to twelve men, and Bargewell had fifty or sixty Delta shooters chomping at the bit to get into the fray. Brotchie was incredulous. Putting ten or twelve men in harm's way, with the only chance of escape using massive firepower from the Air Force, and there wasn't room for one combat controller to orchestrate that support? Downing had always preferred such arguments to be settled below his level, but just as he had in Panama, he backed Brotchie and ordered that every Delta patrol would have a 24th combat controller. In retrospect, it was the smartest decision of the anti-Scud campaign. Virtually every patrol that went deep into Iraq ran into enemy contact. Several patrols encountered significant, determined enemy forces, and only the expert and massive application of Air Force firepower prevented severe U.S. losses—and possibly the complete loss of several patrols.

Still, there were some questionable decisions at ArAr. With the air war raging on, no Rangers had been deployed for Desert Storm, and former Ranger Commander Downing and the current commander, Colonel Buck Kernan, were more than disturbed by that oversight. The heroes of Panama and the finest light infantry in the world were on the sidelines: Schwarzkopf had seen no need for them. Downing and Kernan finally persuaded Schwarzkopf, the "King of Desert Storm," that there might be a need to seize some airfields in western Iraq, and that no unit could seize airfields like the Rangers. Men from the 24th were excited, since the key to airfield seizure was a package of twelve special tactics men integrated with the Rangers. But Schwarzkopf's approval was capped at 150 Rangers, barely a rifle company with some command-and-control overhead, and that included attachments—ergo, no special tactics support. Brotchie was livid. He argued his way up the chain of command and finally found himself in front of Downing, who handed him a phone and told him to call Kernan, since it was his deployment and thus his decision. Kernan's answer was "No!"

The Rangers' work is duly noted in Ranger regimental histories and in that of USSOCOM. There, one can read about a daring night raid into Iraq with helicopter support to attack a secret microwave tower that was supposed to be the key to Iraqi command and control. In reality, the Rangers assaulted a deserted radio tower that was in disrepair, and it's questionable if it was even in Iraq. When Craig Brotchie told me of the Ranger operations, I did a six-mile rucksack march around the ArAr airfield to cool my temper and decided it was time for his group commander to return to the United States. It was the last time I ever carried a rucksack.

In the final analysis, JSOC did some good work keeping Israel out of the war. In the spring of 1991, Defense Secretary Cheney went out of his way at a gathering hosted by the congressional leadership to honor special heroes of the Gulf War to say to one noncommissioned officer from the 24th Special Tactics Squadron, "So you're one of the men who kept Israel out of the war." Much has been argued about whether or not JSOC's forces really found and destroyed any Scuds. It doesn't matter; the fact is that once JSOC got into the fight, the Iraqis never had another effective Scud launch. JSOC had denied Iraq the use of its most effective terror weapon.[1]

At least four special operations teams—some British, some U.S., some joint—had conducted operations to ferret out both fixed and mobile Scud sites and stop them from being fired. Special tactics men also conducted more than eighty-five assault-zone surveys, and they took part in 185 combat infiltration or rescue sorties. The first such cross-border operation took place on February 7 with sixteen special operations men and two vehicles accompanied by the armed Blackhawk Defensive Armed Penetrators. Special tactics men working with the Delta Force squadron headed by Lieutenant Colonel Eldon Bargewell set up one of his "hide sites" 276 miles inside Iraq to search for and destroy Scud missiles and their supporting infrastructure.

Special tactics men like Staff Sergeants Bruce Berry and Brian Shreve and Technical Sergeant Mark "Scrogs" Scholl and Doug Phillips conducted similar clandestine missions all across the border and proved their value in magnificent work to help the Scud-hunting teams evade and escape as, time and again, they were discovered and had to be extracted under fire.

Before the ground war had even begun, for instance, three special reconnaissance teams from the 5th Special Forces Group (Airborne) attempted to infiltrate southern Iraq looking for Scud missile sites. One team's helicopter had to turn around after an Iraqi radar locked onto it. Another landed in an area devoid of cover, found Iraqi movement all around them, and had to call for an exfiltration. The third team found suitable cover and hid there all day, but when they approached their target at night near the Salman airfield, they were so illuminated by bright moonlight reflecting off the desert floor that they too had to exfiltrate.

Special forces and special tactics teams also performed trafficability surveys and other reconnaissance missions in Iraqi territory as a prelude to the ground war launched on February 24. On February 18, for instance, special operations helicopters inserted teams from the 3rd and 5th Special Forces Groups into two sites along VII Corps' planned invasion routes, bringing with them engineers to perform penetrometer tests on the soil and combat camera crews who took still and video photos of the terrain (which proved to be the most valuable data collected). Both VII Corps and XVIII Airborne Corps requested other teams to go deep into Iraq to scout out the terrain for their flanking movements around the Republican Guard concentrations in Kuwait. Three missions covered the main VII Corps routes; two of them infiltrated on February 23 reported regularly on enemy activity in their areas until they linked up with elements of the 1st Cavalry Division on February 27. The third team was inserted among Iraqi forces and had to be withdrawn.

Three other missions supported the XVIII Airborne Corps' enveloping maneuver. One team landed in the middle of a Bedouin encampment and had to call for an emergency extraction. After being picked up, they scouted for alternate sites, saw enemy activity everywhere, but ran into such heavy antiaircraft and surface-to-air missile activity that they had to abort the mission. Another team went into the Euphrates River Valley just before the war began, sent to report on Iraqi military activity along a major highway approaching the corps' flank. During its insertion, one helicopter flew so low to avoid Iraqi radar that its rear wheel tore loose when it hit a sand dune. But the team was in place by daylight and dug a "hide site" in a drainage canal only three hundred meters northwest of Highway 7. The next morning, however, the American troops found the surrounding fields alive with local villagers. They were spotted by several Iraqi children and an adult, who were soon joined by about twenty-five armed villagers and an Iraqi Army company moving toward them. The men called for close air support and an emergency extraction, destroyed their classified gear, engaged in a short but fierce firefight with the Iraqis, and moved to better fighting positions. USAF close support planes dropped cluster munitions and two-thousand-pound bombs within two hundred meters of their position until nightfall. During a lull in the air strikes, two members of the team charged down the canal and eliminated the most threatening Iraqi element. After dark, the team moved another three hundred meters, where they were extracted without further incident.

On another such mission, two three-man teams monitored an area between the Tigris and Euphrates Rivers, but a communications failure prevented one team from reporting on its observations, and it was picked up on the morning of the twenty-seventh. The second team landed in the middle of another Bedouin encampment; they, too, established a hide site along a drainage canal, but it proved to be near a major thoroughfare. The Bedouins failed to notice them until a little girl spotted them. Soon they were being pursued by armed Bedouins and Iraqi soldiers, whom they held off for an hour and a half until F-16s appeared escorting a Black Hawk helicopter from the 160th. Riddled by small-arms fire, the helicopter crew nevertheless pulled off a dramatic daytime rescue.[2]

A team led by Captain T. Eugene Willett, Master Sergeants Larry Rhinehart and Steve Jones, and Technical Sergeant Duane Stanton supported the Marine Corps 1st Division's thrust to capture Kuwait International Airport, swiftly clearing it of debris and mines for immediate use by an inbound, eight-ship special operations assault force.[3] A special tactics team led by Chief Master Sergeant Wayne Norrad was inserted by helicopter and raced up the stairs of the airfield's fourteen-story control tower lugging seventy-five pounds of radio gear to improvise an air traffic control tower. This system worked flawlessly until smoke from burning oil wells lowered visibility to only half a mile.

Other special tactics teams helped Marines liberate the American embassy in Kuwait City, while another four-man team fast-roped from a hovering helicopter onto the fifteen-story British embassy building with men from the SBS who had been given the same mission. Our unique communications net prevented a tragic incidence of fratricide. Still other special tactics men served as frontline combat medics or flew on aeromedical evacuation flights treating wounded coalition personnel.

Of 147 American service members killed in action in the Gulf War, 25 were from special operations units. That 17 percent casualty rate was our lowest in nineteen years, and the one-hundred-hour ground war was probably the shortest in history. Except for the price we paid in men's lives, wars don't come much better.

OPERATION "PROVIDE COMFORT"

Few people realize that combat operations during Desert Storm represented only the beginning of intensive and dangerous American special operations work in Iraq. Our men were soon committed to a truly daunting task, helping to save the lives of tens of thousands of Kurds from among roughly seven million of them who had fled central and southern Iraq in April after an unsuccessful revolt in March that was ruthlessly put down by what remained of Saddam Hussein's military forces. It became known as Operation "Provide Comfort," the largest mass relief effort since the Berlin airlift of 1948–1949.

The Kurds are a non-Arabic people who speak a language related to Persian and adhere to the Sunni Muslim faith, one of seventeen different ethnic groups and 420 tribal groupings that fall within U.S. Central Command's area of responsibility. About twenty million Kurds live in western Iran, central and northeastern Iraq, northeastern Syria, southern Turkey, and southwestern Armenia—an area about as large as France known as Kurdistan, although it is not an internationally recognized separate state. Kurds represent the fourth-largest nationality in the Near East, after the Arabs, Turks, and Persians—but they are virtual Islamic gypsies in the Middle East and South Central Asia, uprooted from their villages and homes so often that they are almost nomads.

Soon after fighting in the Gulf War ended in February, Kurds in Iraq tried to revolt and overthrow Saddam Hussein, who had long suffered their presence with disdain, contempt, and maltreatment—and in 1987 and 1988 had gassed to death fifty to one hundred thousand of them. Saddam quickly crushed the rebellion and retaliated by sending his troops to rid the country of them, killing them by the thousands and driving the rest into northern Iraq and toward southeastern Turkey, where almost eight million of them lived but were almost equally unwelcome.[4]

Their plight became desperate, and the United States decided to intervene. Lieutenant General John Shalikashvili of U.S. European Command (later to become chairman of the Joint Chiefs of Staff) was dispatched to Turkey to protect them from the Iraqis and to handle the humanitarian relief effort needed to care for millions of starving refugees fleeing on foot in freezing weather through some of the harshest, most inhospitable mountain terrain in the world. American fighter-bombers staging from Turkey pounded the Iraqi Army as it tried to pursue and eradicate the Kurds. Eventually, the allied coalition that prosecuted Desert Storm succeeded in establishing a safe buffer zone between the longtime bitter enemies, but thousands of innocent Kurds were dying of hunger, exhaustion, and cold.

Shalikashvili called upon the 24th Marine Expeditionary Unit, headed by Colonel James L. Jones (later to become commandant of the Marine Corps and, late in 2002, the supreme allied commander, Europe), to seal off the buffer zone and begin setting up refugee camps and safe havens for some five million Kurds in northern Iraq. But tens of thousands of Kurds who had fled farther north toward and into Turkey were in desperate straits by May.

Shalikashvili summoned America's special operations forces to avert a disaster. On short notice, MC-130Es led in other aircraft to drop emergency supplies to the Kurd refugees. The first large contingents of USAF MH-53J and some Army special operations helicopters, special forces teams, civil affairs units, and Air Force special tactics troops began arriving at Landing Zone 6, near Cukurca, Turkey, on May 7, 1991. Many of the special tactics troops came from Hurlburt Field's 23rd Special Tactics Squadron and thirty-seven of them from our units in England and Germany. They were generally deployed to the region for about thirty-to-sixty-day rotations and then relieved by others, as were members of the 10th Special Forces Group as well as some from the National Guard's 20th Special Operations Group (from southeastern U.S. states), who had been called to active duty for but were never deployed in Desert Storm.[5] Their work and their experiences varied greatly, from "make work" projects to epic humanitarian adventures, saving hundreds of lives apiece.

One of the first special tactics paramedics there was Staff Sergeant David Moss, who was attached to a Special Forces A-team from the 10th Special Forces Group. In his first eighteen days in a camp that had 130,000 displaced Iraqi Kurds, he found his pararescue training, particularly in doing sutures (which he had only read about, but never done), below par compared to his special forces counterparts. Staff Sergeant Steven L. Moss, a combat controller, arrived about the same time. Between May 8 and May 25, he managed 376 helicopter sorties, most of them to and from a forward operating base at Silopi, Turkey[6]; helped them deliver 122,900 pounds of supplies; ran a Military Airlift Command terminal that delivered 705 "happy customers" (incoming troops); and supervised thirty-four medical evacuations. In his spare time, he trained two special forces members on basic air traffic control procedures to relieve him from time to time. He encountered a few problems: There were no maps of the area; there was confusion over which site would serve as the central control point; there were not enough maintenance people or radio operators to keep his satellite communications net operable; and language barriers between pilots and indigenous workers at the remote base made operations difficult at best.

Master Sergeant Patrick Sinon, a pararescueman from Hurlburt Field, Florida, had arrived the same day as Steven Moss, the combat controller, and was sent by a twelve-hour bus ride to Silopi two days later, where he had to arrange his own billeting. Two days after that he was deployed to Balkoa Bridge in Iraq to work with a company from 40 Commando of the British Royal Marines, charged with securing the bridge and sending the refugees there on their way back "home." He shuttled back and forth between Silopi and the Kani Masi Field Hospital, working with German civilians and a U.S. Army medical team until he was flown to Incirlik, Turkey, and sent back to the States on June 8 after it became apparent that the need was for more combat controllers and not a senior paramedic who had been "force-fed" in and made to "stay busy" instead of being assigned to an area where PJs were really needed.

Technical Sergeant Yonnie F. Schlicht spent from May 7 to May 24 in Silopi and then in field hospitals near Kani Masi, Sirsenk, and Isusoo, Turkey, working with British and Canadian medical personnel. He did everything from evacuating seriously ill patients to treating meningitis and cholera cases, cleaning burns in a trauma clinic, helping doctors during minor surgeries, and organizing medical supplies. He and his fellow American PJs found that British medical technicians were not allowed to do invasive surgery, insert intravenous tubes, or even give shots. The British medical officer-in-charge had no idea of their Air Force medical training and ignored their offers to help until Schlicht provided an in-depth briefing on their capabilities, but even that produced "marginal results," and the British proved reluctant to use their full medical skills. Moreover, he found that certain American medical drugs and supplies were not used in Europe and ended up not being used at all. His proposed solution in a terse after-action report: "We start[ed] work for other organizations when they needed help, and that seemed to be all the time."

Technical Sergeant Ricky L. Weaver encountered similar frustrations. At the first site he was sent to, he found that the medical supplies were intended only for the British Royal Marines and could not be used for the local populace. When more British, Dutch, and Canadian medics arrived, he and his fellow PJs erected a ten-tent hospital, each with a different medical specialty. But patients were not being sorted at any checkpoints until American PJs manned them and culled out those who needed medical care from those who should be sent on to their destinations. The camp had serious diarrhea problems and not enough nurses to staff the various tents handling cases of cholera, trauma surgery, pediatrics, and infant feeding. American pararescuemen, working in three-man teams, filled the voids and augmented civilian personnel from UNICEF, who did not work after 5:00 P.M. As a result, the Americans all worked as medics on the road checkpoints from 8:00 A.M. until noon, then reported to either the supply or surgery tent to instruct, assist, or perform surgical scrubs or work on burns, sutures, stitching, and dispensing medication until 6:00 P.M., at which time some would go to the cholera tent to provide nursing aid until midnight. This was not a uniform schedule, but a typical one.

New problems arose when the British medical officer started to train his support staff for the forthcoming pullout of the Canadian medical team. Even though he was not fully utilizing the skills of the U.S. pararescuemen, he did not want his men performing their present duties so the Americans could handle more serious ones. A British civilian doctor who recognized the Americans' expertise in trauma treatment agreed with the American recommendation, but the officer would not budge. Next, the British officer was asked to prepare care for people wounded in a hostile fire area. But his medics had little understanding of trauma medicine and were asking the Americans how to rig their medical packs and what equipment to bring. The PJs provided the information, but respectfully suggested that the officer substitute his staff for the duties the Americans were performing and take the U.S. PJs with him instead. Sergeant Weaver confronted him on the issue, and the officer said he understood but could not make that "management" decision. By then a chief warrant officer from the Royal Marines had assumed responsibility for all management and placement of assets in the camp. He asked Weaver where his men should be used. Weaver told him that his men were not being properly used and should depart. And they did so, leaving on May 22.

Senior Master Sergeant John Lebold, a combat controller from the 1723rd Special Tactics Squadron, arrived at Silopi on May 8. He was immediately sent to Sirensk, Iraq, to do an airfield survey, since the base had been bombed during the war and the runway, which Navy Seabees were trying to fix, was badly damaged, but needed for C-130 operations. Most of his time was wasted, however, on convoy duty assigned him by the special forces team in charge because there was little combat control work to do. The rest of the time he spent trying to get supplies that he had ordered two weeks earlier but that had never been sent.

Airman First Class Brian D. Hicks, also a pararescueman from the 1723rd, spent nine days on the Turkish side of the Iraqi border at a camp west of Isikveren, "where things were slowing down," while a camp east of him was busy as blazes. He gave measles vaccinations to Kurdish children, assisted by Dutch nurses, distributed food and water, and pulled border duty with two special forces troops who had to watch Turks shake down and steal from Kurdish refugees returning to Iraq, while at another site he was guarding a supply point from which both Turks and Kurds were stealing food. Other days he escorted Kurds down the mountains to buses waiting to transport them to Zakho, Iraq.

Others had far busier experiences. Airman First Class Scott S. Danielson, an air traffic controller from the 1723rd, deployed to Kani Masi on May 17 and was immediately immersed in juggling helicopter traffic in six-hour shifts, moving four to five thousand Kurds every day back to Iraq from the way station in Turkey while also handling numerous medical evacuation flights out of a landing zone that lacked even barbed-wire protection. During his brief tour, Danielson also handled the arrival and movement of two and a half tons of Meals-Ready-to-Eat, four tons of motor oil, two tons of rice, nine hundred pounds of flour, and four sling loads of water blivets each carrying five hundred gallons of fresh, clean water to help the Kurds in their exodus from Turkey. He also had to cope with eleven flights carrying twelve VIPs, seven high-ranking officers, and fifty-nine U.S. and foreign support personnel. He called the training benefits of his hands-on experiences "immeasurable."

Airman First Class Kenneth C. Fournier, a pararescueman, arrived in Turkey on May 2 and was moved forward to Kani Balaw to work with the British Royal Marines setting up a station for Kurds pouring out of the hills who were seeking food, water, fuel, and medical care. He and Technical Sergeant Gary L. Lantrip controlled helicopters into and out of the camp, set up drop zones to air-drop supplies to more distant Kurds, and then worked with the British to set up tents for supplies and medical care. Their biggest challenge was trying to get bug repellent, bug nets, and medicine like Benadryl for about fifty Marines suffering from masses of bug bites. Unable to obtain any such supplies, they had to evacuate two of the Marines to Kani Masi for better medical treatment. Nine days after arriving at Incirlik, Turkey, they were moved to Kani Masi with a troop of Marines to help escort the first convoys leaving there because the trucks had been shot at the day before. He also worked with Technical Sergeant Ricky L. Weaver, another PJ, checking which families waiting for rides might need medical care. Eight of them needed assistance for problems ranging from severe dehydration and malnutrition to abdominal pains and sheer weakness. Many had to be persuaded to come to the hospital for care. The two noncommissioned officers became convinced that several of the babies they treated would not have survived the long trips back to their "homeland."

Fournier returned to Kani Balaw to set up medical supplies that had arrived and then went with the British to different refugee camps to bring Kurds food and water. He saw ailments ranging from chronic diarrhea to back pain, scabies, malnutrition, and dehydration, but there was no interpreter to help discern their problems. He wondered why someone hadn't provided a Kurdish-English dictionary. Next, he went with the British to a valley where four thousand Kurds were going to settle, helped set up a camp for them, worked as a medic with the families already there, and became the camp's primary medic when the Brits' medic was recalled to Kani Masi. Four days later he, too, was returned there to help out in the hospital, which was handling three hundred to five hundred patients a day. He worked in each of the stations—dental, scrub and wound care, trauma, infant care, and cholera—and helped bring in patients from a nearby road. On May 25 he returned to Incirlik and was processed home to Hurlburt Field.[7]

Work like this became almost routine training for our combat controllers and paramedics. No one knows how many Kurd lives we saved, or how many Kurds died in their hapless treks out of and back into Iraq. The operation was rewarding in a humanitarian sense, but frustrating because it was so inconclusive. As President George H. W. Bush told *U.S. News & World Report*, "The battles between the Kurds and the Baath Party have been going on for a long, long time. To solve that problem forever was not a part of the United Nations' goals, nor was it a goal of the United States. We deplore killings, of course. But to tie the Kurdish . . . problem into the handling of the aggression of Iraq is simply a bit revisionistic."[8]

Most of the Kurds were able to return "home," but they remain oppressed and a near-nomadic minority unwelcome in their own homelands. One might liken them to the Palestinians uprooted from Israel and Lebanon, jobless and starving in their native terrain.

Thus, Operation Provide Comfort made us feel good about our work, but also saddened us by its failure to bring closure. In that sense, it was typical of many other humanitarian deployments by our special tactics teams to countries like Cambodia (1975), Zaire (1978), Honduras (1983 and 1988), El Salvador (1989), Liberia (1990), Bangladesh (1991), and Somalia (beginning in 1991). The Kurds have suffered brutally again in recent years. The United Nations reported in early 2000 that Saddam Hussein was again driving unknown thousands of them from government-controlled locations like the oil-producing area around Kirkuk, where there is also a huge military base and airfield in a region Saddam was trying to "Arabize" by resettling about fifty-nine thousand Kurds who lived there to the north.[9]

After twenty-seven years of service, by 1991 special tactics teams had deployed in just about every kind of contingency imaginable. I had been on enough battlegrounds, wars, and humanitarian missions. In 1991, it was time for me to retire—again— and I did so on May 31.

CHAPTER FIFTEEN

MOGADISHU, SOMALIA— "TASK FORCE RANGER"

ragedy befell special operations late in 1993. A team from Task Force Ranger—made up of men from Delta Force, special tactics men, four SEAL snipers, plus a company from the 3rd Battalion, 75th Rangers, a battalion from the 160th Special Operations Aviation Regiment, and soldiers from the 10th Mountain Division—was ambushed by Somali clansmen near the notorious Bakara Market, one of the most heavily armed regions of downtown Mogadishu, while trying to capture warlord Mohamad Farah Aideed and thirty-four of his top lieutenants.[1]

It was the seventh lightning-quick raid that the two-hundred-man team had conducted since August. No force could strike faster, hit harder, or leave more devastation in its wake, and not a single man had been seriously wounded in the previous six raids. Aideed had been on the run for weeks, sleeping in as many as three different places every night, no longer appearing in public, barely traveling during the day. But this raid, on October 3 and 4, ended in the most intense, longest sustained firefight since the end of the Vietnam War, "a 15-hour soldier's nightmare" that lasted twenty hours for some.[2]

There is no such thing as an "average" Ranger, but the young

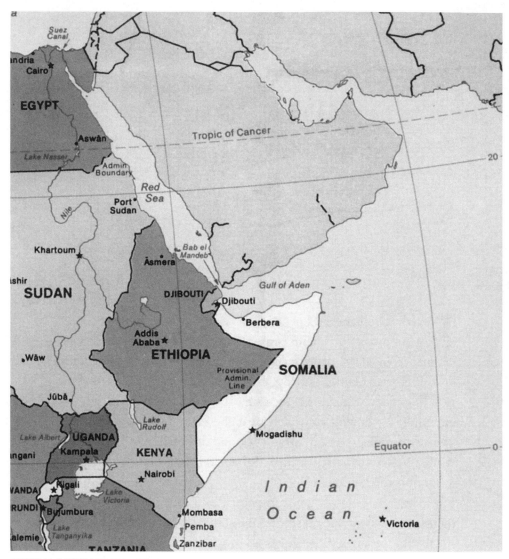

CENTRAL INTELLIGENCE AGENCY

246

soldiers facing this ordeal by fire were typically well-trained but hardly seasoned noncommissioned officers, and they were young: married staff sergeants who were twenty-four to twenty-eight years old with young children and only three to four years of military service. Each had completed airborne and jumpmaster training, graduated from Ranger School and a primary leadership development course or military occupational specialty training such as sniper school, pathfinder training, or the HALO or rappelling master course. Most had served in a Ranger battalion since coming on active duty and served as a team leader, communications NCO, supply sergeant, or training NCO. But few were yet battle hardened.

The Delta Force members were more seasoned and averaged thirty-one and a half years old, a third of which had been spent in uniform. They scored, on average, 118.3 on their intellectual aptitude tests, far above the Army average, and had fourteen and a half years of education. Almost four-fifths of them were married, each with two children.

The SEAL snipers were the youngest and least seasoned of all, but superbly trained. Averaging twenty-three years old, half married, half single, they had been SEALs for about five years, but most of that had been spent qualifying to become one and training for assignment to a SEAL platoon: twenty-six weeks in the brutal BUD/S (Basic Underwater Demolition/SEAL) course, in which about 80 percent of the candidates failed to complete the selection process); three weeks of parachute school; twelve weeks of specialized SEAL training; twelve months in a "workup" with their designated SEAL unit to qualify for their first six-month deployment; and finally completion of the petty officer indoctrination course.[3]

In the next eighteen to twenty hours, eighteen of these men died, seventy-three were wounded, and eleven were injured. One pilot, Chief Warrant Officer Michael Durant, was held captive for eleven days.

Two men from Delta Force, Master Sergeant Gary Gordon and Sergeant First Class Randall Shughart, were awarded the Medal of Honor posthumously. Eleven men from the 24th Special Tactics

Squadron participated in that action. One was awarded the Air Force Cross, the nation's second-highest award for valor; two men won the Silver Star; the eight others all earned Bronze Star Medals, four of them with V devices for valor. These awards finally caused the Air Force to publicly acknowledge the existence of its special tactics units—sixteen years after Brand X was born.

Lieutenant Colonel James L. Oeser was the 24th Special Tactics Squadron commander. At the time his men were alerted for deployment to Somalia, they were out west, off the coast of San Francisco on their biggest exercise to date, "Crafty Kaper." It involved operations over three-fourths of the United States, along with more than seventy aircraft, ships, and boats, and Army, Navy, as well as Air Force units. The total alert package for Somalia was moved to the exercise site to rehearse and "template" or plan operations for Somalia. Their mission would be to dismember the Hawife Aideed tribal faction, whose ten thousand members were the biggest of Somalia's nine major clans and who had killed or mutilated twenty-four Pakistani troops in an ambush the previous June as United Nations Operation Restore Hope got under way.[4]

On a Friday evening, after the plan had come together, men from all three services were in Delta Force's compound for a meal together when General Wayne Downing, then the commander in chief of U.S. Special Operations Command, addressed them, thanked them for their rigorous planning, but said it looked as if they wouldn't be deploying after all. They put the plans on the shelf, and on Saturday Oeser redeployed four to six men back west to press on with the exercise. Suddenly Major General William Garrison, then the JSOC commander, received notice to deploy after all, but decided to use the force that had done the rehearsals instead of handing their plans off to JSOC's normal alert force. Oeser recalled his men, who arrived at Biggs Army Air Field in Texas, where they were met by Major Bob Stephen, Oeser's director of operations, who put them on a plane back to Fort Bragg. Garrison's advance party deployed on August 21, and the main body on August 25. The first "snatch and grab" operations were launched almost immediately.

Master Sergeant Dave Schnoor, a combat controller, was on the first three missions, but Oeser had to send him home because his baby boy had died of medical complications. Oeser replaced him with Staff Sergeant Jeffrey Bray, another combat controller.

Long after the bloody October ordeal, Oeser would tell me of special tactics' harrowing hours in Mogadishu, "Those men held everything together." That action captured the vision that Major General Bill Mall and I had formed for merging combat control and pararescuemen and that Major General Bob Patterson had later championed as commander of 23rd Air Force.

On the afternoon of October 3, around 3:00 P.M., Delta Force's main snatch-and-grab team, accompanied by Rangers, several SEAL snipers, and eleven men from the 24th Special Tactics Squadron, flew into the snarl and confusion of midday traffic in the center of Mogadishu and captured twenty-four militia leaders believed to have led repeated attacks on U.S. and UN forces in Somalia's capital.

Somali gunmen greeted the team members as they fast-roped from their Black Hawk helicopter onto Hiwadag Street, one of Mogadishu's most crowded. "There was a lot of shooting coming at us" as the team moved up the busy street into the thickest concentration of militiamen in the city, going where no one else had dared. The UN peacekeeping force wouldn't send troops anywhere near the area, known as the "Black Sea," nor had any U.S. troops been there. Ten-year-old boys were firing AK-47 Kalashnikov automatic rifles; other militiamen were firing from behind women they were using as shields.

"I was pumped, really pumped," Sergeant Bray would recount later. After joining his Delta Force buddies at the main target building, Bray took up a door security position, firing at gunmen in an alley. Bray realized they needed more firepower and called for an AH-6 Little Bird gunship to cover the target. As the assault team rounded up several suspects, including Ahmed Warsame, one of Aideed's top subordinates, it moved to the courtyard, counted prisoners to make sure they had everyone, and called for a ground reaction force to put the detainees into trucks and move them out. Suddenly a rocket-propelled grenade (RPG) crippled a Black Hawk, call sign Super-61; it crashed with five passengers into a narrow alley about three hundred yards from Bray's position. Bray got a call from Staff Sergeant Ray J. Benjamin, a fellow combat controller in a command-and-control helicopter: "Super-61 is down. Move to crash site." Delta Force and the Rangers with them had rehearsed for just such a contingency; Super-61 had even been used in one of these practice missions.

Two pararescuemen—Master Sergeant Scott Fales, a veteran of Panama and Desert Storm, and Technical Sergeant Timothy A. Wilkinson—were aboard a circling search-and-rescue Black Hawk, Super-68, over the Pakistani soccer stadium northeast of the crash site. (Fales had been selected as one of the Air Force's Twelve Outstanding Airmen of the Year in 1993, but he was unable to attend the Pentagon induction ceremony because he was already in Somalia.) As the pilot brought the aircraft to a hover forty feet above Freedom Road, they threw their litters and medical supplies onto the ground and fast-roped down from opposite sides of the helicopter with their rucksacks on their backs, the last of a fifteen-man search-and-recovery security team out of the aircraft. An RPG slammed into the ship just below the main rotor blades, but instead of transitioning to forward flight and clearing the area—an instinctive reaction in such circumstances—the pilot held hover until Fales and Wilkinson got on the ground. A special forces lieutenant colonel would relate later,

> He put his passengers in the exact position they were supposed to be placed in. In fact . . . , he continued to inform his passengers that they were going down, and also to inform the ground element of this fact. The coolness he had displayed during our other operations had already established the fact that he was unflappable. His calmness and reassuring manner had an immediate effect on all that he talked to and all that could monitor his transmissions.[5]

Fales and Wilkinson heard AK-47 rounds zip past them from three directions. "Bullets don't make the whizzing sound you hear in movies," Fales would recall. "There's a snap, an incredibly loud snap!" Fales and six others ran along the left side of the street and ducked into a courtyard. Wilkinson and his group were caught on the right side of the street and had to dash through a hail of bullets to reach the courtyard.

By then, Bray and a Ranger platoon had started advancing to the crash site, one element on each side of the road, leapfrogging to provide each other cover from Somali forces also racing to the crash site from parallel streets. Rangers caught on the right side of the road were cut down almost instantly. "We took a lot of casualties," Bray would note. Gunfire intensified as they neared the crash and Bray searched for cover. "I saw this little courtyard, actually an uncovered garage with two metal grate doors." Bray hurled himself against the doors ten to fifteen times before they gave in and then stumbled backward into the enclosure, in no position to cover himself. "One of the guys behind me covered me," he said later. "Luckily there was only a family in there." Bray's team detained the family, cleared the house, and set up a casualty collection point. As dusk approached, Somalis swarmed through the streets firing rifles and RPGs at American soldiers barricaded in buildings along Freedom Road. Casualties littered the streets. "We were having trouble recovering some of the bodies," Bray would recall. The Rangers have a tradition of not leaving anyone behind and were keenly aware that some Pakistani peacekeepers had been mutilated by Somali hordes in previous encounters. Bray's position would become a focal point for directing helicopter gunship fire at the Somali militiamen charging U.S. positions. "We knew we were going to be there a long time."

By then, Wilkinson and Fales had reached the downed helicopter, lying on its side with the cockpit folded over. Both pilots were dead, but they didn't know that. Under unrelenting small-arms fire and dodging every few feet, Fales found one of the wounded crew members trying to free his injured crew chief. Suddenly, Somali gunmen unleashed a tremendous volley from a corridor facing the alley, and Fales was hit. "It felt like someone took a hot poker and shoved it through my calf muscle." He took cover behind a pile of rocks and patched himself: "I took my scissors out, cut my pants, and saw what I had. I thought, 'Damn, this should hurt,' but it didn't." He stuffed the muscle tissue back into his leg, packed it with gauze, and put a pressure dressing over it. With a medic's nonchalance, he later observed, "The bullet went through my calf muscle, right beside the tibia. Very luckily, no bone was involved."

Adrenaline and fear kept the pain away, not medicine. "The whole time the firefight was going on, we maintained a really good sense of humor," Fales would insist. "We were cracking jokes back and forth." But there was nothing humorous about their situation. Fales positioned himself between the wounded and enemy fire until a protective barrier of Kevlar pads could be erected from the helicopter wreckage. At one point, he threw himself over two patients to protect them from shrapnel after he saw five grenades flying toward them.

Wilkinson would add that there was a lot of stoic behavior going on:

> I don't think there was any *time* to feel. There was this sense of *fear*, fearing for your life as it's going on all around you. But because of the training you've had, and the task at hand, you put the fear aside and press on. You focus on what you've got to do.

Bray would add, "I don't want to give a false impression. . . . We were in a grave situation. And we knew it. We would occasionally look at one another and say, 'This is bad. Real bad.' "

Wilkinson snuck toward the front of the helicopter as Rangers helped Fales to a triage point near the rear of the aircraft. He and other Rangers managed to free one of the dead pilots and move his body to the collection point, using a Humvee to pull the wreckage apart. Returning to the wreck, Wilkinson and an Army medic helped free the pinned crew chief. "All I could see was his uniform. I started calling to him and saw his finger move, so I knew he was still alive." Wilkinson was handing the dazed crew chief up and out of the aircraft wreckage when the shooting intensified again—a snowstorm of flying shrapnel and small-arms fire from all directions. Metal fragments ripped Wilkinson's face and tore through his lower arm; an Army medic caught some in the hand; the crew chief lost part of his finger.

"There was continuous shooting throughout our ordeal," Wilkinson recalled later. "The volume would change. It would be 'crack-crack-crack,' then a barrage; then it would slow to a 'crack-crack-crack.' Then a rocket-propelled grenade would come in: 'Whomp-boom.' Sort of like a chest freezer door closing, only thirty times louder." The RPGs were the worst threat and caused innumerable casualties. They had felled two helicopters and severely damaged two others. Gunships ignored the scores of Somalis firing rifles and focused their fires on those using RPGs.

While Rangers tried to cover them with protective fire, Fales and Wilkinson treated wounded at the tail of the downed helicopter. Someone yelled from the courtyard across the street, "Medic! Medic! We need a medic over here." Fales said to Wilkinson, "They need a medic, Wilky." Wilkinson grabbed his medical rucksack, waited for Rangers to cover him with more fire, and dashed fifty or sixty yards up the narrow alley. "I felt like I was moving in slow motion. I remember thinking, 'My God, these boots weigh a thousand pounds.' "

Wilkinson made it safely across the intersection, caught his breath, and helped the wounded off Freedom Road into the "safe" casualty collection point in the courtyard. There were four wounded, one of them critically so—but no medical supplies. He called over his intrateam radio to Fales and asked if there were more supplies. Fales said yes, so Wilkinson ran back to the rear of the helicopter, scarfed up the spare medical gear, and ran back across the street: "I had to get those medical supplies back to my patients."

A Ranger, Captain A. Scott Miller, found Wilkinson's back-to-back fifty-yard dashes somewhat more dramatic: "These trips across the open street were at the peak of the battle when enemy fire was at its most intense. We were receiving intense and accurate small arms fire. His repeated acts of heroism saved the lives of at least four soldiers."

During the battle, Task Force Ranger's five-man airfield services detachment worked to refuel and rearm the helicopter armada from the 160th Special Operations Aviation Regiment. In eighteen and a half hours, they loaded more than one hundred rockets and fifty thousand rounds of mini-gun ammunition while pumping 12,500 gallons of fuel in sixty-to-eighty-pound increments to "hot-fuel" the helicopters. It was a hazardous operation that required keen situational awareness, attention to detail, and speed. As helicopters approached the refueling and rearmament pad, pilots had to adeptly position their aircraft in among ordnance, fuel, and soldiers with only feet to spare on each side. Like pit crews at the Indianapolis 500, the five airfield services soldiers took only five to seven minutes to refuel the aircraft and reload their rocket pods and mini guns while rotor blades were turning at idle speed—but still with deadly momentum—only three feet above their heads. Their jobs complete, the soldiers hunched back a few feet, trying to protect their faces from the rotors' downwash and flying debris as pilots hit full throttle and sped off the pad to rejoin the fray. As the evening wore on, the forward-area refueling point team had to drag pilots from their cockpits to get them to eat. Some crews were so "wired" they couldn't eat.

These young pilots, most of them thirty-six-year-old warrant officers third class, were the Army's very best. They averaged almost three thousand cockpit seat hours, a fourth of which had been spent flying on night-vision goggles. They were graduates of grueling search, evasion, and rescue training; parachute or air assault qualified; rated as instructor pilots; and graduates of their combat arms advanced officer courses. Most were married; most had at least associate's college degrees; most had served at least two overseas duty tours after three tours in the continental United States; and they averaged fifteen years of military service. But this was eighteen years after the

Vietnam War ended, and for most, this was therefore their first exposure to combat.[6]

The battle went on though the night, and "time took on a new dimension," as Master Sergeant Philip Rhodes would describe the action three years later in the Air Force's *Airman* magazine.[7]

For the first time since they had fast-roped from their Black Hawk, Fales had looked at his watch and noted, "It was midnight, right straight up. I hollered at everyone, 'Holy s___, guys; it's midnight.' They were like, 'Wow!' "

But the search-and-rescue team, expecting a short mission, had not brought their night-vision goggles—their only distinct advantage come nightfall. Somali gunmen in groups of three or four probed the Ranger strong points. Overhead, however, helicopter gunships with night-vision equipment kept the attackers at bay, thanks to Bray—"Kilo 64"—and his fellow combat controllers, Staff Sergeants Pat Rogers and Technical Sergeant John McGarry. Bray could see only an obstructed view of the friendly positions, but he talked "steel into the targets" all night long.

Chief Warrant Officer Second Class Paul White, one of the gunship pilots, would recall later, "I will always remember the calm demeanor and professionalism [Bray] showed over the radio even as I heard bullets hitting very near his position each time he keyed his radio microphone." Bray came up with an ingenious marking system so the helicopter gunships wouldn't hit friendly troops. Coordinating their defenses over his intrateam radio, Bray contacted all air and ground elements, now in close proximity and in a circle. He directed that emergency strobe lights be turned on and placed on the roofs of the buildings they occupied. People were reaching through the upper walls in spaces between the roofs and the walls and putting infrared strobes on top. From the air they formed a circular perimeter around friendly troops. Bray thus had a reference point from which to direct fire the rest of the night.[8]

Once, Bray had to call in fires almost directly onto his own position. Moving everyone into a covered area, he went to the open courtyard and told the gunship crews, "Danger close" (meaning they were extremely close to the line of fire), as the armed heli-copters fired on Somalis only ten meters away. Spent shell casings fell on Bray's head. Time and again, he called for more fire, finally clearing them to use rockets instead of their Gatling-like mini guns. "I think they expelled 60,000 rounds and 63 rockets on our targets," Bray would remember. While that finally cleared most of the threat to Bray's position, Somalis closed in on his group, which had moved from the alley into a building when night fell. "They pounded our building with RPGs until it nearly collapsed. We didn't have a way out." Fales had never experienced worse fighting, which he would label a nine on a scale of one to ten. "The only way it could have been more intense is if we fought to the last man and all per-ished. At one point, we figured we'd run out of ammunition and have to."

Finally a Ranger blew a hole in a wall into a courtyard and then into another building, where Fales and his Rangers moved the wounded to safe refuge. "Things settled down for about an hour be-cause the Somalis didn't know where we were." But then a heavy machine gun raked the building from across the street, a line of fire with tracers for about every fifth round streaking through the wall four feet off the ground as Fales and the Rangers dove for cover. "The light was catching people in stop-frame action. . . . People were flying everywhere," Fales said later of that five-minute siege.

Still, attacks continued sporadically, almost relentlessly, through-out the night. Bray and Wilkinson fought off repeated RPG attacks, two of which made direct hits on one of their rooms. While Wilkin-son stayed with his immobilized patients, Bray repeatedly exposed himself to enemy fire to direct helicopter gunship fires.

At about 4:00 A.M., the men heard explosions and other gunship fire in the distance: A relief column headed by Lieutenant Colonel Danny McKnight, commander of the 3rd Ranger Battalion, was fi-nally approaching, faithful to the Ranger Creed never to "leave a fallen comrade to fall into the hands of the enemy."[9] But the convoy kept getting lost as it, too, came under heavy fire. Fales's gunshot wound started bleeding, and he had to give himself an intravenous solution to fight off shock. That worked only intermittently as he lapsed into and out of consciousness. At last he heard an armored personnel carrier approach. (It had to be borrowed from a Pakistani "peacekeeping" contingent, since Defense Secretary Les Aspin had turned down Task Force Ranger's request weeks earlier to deploy AC-130 gunships, tanks, and armored personnel carriers after the Mogadishu fighting had begun intensifying.) Fales would recall, "I knew they were here to get us. They came in and told us to move our casualties."

One of the men in the relief column was Air Force Staff Sergeant Daniel G. Schilling, a combat controller who was one of Wilkinson's best friends. The column fought its way "through streets hopelessly jumbled in an impenetrable maze," Schilling would write years later.[10]

A special forces master sergeant was providing security for the ground reaction force as it moved to the site of the downed aircraft when the driver of the vehicle to his front was wounded. The NCO immediately gave emergency medical care to the driver and took his place to keep the force moving. Almost immediately another Ranger was wounded. The master sergeant left his vehicle and began lifesaving measures on the wounded soldier, under heavy fire the entire time. He returned to his vehicle and began to drive the casualties out of an intense kill zone when he was hit by an RPG, a fatal wound. His fellow Rangers would say of him later, he "exemplified the third stanza of the Ranger Creed: 'Never shall I fail my comrades. . . .' "[11]

A SEAL provided valiant fire support to the ground reaction force. Although wounded twice with gunshot wounds to the leg, he stayed in the fight despite heavy, continued contact and provided critical fire that in the end saved lives and casualties.

Three of the five men in Schilling's Humvee were shot. Two bullets came through his "bulletproof" door and hit him in the chest. McKnight was wounded, too, and when more than half the men in his convoy were either dead or wounded and running low on ammunition, the convoy turned back, regrouped for another try, loaded new ammunition into their magazines, and returned to the battle. They fought all through the night trying to collect their wounded comrades. In some cases, it was hopeless: At the second crash site, there was no sign of the men who'd gone down with the helicopter. Schilling found Wilkinson and offered him a ride in his Humvee, and to his surprise, Wilkinson accepted instead of the two-minute ride by helicopter. They rode in the open back of the last vehicle in the convoy as it made another run for safety through the carnage.

About 7:00 A.M., after fighting their way *out* of the city, the relief column carried Fales, Schilling, Wilkinson, and Bray to a temporary aid station inside the Pakistani soccer stadium. The airport where U.S troops had been headquartered was too far from the battle to function as a triage and evacuation site for the wounded. Schilling's was the last vehicle in the convoy. It rolled into the airport at noon the next day after fighting its way there for nearly twenty hours.

At the airport the previous night, a helicopter crew had brought in their aircraft, crippled beyond repair by enemy fire, and immediately ran to a spare helicopter and returned to the battlefield. They flew the rest of the night and into the morning trying to locate those missing in action. When they were finally relieved about ten o'clock the next morning, tears were rolling down the pilot's cheeks because there was nothing more he could do to find his fallen comrades and members of his command. "All this from a man who had just flown over eighteen hours in combat."

In the early-morning hours, the airfield services detachment elected to pass up their breakfast—omelettes and bacon a staff sergeant had managed to get them—in favor of feeding the exhausted pilots. At another hot-refueling point operated by the 10th Mountain Division, two more soldiers from the airfield services detachment pumped more than fifteen thousand gallons of gas into the helicopters that rotated through, all the while watching tracers and exploding RPG explosions around the helicopters engaged in mortal combat over the city. Throughout the night, the men helped litter teams pull scores of wounded off a seemingly endless stream of medevac helicopters.[12]

Fales had given in to shock, fatigue, and dehydration and was evacuated to a hospital for immediate surgery. Later, he said of the harrowing mission:

> There were a lot of heroes out there. Everyone did more than their job. It was probably the greatest team effort I've ever seen. I'm proud to have been a part of Task Force Ranger.

Bray would add, "The way I see it, we went into the tiger's cage. We took his bone. And we came out."

In early 1994, Wilkinson was awarded the Air Force Cross. The thirty-six-year-old became the first Air Force enlisted man to receive the nation's second-highest award for valor since the *Mayaguez* rescue mission after the Vietnam War ended in 1975.[13] Fales, thirty-five, another pararescue "technician," and Bray, twenty-seven, a combat controller, earned Silver Stars. Four other combat controllers—Master Sergeant Jack L. McMullen, Staff Sergeants Daniel G. Schilling and John L. McGarry, and Sergeant Patrick C. Rogers—earned Bronze Star Medals with Valor devices. Another pararescueman, Senior Master Sergeant Russell J. Tanner, and two combat controllers, Master Sergeant Robert G. Rankin and Staff Sergeant Ray J. Benjamin, earned Bronze Stars—a special tactics team extraordinaire. Five special tactics men earned Purple Hearts for battle wounds.

Lieutenant Colonel James L. Oeser also earned a Bronze Star for his part in the actions while commanding the 24th Special Tactics Squadron. He said at the awards ceremony, "I firmly believe you could have put any PJ or combat controller in their positions, and they would be here receiving medals at this time. Everyone in the unit is equally qualified. There are no superstars."

About 500 Somalis died in the gun battles and another 750 to 1,000 were probably wounded. From that day forward, the Clinton administration ceased operations in Mogadishu, and all U.S. forces were withdrawn within three weeks. Mohamad Farah Aideed went free and died in Mogadishu in clan fighting in 1996.[14]

CHAPTER SIXTEEN

HAITI—"RESTORE DEMOCRACY," COMMANDING A STOVE, AND COLLEGE FOR 320 KIDS

B arely had our special operations forces been withdrawn from Somalia when they took the lead again in another country in
upheaval far closer to home—Haiti.

The people of Haiti had endured political oppression for hundreds of years when Jean-Bertrand Aristide was freely elected president in 1990. But an army coup wrested power from him in late
1991 and chaos ensued: Tens of thousands of Haitians fled the
country by boat and flooded Guantanamo Bay, Cuba, and the
Florida coast with refugees. Attempting to reestablish the Aristide
government, the United Nations imposed economic sanctions in
mid-1993, but to little avail. Embargoed goods were smuggled into
the island nation's shallow coasts and from the neighboring Do-
minican Republic. In mid-1994, the Clinton administration sought
and won UN Security Council approval for an invasion and occu-
pation of the country.[1] Special operations forces had primary responsibility for the invasion, supervised by Lieutenant General
Hugh H. Shelton, then commander of XVIII Airborne Corps (and
later to become chairman of the Joint Chiefs of Staff). His plan
envisioned the special operations' takedown of key governmental
sites, followed by a linkup with up to fifteen thousand conventional

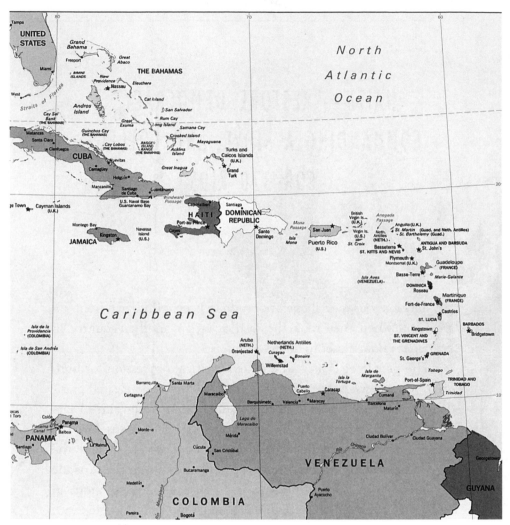

CENTRAL INTELLIGENCE AGENCY

262

forces, similar to the scenario executed in Panama, while special forces teams would secure the countryside. Subsequently, six thousand UN troops would train a new Haitian police force to maintain order.

Just before the planned invasion on September 19, former President Jimmy Carter, Senator Sam Nunn, and retired General Colin Powell brokered a last-minute deal with the Haitian military to turn over power peacefully.

Shelton radioed his special operations forces, concentrated on the carrier *America*, a prearranged message that their forced entry would become a peaceful, uncontested landing. The invasion became a humanitarian mission. Conventional forces from the 10th Mountain Division (and later the 25th Infantry Division) secured Port-au-Prince, the nation's capital and center of gravity for the political and economic struggle ahead, while special operations troops headed by Brigadier General Richard Potter fanned out into the countryside.

Three battalions from the 3rd Special Forces Group (Airborne), which covers Latin and Central America, deployed over 90 percent of the country and became the only source of law and order as Haitians in more than 730 villages called on special forces captains, warrant officers, and sergeants to act as policemen, judges, and juries to settle countless disputes, many of which had festered for years. Those men are *very* well trained, soft spoken and highly disciplined, not the hip-shooting, swashbuckling, hellbent-for-leather, cocky renegades that Hollywood used to portray in films like *Rambo*.

About one-fourth of all special forces members are medically trained to the skill level of an emergency medical technician or physician's assistant and able to treat trauma wounds, deliver babies, even perform emergency surgeries. All special forces members learn a foreign language spoken in their assigned area of operations, some of them the toughest in the world to learn. About fourteen languages are taught today at Fort Bragg's John F. Kennedy Special Warfare Center, including Persian Farsi, Afghan Dari and Pashto, Urdu, Russian, Czech, Polish, Korean, Thai, Vietnamese, Indonesian, and Philippine Tagalog. Soldiers who have earned their special forces tabs and green berets but can't pass their language exams have to turn in their green berets and are sent back to conventional units. In addition, each special forces group has its own language training; these are not just refresher and proficiency courses. The 3rd Group, for instance, teaches French-Creole and Haitian-Creole, which paid huge dividends in Haiti.[2]

Schooled in local Haitian cultures, special forces teams used their linguistic, civil affairs, rural development, and medical talents to help Haitians transition back to democracy. They precluded bloody reprisals against corrupt police thugs; opened a road system that had become impassable; taught villagers to restore power and water systems that hadn't operated in years; and helped rebuild a public school system that, as Army Colonel Mark D. Boyatt would later describe, "was basically gone." The schools had "no roofs, no desks, no chairs, no books, no paper or pencils, no chalk boards or chalk, and teachers hadn't been paid in over a year," Boyatt would note. Special forces didn't go to Haiti to run the country; they went to let the Haitian people regain control of it. As one sergeant stressed, "We tried never to start a job the local populace couldn't finish."

Throughout this work, men from our special tactics teams were right at their side, an integral part of their work. In addition, the 4th Psychological Operations Group from Fort Bragg conducted an intensive PsyOp campaign that stressed cooperation with U.S. forces and avoided bloody confrontations with the hated, illegal regime. (Long before the invasion, EC-130E Commando Solo planes from the Pennsylvania Air National Guard had been broadcasting daily four-hour programs trying to reduce the volume of refugees fleeing the country and to help increase support for the return of Aristide to power.) In the final weeks prior to U.S. intervention, Air Force Special Operations Command aircraft dropped 8.4 million leaflets across the country with similar messages.[3] Teams from the 96th Civil Affairs Battalion assessed Haiti's creaking infrastructure and worked to lift the country from endemic poverty and chaos, restoring electricity to many towns for the first time in years.

Having retired, I missed the operations in Somalia and Haiti but followed the work of our special tactics teams with as much interest—and pride—as ever. But new challenges preoccupied me.

MY LIFE OVER A STOVE

For twenty-three years, I had relieved stress by cooking up special dishes after an exercise or real-world operation. Friends said I was a good cook, although a few joked that I was actually practicing assassination: I was going to poison my next targets. I was tired of danger, excitement, and travel. I was tired of fighting off sister service members for roles and missions and constantly reinventing the wheel. We were a long way from being a truly joint team. I decided to become a professional chef. Brigadier General Jerry Boykin, a former Delta Force commander, heard about this and said to me, "I can't figure you out, Carney; you can't decide if you want to shoot somebody or make a soufflé." My wife, Cindy (a fabulous cook in her own right), encouraged me to sign up for the CIA—the Culinary Institute of America. I wanted nothing to do with any outfit by that name, so I signed up for the Johnson & Wales chef's school in Charleston, South Carolina.

I thrived on my budding new career. I loved everything about Charleston—except the tuition, which was astronomical. I loved peeling potatoes and dicing onions; I loved washing pots and pans; I loved wearing my white toque while driving to class in my new convertible. I graduated at the top of my class and won a six-month internship at Mr. B's Bistro in the old French Quarter, owned and operated by New Orleans's Brennan family, where they made me a line cook. I fell in love with Cajun food.

My yearlong introduction to the restaurant business offered some dramatic contrasts to the (generally) disciplined life I had experienced in special tactics. Restaurant workers were not as motivated, reliable, or honest, I learned. A lot of them had no real work ethic.

Still, Cindy and I decided we would open our own restaurant

near my old stomping grounds in Fort Walton Beach, Florida, next to Hurlburt Field. We would set our own standards. We built a new home on the beach and set about planning our new life.

Three ingredients make a restaurant successful: a skilled owner-chef, the right location, and a memorable menu. While Cindy scouted out locations, I worked on the menu. The Brennans had taught me it would take six months to learn to combine the right luncheons and dinners so that no leftovers would ever be wasted. Profits had two components: booze and leftovers. It took me a month to come up with my first dish, a dinner appetizer I called Chicken Ya Ya. I spent the next month perfecting it, an already perfect dish that was a signature meal at Mr. B's Bistro, and the third month sitting back in my recliner in our new home awaiting inspiration for the next recipe. It never came. Instead, Hurricane Opal arrived and blew our home away. The only things left were our fireplace and my recliner. I gave up worrying about menus and soon found myself immersed once again in special operations.

Travel always generated new mental isometrics for me. I accepted more and more speaking invitations from U.S. Special Operations Command to teach lessons learned and tricks of the trade at various units, headquarters, and service schools around the world.

Booz, Allen & Hamilton, Inc., a for-profit think tank (one of the firms often referred to as "Beltway Bandits"), was then focusing a major new business initiative on the burgeoning special operations world and offered me a very appealing job managing its Fort Walton Beach office, which catered to headquarters, Air Force Special Operations Command. I spent most of my time helping to write proposals for new business and briefing studies we had completed. Business boomed.

Booz Allen then asked me to head a regional office it had set up near U.S. Special Operations Command headquarters in Tampa. My first job was as assistant program manager; a year later I became program manager. By my standards, the salary was enormous—plus profit sharing and an annual bonus based on increases in our business base. We won a multimillion-dollar, multiyear contract managing the command's contract support—and soon won add-on contracts to increase that business by 50 percent. At the end of two years, I was fifty-nine years old and bored. I needed a new challenge.

FINDING SCHOLARSHIPS FOR 320 KIDS

Cindy and I decided I should accept a new job—helping some very special children.

Special operations had been very good to me, and I decided it was payback time. My son, Sean, was flying Black Hawks in the Army, and my daughter, Michele, was an Air Force medical technician. That left just Cindy and me. Cindy had tucked away enough savings for us not to worry too much about money, and she didn't flinch when I told her I wanted to take a pay cut (and give up all my perks) to become president of a little-known nonprofit foundation. Its sole purpose was to offer college scholarships to the children of all special operations personnel killed on real-world missions or while training for them. Despite their disproportionate casualty rates, there are no special survivors' benefits for people in special operations, and few of their children could afford a college education. At that time, mid-1999, there were 320 such children. We were determined to help every child get the higher education his or her lost parent surely would have wanted for them. Our scholarships were all grants, not loans, and covered all college expenses— tuition, room, board, books, travel, and even living expenses when necessary.

We also knew that the foundation's work was important to unit morale; it helped the men focus on their missions instead of worrying about their families. It let them operate at peak performance when their country needed them at their very best.

There were only a few problems. The foundation had about $700,000 in the bank, but projected that it would cost about $3.2 million to pay for the scholarships it had already committed to. Even that sum, however, failed to consider that peacetime special operators died in training accidents or on real-world missions at a rate of about fifteen a year, leaving behind roughly eighteen more children. Over the next twenty years, one projection showed, the new children we would be helping would require another $2.2 million in scholarship money.

Another problem was even more daunting: In two of the preceding five years, the foundation had failed to raise even a single penny of new scholarship money. I leaped at the chance to tackle the challenge. It was time to give something back to all the people who over the years had stuck their necks out for me. I had never raised money before, but I vowed that these special children surviving America's largely unsung heroes would get the same chance at a better life that my mentors had given me.

Again, there would be no room for error. Within a year and a half, our family grew to 336 children. I gradually changed the makeup of our board of directors and recruited dedicated, seasoned, but soft-spoken businessmen with proven track records in the philanthropic world. Within two years, they helped raise more than two million dollars of new scholarship money. Our biggest boost came from Mr. George Steinbrenner of the New York Yankees during a telephone conference with his son, Hal, whom I had asked to join our board. I told Mr. Steinbrenner that I lay awake nights worrying about having enough money to provide for the education of all those children. Mr. Steinbrenner replied quietly, "Well, I think you will sleep better now. I will have Hal fill you in later."

A few weeks later, in the fall of 2001, the New York Yankees' owner sent the foundation his personal check for five hundred thousand dollars with a promise to match it within a month or so—a million-dollar gift! He then invited me and one of our new directors, General Peter J. Schoomaker, who had just retired as commander in chief of U.S. Special Operations Command, to a special buffet and informal reception in his Yankee Stadium skybox. He had also invited thirty or forty of his closest friends—including New York Mayor Rudolph W. Giuliani—and told each of them to come prepared to write a big check to a very special charity. Mayor

Giuliani made a short but moving speech about how much he believed in the Warrior Foundation's work, while General Schoomaker added some brief remarks to tell people what special operations was all about. Within a month, Mr. Steinbrenner's guests had sent us checks totaling more than three hundred thousand dollars. One couple invited us back to New York for a private dinner party in their home with another twenty guests, who donated two hundred thousand dollars more.

CNN-TV aired a low-key half-hour public service special on January 20, 2002, about the foundation, summarizing the harrowing firefight in Mogadishu in October 1993. The closing minutes of that broadcast featured one of our scholarship children, Stephanie Matos, who said she never could have enjoyed the college education she had just finished had it not been for the foundation's help. We almost never let the children publicize our work, but in this case the girl had insisted on a chance to speak publicly on what the Foundation's stewardship meant to children like her.

That exposure prompted one of the most moving donations imaginable. Catherine Cartwright, an eighteen-year-old from Bonita Springs, Florida, had just started her rookie year as a professional golfer on the LPGA tour, something that had been her dream since she was ten years old. She held a special press conference on Valentine's Day and announced that she had decided to adopt the Warrior Foundation as her philanthropic cause. She was donating her first LPGA tournament check to the foundation—and henceforth would send a twenty-five-dollar check for every birdie she made on the tour. She invited her fellow professional golfers to join her in donating twenty-five dollars per birdie to help the children of fallen service members pursue their dreams.

By the mid-summer of 2002, after thirty-two special operations men had been lost in Afghanistan, we were caring for more than 370 children. On July 8, Jody Powell, President Carter's former press secretary and an early booster of the Bull Simons Scholarship Fund, hosted a special fund-raising dinner in Washington with another of our directors, Earl Lockwood, a consultant who had helped

Charlie Beckwith set up Delta Force. At that event, Aegon USA, Inc., presented us with a check for $400,000. That raised our endowment to over $4 million. Cindy and I no longer lay awake nights worrying that we'd never get more than 370 kids through college, much less the 180 to 250 others whose fathers, past statistics suggested, might be lost over the next ten years.

AMERICA'S FIRST SPECIAL OPERATIONS WAR—"ENDURING FREEDOM"

A merica is not good at predicting its next wars. When Defense Secretary Robert S. McNamara underwent his confirmation hearing before the Senate Armed Services Committee in 1961, no one mentioned Vietnam. The war there consumed his term as secretary. When Defense Secretary Donald Rumsfeld appeared for his own Senate confirmation hearing in January 2001, not one senator mentioned Afghanistan or the Taliban or the al-Qaeda terrorist network; nor did Rumsfeld.[1]

Nine months later, U.S. bombers were pounding Afghanistan relentlessly and American special operations forces began organizing Northern Alliance anti-Taliban forces for all-out war against the repressive Taliban regime and the al-Qaeda terrorists it was harboring.

Afghanistan is one of the most primitive, inhospitable countries in the world. The monthly newsletter *International Living* publishes an annual "Quality of Life Index": Of the 206 countries it rated in January 2002 on ten factors—cost of living, culture, recreation, economy, environment, freedom, health, infrastructure, safety and risk, and climate—Afghanistan rated dead last (even though the horrific events of September 11, 2001, had no influence on the statistics,

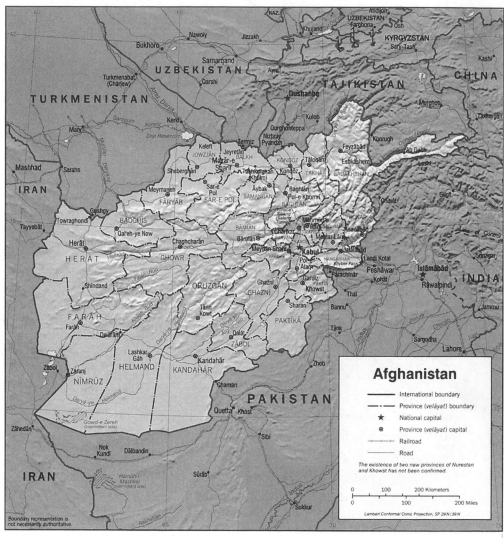

Afghanistan

International boundary
Province (velāyat) boundary
★ National capital
◉ Province (velāyat) capital
Railroad
Road

The existence of two new provinces of Nurestan
and Khowst has not been confirmed.

| 0 | 100 | 200 Kilometers |
| 0 | 100 | 200 Miles |

Lambert Conformal Conic Projection, SP 29 N / 39 N

Boundary representation is
not necessarily authoritative.

CENTRAL INTELLIGENCE AGENCY

all compiled from official government sources). On a scale of 100, the United States rated first with a score of 86.65; Afghanistan earned a score of 20.7, just below Somalia.[2]

American special operations forces found out in mid-September 2001 why Afghanistan rated so low among places one might want to visit, when a twelve-man special forces A-team, accompanied by two special tactics personnel, began operating in the country with Northern Alliance tribesmen against the Taliban. By November 5, Defense Secretary Rumsfeld acknowledged that such teams were operating in "four locations ... maybe more."[3] They worked in primitive conditions, usually wearing Afghan garb instead of special U.S. cold-weather gear, in freezing plains and mountain ranges averaging more than nine thousand feet but with some reaching over twenty-one thousand feet.

Over the ensuing months, some 190 men—70 percent of all special tactics personnel based in the United States, plus many others from such units in Europe—would deploy to Afghanistan to fight with four regional warlords against al-Qaeda and the Taliban. By late January 2002, combat controllers and paramedics from five special tactics squadrons were engaged in Operation Enduring Freedom, spread among three special operations task forces and five joint task forces supporting the efforts of eight different regional warlords. By then, special tactics teams from the 720th Group had completed twenty-one austere airfield surveys (including four in Pakistan); managed air traffic control at fifteen expeditionary airfields; controlled 8,143 sorties or individual flights from them; taken part in more than thirty SEAL and Special Forces operations with coalition forces; controlled over 90 percent of all terminal guidance control for precision-guided munitions; called in more than 630 close air support sorties, dropping over forty-four hundred bombs; and provided weather forecasts for worldwide dissemination from four locations (Mazir-i-Sharif, Kandahar, and Bagram air bases plus a forward operating base at Kandahar).

In one operation, they had directed air strikes while at full gallop on horseback to prevent General Abdul Rashid Dostum's

"Tiger 02" task force from being overrun by Taliban fighters, and then controlled three-fourths of all close air support missions supporting another warlord, General Muhammad Fahim Khan of the Eastern Alliance as his forces pushed the Taliban from Gardez to Kabul. Later, special tactics teams controlled more than seventy thousand pounds of bombs dropped in a forty-eight-hour period during a fierce battle at Tora Bora.[4]

Although it took weeks for them to sort out which clans warranted U.S. support and to earn their trust, the punishing air strikes they called in against Taliban forces won them special respect. Those special operations forces had grown to "several hundred" by mid-November of 2001[5] and to less than three hundred special forces, special tactics, and Navy SEAL team members over the next three months, but proved to be "force multipliers" far beyond their meager numbers. As Defense Secretary Rumsfeld told a National Defense University audience on January 31,

> In Afghanistan we saw composite teams of U.S. Special [Operations] Forces [sic] on the ground, working with Navy, Air Force, and Marine pilots in the sky to identify targets, communicate targeting information, and coordinate the timing of air strikes with devastating consequences for the enemy. . . . Precision-guided bombs from the sky did not achieve their effectiveness until we had boots on the ground to tell the bombers exactly where to aim.[6]

SEALS

Except in their hometown of San Diego, California, just north of their Coronado Island headquarters and training base, SEALs from the Naval Special Warfare Command received little attention for their role in Afghanistan. But they, too, played central roles. In fact, it was a SEAL, Rear Admiral Bert M. Calland, who commanded all of U.S. Central Command's special operations forces in the region for the first eight months of the war.[7] His SEALS first made the public dispatches for an operation that lasted more than a week in January 2002 in a vast complex of about seventy caves and sixty structures in a nine-square-mile area called Zawar Kili, south of the Tora Bora mountains in southeastern Afghanistan, an area that had been hotly contested in December. A platoon of sixteen SEALs, sent in with an Air Force special tactics team, went to Zawar Kili on what was expected to be a twelve-hour mission, combing some al-Qaeda caves that had gone unsearched. Instead, they spent nine days finding "unbelievable cave complexes . . . fully-equipped underground hospitals and vehicle-storage areas," countless intelligence documents, and enormous caches of weapons and munitions, according to the unnamed Navy lieutenant leading the mission. "It was mind-boggling how far they go into the mountains," he said. Most of the caves and structures had been abandoned, but the team took eight prisoners—and liberated a dog.[8]

The SEALs found the pup tied up in a house adorned with a poster of Osama bin Laden. Ready to call in F-18 air strikes to destroy the weapons and close the caves, they released the dog. "But he kept following us the whole day, even though we had to hump up and down mountains," the lieutenant reported. As they neared their helicopter extraction site, the mongrel all but collapsed trying to keep up. A young petty officer carried him the last few hundred yards for the trip back to their Kandahar base camp. The SEALs kept the dog as a mascot and planned to take him home to San Diego when their tour ended in a few weeks. They named him Jay-DAM, after the JDAM (joint direct attack munitions) used to pummel the complex they had just searched. "Since he had had such a tough day," the lieutenant explained, "we figured . . . that he had earned the right to be extracted."

In late January, an unmanned but armed CIA Predator reconnaissance vehicle loitering near the same Zawar Kili area fired a missile at a suspected al-Qaeda complex, killing a number of Afghans while special operations troops captured twenty-seven others, all of whom were later alleged to have been mistakenly identified. A fifty-man special operations team searched the site, having had to remove three to four feet of snow over a two-hundred-yard radius, to find some documents, ammunition, weapons, a tailfin from the missile, and small pieces of human bones and flesh. The materials were sent to the United States for further analysis and forensic tests, since one of the individuals attacked was tall, bearded, and thought to resemble Osama bin Laden. The twenty-seven prisoners were released to Afghan authorities on February 6 while investigation of the possible mishap continued.[9] It proved inconclusive, but no DNA evidence suggested that Osama bin Laden had been killed in the strike.

Findings conflicted about a similar firefight that took place on January 24 in the nearby mountains of Oruzgan province in two compounds in an area called Hazar Qadam. General Tommy Franks of Central Command and Defense Secretary Rumsfeld became persuaded that while U.S. forces had had the complex under surveillance for weeks and had good intelligence that both Taliban troops and members of al-Qaeda were hiding there, this was not enough to justify an air strike. Both U.S. leaders said the Afghans had opened fire first. The Pentagon said sixteen people were killed. Local Afghans later insisted that twenty-one people had died, some shot in the back or backs of their heads, and claimed that the Americans had been misled by local tribal chiefs caught in a feud. One Afghan who had found bodies hours after the raid said that at least eight of the dead Afghans had their hands tied behind their backs with the white plastic binding that special forces teams use as handcuffs. (It was standard special operations procedure to handcuff the wounded to make sure they did not grab weapons.) Some weapons and vehicles were seized that belonged to a senior Taliban commander and the Taliban's former minister of public health, Mullah Mohammed Abbas. He had been in the complex weeks earlier, but had fled six or seven weeks before the American raid. Local officials believed the Americans had been fed false information in a complex ploy by the former district chief, Muhammad Yunas, trying to regain control of the village. He had not been seen in Oruzgan since mid-February, when he was ordered to disarm. Local leaders were determined to find who had supplied the false intelligence to the Americans, fearing that relatives of the dead would take matters into their own hands, and provincial officials arrested a man said to have been the messenger between Yunas and government officials in Kandahar in contact with the Americans.[10] Given the prevalence of tribal rivalries and shifting allegiances in Afghan culture, the truth behind the raid might never become known.

ALLIED HELP

In time, troops from at least seven other nations would join the U.S. forces fighting in Afghanistan—special tactics men plus Special Forces teams from the 5th Special Forces Group at Fort Campbell, Kentucky, and the 3rd Special Forces Group from Fort Bragg, North Carolina; as well as several thousand conventional troops, first from the 10th Mountain Division at Fort Drum, New York, and then from the 101st Airborne (Air Assault) Division out of Fort Campbell, Kentucky, who were deployed late in January to relieve the 15th and 26th Marine Expeditionary Units to secure Bagram airfield near Kandahar as the central base for American operations and who had been "on the hunt" for the Taliban as well; and in July from the 82nd Airborne Division at Fort Bragg.

British special operations forces (from the famous Special Boat Service) were the first allied troops to join the fighting, followed by one thousand seven hundred men from the United Kingdom's Royal Marines. Soon, troops from Australia, Bulgaria, France, Denmark, Germany, India, Italy, Poland, Romania, South Korea, and Turkey either joined them or shipped equipment. Canada deployed more than a thousand men from the Princess Patricia Canadian Light Infantry Battle Group, who in late spring of 2002 scoured the 10,000-to-12,000-foot mountain ridge known as the Whale's Back overlooking the Shar-i-kat valley in southeastern Afghanistan for al-Qaeda and Taliban holdouts in Operation Harpoon. They were supporting troops from the U.S. 101st Airborne Division (Air Assault). Canadian snipers carrying 110-pound rucksacks in thin air along heights reportedly scored over twenty kills at long ranges, including one unconfirmed but widely reported chest shot at 2,400 meters against the driver of a resupply truck. If validated, it would be the record for the longest shot made by a military sniper in combat.[11] In addition, an undisclosed number of personnel from Canada's equivalent of Delta Force and the SAS, JTF-2 (Joint Task Force Two), saw action in Afghanistan.

Because of Afghanistan's historically hostile reception to foreign troops, the United States worked hard to keep its footprint small (about seven thousand five hundred U.S. troops in all by the end of July 2002, although several thousand of those resulted from the overlap between the 101st and 82nd Airborne Divisions as the former rotated back to the United States.) The U.S. kept the allied footprint small as well (another eight thousand coalition troops, including the International Security Assistance Force in Kabul).

In all, the coalition in the war on terrorism grew to more than sixty-eight nations, nineteen of which deployed sixteen thousand troops in Central Command's area of operations, atop sixty thousand from the United States. (Many of the allies were aboard ships or flying surveillance aircraft sent to help interdict Taliban fighters and al-Qaeda terrorists from fleeing to safe havens such as Iraq, Chechnya, Sudan, Somalia, Yemen, Malaysia, and Indonesia.) Most of the countries sending military forces were NATO allies—the United Kingdom's Royal Air Force refueling tankers, for instance, could service Navy aircraft, which strangely U.S. Air Force tankers could not do. But other countries, notably France, Jordan, Germany, Italy, Australia, Romania, Spain, and Turkey also had significant forces in the region, according to Deputy Defense Secretary Paul Wolfowitz. Thirty-three nations had established national liaison elements in trailers outside Central Command headquarters at MacDill Air Force Base, Florida.[12] And by the end of January 2002, twenty-two hundred conventional British troops were patrolling the streets of Kabul as peacekeepers, replaced in early summer by four hundred Italian troops as part of the International Security Assistance Force.

But Operation Enduring Freedom was far from over. Late in January, interim Prime Minister Hamid Karzai appealed to the United Nations, the United States, and Great Britain to dispatch about three thousand more peacekeepers to maintain order among feuding warlords throughout Afghanistan and to capture whatever Taliban and al-Qaeda cells lingered there. By then, close to 600 captured members of the Taliban and al-Qaeda were being detained for questioning (and, possibly, trials before military tribunals) at the U.S. naval base in Guantanamo, Cuba, with other prisoners being held at Kandahar and Bagrem Air Bases in Afghanistan. And President George Bush showed the *Washington Post* a "scorecard" he kept in his Oval Office desk with an X crossing off those leaders of Osama bin Laden's al-Qaeda network who had been captured or killed: It showed that sixteen of the top twenty-two terrorists remained at large.[13]

Within days, Defense Secretary Rumsfeld warned that the war on terrorism was a year or more from being finished; although CIA Director George Tenet revealed in congressional testimony that "nearly 1,000 Al-Qaeda operatives" had been arrested, yet that many again might be lying in wait in over sixty countries, "sleepers" ready to strike new targets.[14] (In Arabic, al-Qaeda means only the "base.") General Tommy Franks of Central Command told the Senate Armed Services Committee, "We will not reach a military end state in Afghanistan as long as there is a credible threat from puddles or pockets of al-Qaeda or residual, hard-core Taliban."[15]

Operation Anaconda illustrated vividly by late July 2002 how much progress had been made in Afghanistan in only nine months; how much remained to be done; and how effective American special operations forces had become in recent years.

In the heavy fighting of November 2001, Chief Warrant Officer David Diaz, an Arabic-speaking soldier who led the first special forces team into Afghanistan, radioed excited Taliban leaders being pummeled by a U.S. air strike, "How far were the bombs from you?" Assuming they were speaking to one of their own, the Taliban answered him. The next round of bombs fell on their doorstep. Diaz explained later, "They would assume that since we were speaking Arabic, we were part of their forces. They would tell us, 'The command headquarters is fine; the bombs hit 500 meters to our left.' We continued to call on the radio until the command was eliminated."[16]

In November 2001, an American special tactics team headed by Master Sergeant Bart Decker of the 23rd Special Tactics Squadron radioed urgently for close air support and AC-130 gunship fires against Taliban and al-Qaeda fighters, whose withering fire from the rugged mountain cave complexes of Afghanistan's southeastern Paktia province was raking the U.S.-led Northern Alliance forces. A female navigator aboard an orbiting AC-130 gunship responded instantly that it would open fire within seconds; precise fires from its side-firing 105-millimeter howitzers and 40- and 20-millimeter cannons quickly decimated the attacking enemy. Puzzled at first by the sound of a woman's voice responding from the gunship, General Abdul Dostum, the Northern Alliance leader who had monitored the radio transmissions on a U.S.-supplied radio, quickly picked up a Taliban radio left on the ground by dead and fleeing troops. He keyed it to a frequency the Taliban had been using, played back an instant recording of the navigator's response, and then transmitted this message: "See what the Americans think of you? They send their *women* to kill you! We call her 'the Angel of Death.' "[17]

Retired Army General "Stormin' Norman" Schwarzkopf summed up that kind of work when he was asked in mid-February if he thought there was any room for forgiveness for the perpetrators of the September 11 attacks on the World Trade Center and the Pentagon. He replied, in effect, "They want to meet Allah, and we just make the appointments for them."

By the end of June 2002, after repeated, exhausting ten-day and three-week sweeps by U.S., British, Australian, and Canadian troops through the rugged mountains in southeastern Afghanistan and northwestern Pakistan, Osama bin Laden had still not been found, dead or alive, nor had half of his top thirty or so lieutenants—just more caves, weapons caches, al-Qaeda documents, and dismembered, rotting bodies, some in tunnels lined by brick and mortar and cut a thousand feet deep into terrain where more than twenty separate mountains exceed 11,000 feet in height (some reach to 24,000 feet, 10,000 feet higher than Pikes Peak in the U.S. Rocky Mountains), all within an area the size of Montana and all separated by deep, precipitous valleys. That Hindu Kush mountain range translates to "Indian Killer" in English. As Deputy Defense Secretary Paul Wolfowitz testified to the Senate Foreign Relations Committee on June 26, "You don't seal borders there."[18]

Had America "lost" the war on terrorism—or bogged down in a stalemate? By the end of August 2002, the U.S. had forty teams of Special Forces and Special Tactics men still hunting the al-Qaeda and Taliban holdouts. Had bin Laden escaped to safe haven across Afghanistan's 1,700-mile-long borders with Pakistan?

It was far too soon to tell. Between March and August of 2002, U.S., British, Canadian, and Australian troops had swept the area repeatedly but made little contact with al-Qaeda or Taliban forces, nor had they found any trace of body parts that could be linked by DNA forensics to Osama bin Laden. But no such evidence may *ever* be found: *Nine months* after the September 11 World Trade Center attacks in 2001 and the examination of more than 19,500 body parts collected in that formidable terrain, the remains of only 1,102 of the 2,819 people who perished that day had been positively identified—only 39 percent of the victims for whom U.S. and New York City authorities had far better DNA samples.[19]

Remember, too, that it took years for U.S. and Bolivian special forces to track down and kill the famed Marxist terrorist Che Guevara in 1967. Nor could the United States Central Command, U.S. Special Operations Command, and their coalition partners forget that more than fifteen months passed *after* Pablo Escobar escaped from his palatial, self-designed mountaintop jail—from September

1992 until December 1993, while he murdered, assassinated, and slaughtered thousands of his countrymen—before the Colombian national police finally hunted down and killed the infamous, elusive drug lord, working diligently with American-flown airborne signals intelligence planes and helped by a handful of patient, tireless men from Delta Force (never acknowledged by the U.S.), as well as with countless tips from Escobar's rival Cali drug cartel.[20]

In remarks around the July 4th Independence Day weekend, President Bush was asked about his "take" on Osama bin Laden's fate. He replied, in effect, "He may be dead, or he may be alive. But it doesn't make much difference. If he's dead, we got him. If he's still alive, we'll get him."

The 2001–2002 war on terrorism marked the penultimate "graduation test" for special tactics. They had grown from a six-man, ad hoc pickup team in 1977 into a cohesive, permanent, squadron-sized cadre that, more often than not, had to fight their way onto the battlegrounds to lead American forces into harm's way throughout the 1980s and 1990s. Now they were an Air Force group of seven squadrons deployed worldwide, truly the very tip of America's spear, winning a major war while helping only a few hundred of their fellow special operators decimate a ruthless enemy in the world's most inhospitable environment. Unlike previous forays where they had to beg for an invitation to get into the fight, at the turn of the twenty-first century America's military hierarchy looked to special tactics to win the day. And so did America's allies, as governments from the Philippines to Colombia, Georgia, and Pakistan urged the United States to lend them just a few of these unsung heroes to help rid their nations of the scourge of terror.

SPECIAL OPERATIONS COMBAT FATALITIES COMPARED TO CONVENTIONAL FORCES, 1980–2002*

OPERATION	YEAR	COUNTRY	TOTAL KILLED IN ACTION	SOF KILLED IN ACTION	SOF AS % OF TOTAL KIA
Desert One	1980	Iran	8	8	100%
Urgent Fury	1983	Grenada	19	9	47%
Just Cause	1989	Panama	23	11	48%
Desert Storm	1991	Kuwait/Iraq	147	25	17%
Task Force Ranger	1993	Somalia	29	18	62%
Allied Force	1999	Kosovo/Serbia	2	0	0%
Enduring Freedom	2001–02*	Afghanistan	51	32	63%
Total or Average			279	103**	37%

* Special Operations Warrior Foundation demographics as of August 20, 2002.
** Plus thirty-five men lost on less prominent real-world missions in seventeen other countries.

SPECIAL OPERATIONS WARRIOR FOUNDATION

Ten years after the 1970 Son Tay prisoner-of-war raid, eight American airmen died at Desert One in Iran in a valiant but ill-fated attempt to rescue fifty-three Americans held hostage by militants who had seized the American embassy in Tehran. Those men left behind seventeen fatherless children. Members of the rescue team passed the hat to help start a scholarship program to provide these children college educations. That effort, established by the units that went to Desert One and with the help of my coauthor, Ben Schemmer, was called the Colonel Arthur D. "Bull" Simons Scholarship Fund.

Sixteen years after the Son Tay raid and six years after the 1980 Iranian rescue mission, two visionaries in the U.S. Senate, Sam Nunn and William S. Cohen, created legislation forming the U.S. Special Operations Command. America owes them a debt of gratitude, for never again will ad hoc rescue forces have to be cobbled together to meet the kind of time-urgent crisis that the Son Tay and Iranian rescue missions represented. We now have superbly trained standing units to handle such contingencies, as well as to lead the wars on drugs, terrorism, and transnational unrest and to help stem the proliferation of weapons of mass destruction. But this is dangerous work, and by its very nature training for it is even more hazardous.

Even though they make up barely 2 percent of all America's armed forces, the volunteers who serve in its elite special operations units suffer more than 37 percent of all combat casualties. Since 1980, 371 of these soldiers, airmen, and sailors (including the three Marines who died at Desert One) have made the ultimate sacrifice for our country. By the end of June 2002, eight months into Operation Enduring Freedom in Afghanistan, 139 special operators had died on real-world missions in twenty-six countries, suffering more than fifteen times the combat casualty rate of America's conventional forces; 232 other men had died in training accidents preparing for such missions. Yet there are no special survivors' benefits for special operations families. Thus, there is an urgent need to relieve these courageous volunteers of the one concern—their families— that could distract them from peak performance when they need to be, and when America needs them, at their very best.

The brave men and women in our special operations units have left behind some 386 children, most of whose families cannot afford a college education for them. Today the Bull Simons Scholarship fund continues on a far larger scale as the Special Operations Warrior Foundation, a nonprofit, tax-exempt, 501(c)(3) educational organization. Its sole mission is to provide college educations, based on need, for children surviving special operations personnel killed on real-world missions or in training accidents.

All of the foundation's scholarships are grants, not loans, and cover full college costs—not just tuition and books but also room, board, and, when necessary, even travel and living expenses. Through a unique financial aid counseling program provided free to all surviving families as children approach college age, the foundation helps qualify each student for every other form of scholarship aid available. On average, the foundation finds each child almost four dollars in outside aid for every scholarship dollar it lays out. In 2001, for instance, the foundation qualified the average student for $8,337 in federal, state, and college grants plus scholarships from other philanthropies, leaving $1,988 to be paid by the Warrior Foundation, a 4.19-to-1 ratio. With its donor dollars doing more than triple duty, the foundation offers a rare philanthropic bargain.

To donate, please send your tax-deductible contribution to:

The Special Operations Warrior Foundation
P.O. Box 14385
Tampa, FL 33690

The Warrior Foundation's tax-exempt number is 52-1183585. It is accredited as part of the Combined Federal Campaign under donor number 2124. You may contact the foundation by phone at (813) 805-9400, by fax at (813) 805-0567, or by e-mail at warrior@specialops.org. You can also check it out on the Internet at http://www.specialops.org.

NOTES

INTRODUCTION

1   From a classic 1982 address at the Air Force Special Operations School at Hurlburt Field, Florida.

CHAPTER I: TUNGI, AFGHANISTAN

1   Telephone interviews with Sgt. William "Calvin" Markham, May 2002.

2   Dr. Nilan Vego, "What Can We Learn from Enduring Freedom?" U.S. Naval Institute *Proceedings*, July 2002, page 30.

3   Molly Moore and Kamran Khen, *Washington Post*, November 2, 2001, page A-21.

4   Andrew J. Bacevich, "Not-So-Special Operation," *National Review*, November 19, 2001, pages 20–21.

5   Testimony of Army General Tommy R. Franks before the Senate Armed Services Committee, February 7, 2002.

6   David Rohde, "A Nation Challenged: Transfer of Power; Afghan Leader Is Sworn In Asking Help to Rebuild," *New York Times*, December 23, 2002, page 1.

7   Department of Defense, Transcript of news briefing by Defense Secretary Donald Rumsfeld and JCS Chairman General Richard Myers, November 1, 2001.

8   The White House, "The Global War on Terrorism—The First 100 Days": http://www.whitehouse.gov/news/releases/2001/12/100dayreport.html.

9   "Comparing Air Campaigns," *New York Times*, April 2, 2002, page A-14.

10   Department of Defense Transcript of News Briefing, Secretary of Defense Donald Rumsfeld, November 19, 2001.

11   Rajiv Chasndrasekaran, "Lives Spared, Targets Destroyed," *Washington Post* Foreign Service, November 23, 2001.

12   Department of Defense, text of Deputy Defense Secretary Paul Wolfowitz's remarks at the Fletcher conference, November 14, 2001.

13   *Ibid.*

14   "Rumsfeld on Fighting 'Modern War,' " On Politics (Washingtonpost.com), January 31, 2002.

15   Wolfowitz, Fletcher remarks, *op.cit.*

16   Sergeant First Class Kathleen T. Rhem, U.S. Army, "Two Soldiers Killed; Special Forces Assault Taliban Sites," American Forces Press Service, October 20, 2001.

17   Jim Garamone, "U.S. Ground Forces Helping Northern Alliance," Armed Forces Press Service, October 30, 2001.

18   Department of Defense news transcript, "DoD News Briefing—ASD [Assistant Secretary of Defense] Clarke and Lt. Gen. Newbold," October 16, 2001.

19   Defense Department transcript, "Gen. [Richard B.] Myers interview with *Meet the Press*, NBC TV," November 4, 2001.

20   Transcript, CNN *Newsnight* with Aaron Brown, December 6, 2001.

21   Thom Shanker, "Conduct of War Is Redefined By Success of Special Forces, *New York Times*, January 21, 2002, page 1. (Comer has since been promoted to major general.)

22   Transcript of testimony before the Senate Foreign Relations Committee on June 26, 2002, Federal News Servce, 27 June 2002.

23   Telephone interview with Colonel Craig D. Rith, Commander, 720th Special Tactics Group, July 31, 2002.

24   Gerry L. Gilmore, "Bin Laden Is 'A Man on the Run,' " American Forces Information Service, November 21, 2001.

25   Transcript, NBC-TV, *Meet the Press*, January 20, 2002.

26   Karzai interview, CNN, *Wolf Blitzer Reports*, January 28, 2002.

27   John F. Burns, "Warlord Fends Off Warlord, Echoing Afghans' Bitter Past." *New York Times*, February 1, 2002, pages A-1 and A-11.

28   Fox News Channel, *The O'Reilly Factor*, January 31, 2002.

29   Secretary of the Army Thomas White's press conference, January 21, 2002.

30   The White House, "The State of the Union Address," January 29, 2002.

31   Transcript, White House Press Office, February 1, 2002.

32   Transcript, Department of Defense, Secretary Rumsfeld's Remarks at National Defense University, January 31, 2002.

33   Dexter Filkins, "British Warn of Plot to Assassinate Former Afghan King," *New York Times*, April 21, 2002, page 16.

34   Philip Shenon, "Qaeda Leader Said to Report A-Bomb Plans," *New York Times*, April 23, 2002, page A-9.

35   Dexter Filkins and Eric Schmitt, "British Commandos in a High-Altitude Operation to Hunt Taliban and Al-Qaeda," *New York Times*, April 17, 2002, page A-10.

36   Retired Army General Carl W. Stiner subtitled his 2002 book with Tom Clancy and Tony Koltz, *Shadow Warriors,* as *Inside the Special Forces* (not Special Operations Forces), and throughout it he refers to the Joint Special Operations Command as the "Joint Special Operations Task Force," even though as a major general he commanded JSOC in 1984 and 1985, two of its busiest

years. Oddly, neither outfit is mentioned in the book's nine-page fine-print index. Stiner went on to command the XVIII Airborne Corps, planned and led the 1989 invasion of Panama, and in 1990 became a four-star general and commander in chief of U.S. Special Operations Command. Nor does his book's index refer once to special tactics. Still, I was deeply honored that he inscribed one of the first copies to me: "To John Carney—With great respect to one of the most professional and bravest Special Operators I have ever known. . . . Many thanks for what you have done for me while we were involved in some of these challenging missions."

CHAPTER 2: WHO *ARE* THESE WARRIORS?

1   Ronald Reagan, *An American Life* (New York: Simon and Schuster, 1990), pages 449–458 and 508–509.
2   The rare Army references to 1st SFOD-D and Delta Force are inconsistent both with respect to time frames and unit designations.
3   Joint Staff message 061651Z, December 1999, Subject: Global Military Force Policy (GMFP), Change 4, quoted in Robert P. Haffa Jr. and Barry D. Watts, "Brittle Swords: Low-Density, High-Demand Assets," *Strategic Review*, fall 2000, page 43.

  The eighteen special operations units included: Army Special Forces Detachments (ODA/ODB), 75th Ranger Regiment, Active [duty] Civil Affairs Units, Active [duty] PsyOps Units, 112th Special Operations Signal Battalion, and the 160th Special Operations Aviation Regiment; Air Force Special Tactics Squadrons, MC-130H (Combat Talon) Squadrons, AC-130U (Spectre gunship) Squadrons, EC-130E (Commando Solo) aircraft, and HH-60G Pave Hawk rescue helicopters; and Navy SEAL platoons, Patrol Coastal Ships, Rigid Inflatable Boat (RIB) Detachments, Mark V Special Operations Craft (SOC), and SEAL Delivery Vehicle Task Units.
4   The other principal systems were the U-2, RC-135V/W Rivet Joint, JSTARS Joint Surveillance and Reconnaissance System, Predator surveillance unmanned aircraft, HC-130 refueling aircraft, the 7th Chemical Company (to detect biological agents), E-6A/B and H-130H Compass Call electronic warfare aircraft, and Patriot air defense missile systems.
5   Jim Garamone, "Flexibility, Adaptability at Heart of Military Transformation," American Forces Press Service, January 31, 2002.
6   E-mail message of May 13, 2002 from Lieutenant Commander Edie Rosenthal, U.S. Special Operations Command Public Affairs Office.
7   Special Operations Warrior Foundation, Demographics, August 20, 2002; (http://web1.whs.osd.mil?MMID/CASUALTY/Table13htm; November 6, 2000); U.S. Special Operations Command, Casualty Roster, 1980–2002.

  The disproportionate scale of these losses is all the more striking when compared in the tabular form shown in Appendix I.
8   Lieutenant Commander Edie Rosenthal, U.S. Special Operations Command, Public Affairs Office, May 13, 2002, plus Benjamin F. Schemmer, "Special Book, Special Movies—Special Ops, Special People," *Strategic Review*, Summer 1997.

CHAPTER 3: "BRAND X"

1   Colonel William G. Boykin, "Special Operations and Low-Intensity Conflict Legislation: Why Was It Passed and Have the Voids Been Filled?" U.S. Army War College, April 12, 1991, page 4.

2   Colonel Rod Lenahan, USAF-Ret., *Crippled Eagle: A Historical Perspective of U.S. Special Operations, 1976–1996* (Charleston, South Carolina, and Miami, Florida: Narwhal Press, 1998), page 13.

CHAPTER 4: JUMPING INTO COMBAT CONTROL

1   Benjamin F. Schemmer, *The Raid* (New York: Harper and Row, 1976), pages 2, 304, and 305. Revised and expanded by Ballantine Books in 2002 with a new hardback edition by Military Book Club and an abridged audio cassette version by Random House Audio Publishing Group.

2   His father, Chief Master Sergeant Jim Howell, was a legend in combat control who had been a great mentor to me over the years. He also happened to be the first man to test the ejection seat of a supersonic F-106 interceptor.

3   Jump details clarified by retired Chief Master Sergeant Nick Kiraly, memorandum for the authors, May 14, 2002.

4   Task Force 160 became the 160th Special Operations Aviation Regiment after U.S. Special Operations Command was formed in 1987.

5   The unit became the 16th Special Operations Wing but may be redesignated as the 1st Special Operations Wing. When Tactical Air Command formed an F-15 fighter wing at its home base, Langley Air Force Base in Virginia, TAC's commanding general thought that wing should be designated the Air Force's *First* Whatever, and the 1st SOW lost its heritage.

6   Susan L. Marquis, *Unconventional Warfare: Rebuilding U.S. Special Operations Forces* (Washington, D.C.: Brookings Institution Press, 1997), page 68.

7   Lenahan, *Crippled Eagle*, pages 19–20.

CHAPTER 6: DASHT-E-KAVIR

1   General Edward C. Meyer, Oral History transcript draft, U.S. Army Military History Institute, October 10, 2001.

2   Colonel Charlie A. Beckwith, USA.-Ret., with Donald Knox, *Delta Force* (New York: Harcourt Brace Jovanovich, 1983), pages 123–127 and 142.

3   *Special Operations in Peace and War*, USSOCOM Pub. 1, United States Special Operations Command, January 25, 1996, page 2–15; plus 1980 conversations with Major General James Vaught.

4   Retired Army Lieutenant Colonel L. H. Burruss, memorandum to the authors, May 18, 2002; Lenahan, *Crippled Eagle*, page 124.

5   Lest it contact the ground before the MC-130 comes to a stop, the rear loading ramp is not fully lowered in flight. The procedure is to open the cargo door (the aft ramp top door); disconnect the grasshopper arms that keep the ramp from going beyond parallel; lower the bottom half of the ramp to parallel on the landing rollout; and then lower it the rest of the way to the ground once the plane stops.

6   Vance's objection to mounting a rescue obviously hinged on his concern for the safety of the hostages and on diplomatic considerations, but they were at

odds with his own philosophy. When he was the deputy secretary of defense, he reminded one of the authors of this book late in 1967, in conjunction with another venture that posed a high risk of failure, "Just remember this: There is no failure in failing; there is only failure in failing to try."

CHAPTER 7: DESERT ONE—OPERATION "EAGLE CLAW"

1   Special Operations Review Group, *Rescue Mission Report* [Holloway Commission] Washington, D.C., Department of Defense, 1980.
2   Colonel James H. Kyle, USAF-Ret., *The Guts to Try* (New York: Ballantine Publishing Group, 2002)., page 74.
3   William J. Daugherty, *In the Shadow of the Ayatollah: A CIA Hostage in Iran* (Annapolis, Maryland: Naval Institute Press, 2001).
4   Kyle, *The Guts to Try*, pages 129, 244.
5   Lenahan, *Crippled Eagle*, page 227.
6   Lenahan, *Crippled Eagle*, page 123; Jimmy Carter, *Jimmy Carter: Memoirs of a President* (New York: Bantam Books, 1982), page 509; Beckwith, *Delta Force*, pages 221–224.
7   Retired Master Sergeant James W. McClain Jr., memorandum for the authors, May 10, 2002.
8   Kyle, *The Guts to Try*, pages 275–281; Lenaham, *Crippled Eagle*, pages 134–139.
9   McClain, memorandum.
10   Kyle, *The Guts to Try*, pages 275–81; James R. Locher, *Victory on the Potomac* (College Station, TX: Texas A&M University Press, 2002), page 47.
11   *Ibid.*, pages 288–297.
12   Marine Corps Staff Sergeant Dewey L. Johnson, age thirty-one; Marine Corps Sergeant John D. Harvey, age twenty-one; Marine Corps Corporal George N. Holmes, age twenty-two; Air Force Major Harold L. Lewis Jr., age thirty-five; Air Force Major Richard L. Bakke, age thirty-three; Air Force Captain Lyn D. McIntosh, age thirty-three; Air Force Captain Charles T. McMillan II, age twenty-eight; and Air Force Technical Sergeant Joel C. Mayo, age thirty-four.
13   The loadmasters had had to use wooden plugs to seal up the leaks during taxi and en route to Desert One.
14   None of these four men or the eight men killed at Desert One was awarded the Purple Heart, since it is awarded only to those wounded or killed "in combat." Military peronnel wounded or killed in terrorist attacks, however, are eligible for this medal.
15   Kyle, *The Guts to Try*, pages 270 and 272.
16   Daughterty, *In the Shadow of the Ayatollah*, page 189.

CHAPTER 8: DESERT TWO—OPERATION "HONEY BADGER"

1   The quote is from Cyrus Vance; see chapter 6, note 6.
2   Daughterty, *In the Shadow of the Ayatollah*, page 139.
3   *Ibid*, page 202.
4   Lenahan, *Crippled Eagle*, pages 180–183.

5   Jack Higgins, *Solo* (New York: Stein & Day, 1980.)
6   Between 1977 and 1992, the unit would have between six and eight different designations, depending on how one counts its classified "cover" names.

CHAPTER 9: GRENADA—"URGENT FURY"

1   Ronald H. Cole, "Operation Urgent Fury: Grenada" (Washington, D.C.: Joint History Office, Office of the Chairman of the Joint Chiefs of Staff, 1997), page 6.
2   Ronald Reagan, *An American Life* (New York: Simon and Schuster, 1990), page 455.
3   Cole, "Operation Urgent Fury."
4   Department of the Army, Office, Chief of Military History, "Casualties in Operation Urgent Fury (Grenada 1983)"; Special Operations Warrior Foundation, Demographics, May 26, 2001 (http://www.army.mil/cmh-pg/faq/cas;.htm;).
5   *World Factbook*, Central Intelligence Agency, 1982, page 121.
6   New Joint Endeavor for Welfare, Education and Liberation. Cole, "Operation Urgent Fury," page 9.
7   John F. Lehman Jr., *Command of the Seas* (New York: Charles Scribner's Sons, 1988), page 293.
8   Remarks on Central America and El Salvador at the Annual Meeting of the National Association of Manufacturers, March 10, 1983 (Washington, D.C.: Papers of the Ronald Reagan Presidential Library (http://www.reagan.utexas.edu/resources/speeches/1983/31083a.htm).
9   Address to the Nation on Defense and National Security, March 23, 1983 (Washington, D.C.: Papers of the Ronald Reagan Presidential Library, http://www.reagan.utexas.edu/resources/speeches/1983/31083a.htm).
10   Cole, "Operation Urgent Fury," page 11; Lehman, *Command of the Seas*, page 292.
11   Cole, JCS Historical Collection, "Operation Urgent Fury: Grenada" (Washington, D.C.: Joint History Office, Office of the Chairman of the Joint Chiefs of Staff, 1997), pages III-1–III-3. [This volume is a much more detailed one than the one cited above, although the two versions differ markedly in many details.] Also, Cole, "Operation Urgent Fury," pages 10–14.
12   21st Air Force logs made available to the authors.
13   JCS Historical Collection, page III 1-3; Cole, "Operation Urgent Fury," pages 10–14.
14   Cole, "Operation Urgent Fury," page 20.
15   James R. Locher III, *Victory on the Potomac: The Goldwater-Nichols Act Unifies the Pentagon* (College Station: Texas A&M University Press, 2002).
16   JCS Historical Collection, pages III-3–III-4.
17   *Ibid.*; Cole, "Operation Urgent Fury," pages 18, 73.
18   Reagan, *An American Life*, pages 449–450.
19   JCS Historical Collection, pages III-3–III-4; Cole, "Operation Urgent Fury," pages 18–20.
20   Cole, "Operation Urgent Fury," page 22.
21   Reagan, *An American Life*, page 450.

22   Former Defense Secretary William S. Cohen, remarks before the Naples–Fort Myers Town Hall, Naples, Florida, February 22, 2002.

23   Fourteen pages of undated, unpublished briefing notes compiled by USMC Lieutenant Colonel G. W. T. "Digger" O'Dell, JSOC J-3 training officer; seven pages of handwritten, unpublished after-action notes by Air Force Master Sergeant John Pantages; author's lecture notes.

Note that neither JCS official history (Cole or Joint Military Operations Historical Collection) makes any mention of Vessey's phone call to JSOC or General Scholtes, even though Cole's history is based on multiple, classified interviews with Vessey and even though Cole apparently had access to all JCS message traffic and logs about the operation (although he does not specifically mention "logs" of Vessey's traffic). JSOC worked for the National Command Authority, the president, and the secretary of defense; since Defense Secretary Weinberger delegated all authority for operational planning about Grenada to Vessey, Vessey is the one person who should and would have called Scholtes. Neither Vessey nor Scholtes has written a memoir. However, the JCS official history (Cole's) notes that on the evening of October 19, the JCS director of operations or J-3 sent CINCLANT a warning order "signed by General Vessey" requesting alternative courses of action for a three- to five-day noncombatant evacuation. One of the alternatives was to include an option for "combat operations to defend the evacuation." The history makes clear that LantCom was to be the supported command for all operations, contrary to what Vessey told Scholtes on October 20. There is no hint that LantCom was told of JSOC participation until Vessey sent Lant-Com new instructions on October 21 "to plan for the most demanding contingencies" and to "reduce the time to airlift JSOC and Ranger forces to the island." Vessey reemphasized the "close hold" nature of all planning, directed "special category" restrictions on all such traffic, and limited coordination to secure teleconferences. By that time, however, CBS had learned that warships had been diverted to the area and broadcast that information on its late-evening news.

24   O'Dell, briefing notes, page 2.

25   Ibid., page 3.

26   Cole, "Operation Urgent Fury," pages 17, 27, and 35.

27   General H. Norman Schwarzkopf, with Peter Petre, It Doesn't Take a Hero: An Autobiography (New York: Linda Grey—Bantam Books, 1992), page 247.

28   Marquis, Unconventional Warfare, page 91; Robert A. Gormly, Combat Swimmer: Memoirs of a Navy SEAL (New York: Dutton, 1998), page 207. Gormly states incorrectly that "Up until now [October 23], the Marines had not been involved in Urgent Fury; the initial assault was a Joint [Special Operations Command] Headquarters show, with the 82nd Airborne Division and other forces coming in later."

29   O'Dell, briefing notes, page 3.

30   JCS Historical Collection, page III-3.

31   Cole, "Operation Urgent Fury," page 75.

NOTES

32 JCS Historical Collection, page III-11.

33 Locher, *Victory on the Potomac*, page 313.

34 Cole, "Operation Urgent Fury," page 14.

35 JCS Historical Collection, pages III-4 and 5.

36 Ibid., page III-11.

37 Cole, "Operation Urgent Fury," page 36; JCS Historical Collection, page III-4.

38 JCS Historical Collection, pages III-4 and 5; Cole, "Operation Urgent Fury," page 30.

39 O'Dell, briefing notes, page 4; Pantages, after-action notes, pages 2–4; Gormly, *Combat Swimmer*, pages 204–207.

40 Steven Emerson, *Secret Warriors: Inside the Covert Military Operations of the Reagan Era* (New York: G. P. Putnam's Sons, 1988), page 145. When Atlantic Command was alerted about the mission, it refused to speak to the Army liaison officer sent to advise them of the planned CIA-Army insertion on the basis that it had never heard of ISA (Intelligence Support Activity), the clandestine unit involved, and because Admiral McDonald was "busy with other things."

41 JCS Historical Collection, page III-7.

42 Pantages, after-action notes, pages 1 and 5; O'Dell, briefing notes, pages 6 and 8.

43 O'Dell, briefing notes, page 6.

44 Ibid.

45 Locher, *Victory on the Potomac*, page 307.

46 Cole, "Operation Urgent Fury," pages 12 and 13.

47 Ibid., page 44.

48 "Lessons Learned, Operation Urgent Fury," Department of the Navy, 1988, page C-7. In a classic understatement, as if it were referring to a shortage of ketchup in some wardroom, the admissions about map shortages began: "The initial shortage of maps was eventually overcome by the short-fuzed production of 1:25,000 scale tactical maps by the Defense Mapping Agency (DMA). Unfortunately, DMA was not tasked to produce the maps until 25 October. . . ."

49 O'Dell, briefing notes, pages 6–8.

50 Gormly, *Combat Swimmer*, page 208.

51 Ibid.

52 Ibid., pages 208–209; O'Dell, briefing notes, page 7.

53 O'Dell, page 7.

54 Recollections of Major General Robert Patterson, USAF-Ret., in five-page memo to the authors, July 23, 2001.

55 Schwarzkopf, *It Doesn't Take a Hero*, pages 245–247.

56 Ibid., page 248.

57 O'Dell, briefing notes, page 8.

58 Lehman, *Command of the Seas*, page 299.

59 O'Dell, briefing notes, page 8.

60 Reagan, *An American Life*, page 254.

61 O'Dell, briefing notes, page 8.

62   Patterson, memo to the authors.
63   *Ibid.*
64   Reagan, *An American Life,* page 254.
65   O'Dell, briefing notes, page 9; Pantages, after-action notes, pages 2–6; Gormly, *Combat Swimmer,* pages 209–210.
66   Schwarzkopf, *It Doesn't Take a Hero,* page 265.
67   O'Dell, briefing notes, page 11.
68   The unit, known as the "Night Stalkers"—because that's when it operates best—has a motto, "Night Stalkers Don't Quit," that refers obliquely to the performance of Marine helicopter pilots during the Desert One rescue attempt.
69   O'Dell, briefing notes, page 10.
70   *Ibid.;* Gormly, *Combat Swimmer,* pages 212–216.
71   O'Dell, briefing notes, pages 10–12.
72   Ibid., page 12.
73   Orr Kelly, *From a Dark Sky: The Story of USAF Special Operations* (Novato, California: Presidio Press, 1996), page 265.
74   Technical Sergeant Rick Caffee's handwritten, unofficial after-action notes, page 4.
75   Recollections of Air Force Master Sergeant Michael I. Lampe in telephone interviews of August 7 and 8, and in memorandum to the authors, August 19, 2001.
76   Schwarzkopf, *It Doesn't Take a Hero,* page 250.
77   Caffee, after-action report, page 4.
78   "JCS Analysis of the 'Lind Report' " and "JCS Reply to Congressional Reform Caucus' Critique of the Grenada Rescue Operation," *Armed Forces Journal International,* July 1984, pages 12–14, 18, and 99.
79   Cole, "Operation Urgent Fury," pages 44 and 45; JCS Historical Collection, page III-8.
80   Marquis, *Unconventional Warfare,* pages 100–101; Cole, "Operation Urgent Fury," page 44; JCS Historical Collection, page III-8; O'Dell, briefing notes, page 12.
81   "JCS Analysis of the 'Lind Report' " and "JCS Reply to Congressional Reform Caucus' Critique of the Grenada Rescue Operation," page 99.
82   Details of the Richmond Hill prison assault are based on a memorandum to the authors from retired Army Lieutenant Colonel L. H. Burruss, May 15, 2002.
83   Gormly, *Combat Swimmer,* page 218.
84   Ibid., pages 214–216; O'Dell, briefing notes, pages 12–13; JCS Historical Collection, page III-8; Cole, "Operation Urgent Fury," page 44.
85   "JCS Analysis of the 'Lind Report' " and "JCS Reply to Congressional Reform Caucus' Critique of the Grenada Rescue Operation," page 18.
86   O'Dell, briefing notes, pages 12, 13; JCS Historical Collection, pages III-8, 9; Cole, "Operation Urgent Fury," pages 42, 47, 49, 57, and 75; Gormly, *Combat Swimmer,* pages 220–223; Schwarzkopf, *It Doesn't Take a Hero,* page 250.
87   Cole, "Operation Urgent Fury," page 43.
88   *Ibid.*

89　O'Dell, briefing notes, pages 12, 13; Cole, "Operation Urgent Fury," pages 43, 44; Gormly, *Combat Swimmer*, pages 217–223.

90　Cole, "Operation Urgent Fury," pages 44, 45; Schwarzkopf, *It Doesn't Take a Hero*, pages 255–256.

91　Cole, "Operation Urgent Fury," page 45; Schwarzkopf, *It Doesn't Take a Hero*, pages 252–253.

92　O'Dell, briefing notes, page 13.

93　Cole, "Operation Urgent Fury," pages 46–49; Schwarzkopf, *It Doesn't Take a Hero*, pages 253–256; JCS Historical Collection, page III-9.

94　Cole, "Operation Urgent Fury," pages 52–53; JCS Historical Collection, pages III-9–III-10.

95　Schwarzkopf, *It Doesn't Take a Hero*, pages 254–256.

96　"JCS Analysis of the 'Lind Report' " and "JCS Reply to Congressional Reform Caucus' Critique of the Grenada Rescue Operation," page 14.

97　In the course of thirteen months, almost twenty Freedom of Information Act requests asking how many friendly casualties were from enemy fire and how many from friendly fire were filed with the Departments of Defense, Army, Navy, and Air Force. All of the responses referred the authors to some other source within that department or relayed our request for information elsewhere. The efforts were fruitless: Not one of the military departments could produce one record showing even rough estimates of the number of casualties from friendly fire. As of early March 2002, all were "still searching" for such data. None had arrived by the end of August 2002.

98　Cole, "Operation Urgent Fury," page 54.

CHAPTER 10: GRENADA IN A REARVIEW MIRROR AND "SHOOT-OUT" IN A NUCLEAR POWER PLANT

1　Gormly, *Combat Swimmer*, page 206.

2　Henry Cunningham, "Schoomaker Retires," *Fayetteville (North Carolina) Observer*, November 30, 2000.

3　Taped report made by USMC First Lieutenant John P. DeHart aboard the USS *Guam* en route from Grenada to Lebanon, November 17, 1983.

4　Lieutenant Colonel John P. DeHart, USMC-Ret., letter to the coauthor, May 19, 2001.

5　Cole, "Operation Urgent Fire," page 47; O'Dell, briefing notes, page 14.

6　Robert M. Gates, *From the Shadows: The Ultimate Insider's View of Five Presidents and How They Won the Cold War* (New York: Simon and Schuster, 1996), pages 248 and 274–275.

7　Cole, "Operation Urgent Fire," pages 10–13.

8　Myriad explanations and excuses have been made for the lack of human intelligence about Grenada, a situation General Vessey later called "inexcusable." The fact is that the CIA had closed its Grenada station during the Carter presidency, over the objections of then CIA Deputy Director Frank Carlucci. Years after the invasion, the CIA's Gates would claim that the "CIA had placed a woman on the island who provided troop and weapons information to a 'pleasure yacht' offshore." But the Agency, he said, was concerned about the visibility of the boat and asked a close U.S. ally—"for whom we had done much in the past"—to get to the woman a more powerful radio that would reach Florida, thus allowing the boat to leave. "Our ally turned us down flat," Gates said, and the United States "had to withdraw the woman" (Gates, *From the Shadows*, page 275).

That is an implausible, unlikely, story—even absurd. How could a pleasure yacht have stood out like a sore thumb in an island chain where hundreds—perhaps thousands—of such vessels cruise year-round? If the woman had indeed "provided troop and weapons locations" to the yacht, why didn't the yacht relay that information to Washington, or to CIA stations in Barbados or Miami, or to a U.S. naval vessel or American signals intelligence aircraft in the Caribbean? The fact is that none of the information Gates said she provided—if indeed any such agent provided any—reached any American planners or troops until minutes before the assault began.

Another source has written that the United States did get a woman agent on the island, but that she left because she deemed it too dangerous. Still another source claims that a German-born, retired member of the CIA's clandestine service who spoke fluent Spanish was hastily recalled to duty as a "contract employee" and sent to the island through Barbados from Germany. Allegedly, he was quickly able to pinpoint every major antiaircraft gun on Grenada, get a good estimate on the number of Cuban military and armed construction workers and their respective locations, and somehow managed to find his way aboard Admiral Metcalf's flagship. Once there, however, no one would believe he was a CIA agent, and he was treated inhospitably until he finally persuaded Metcalf or someone on his staff to check his bona fides with Washington. By that time, the invasion was only minutes away.

An even more implausible version of this third account appeared in the 1988 book *Secret Warriors*, written by Steven Emerson, a senior editor of *U.S. News & World Report*. Emerson wrote that at the time the Joint Chiefs were planning the invasion, the closest CIA informant was on Barbados. He said that "at four o'clock on Friday afternoon, October 21, the CIA had contacted retired Army General Richard Stilwell, the Deputy Under Secretary of Defense for Policy [a post focused mostly on intelligence matters], and urgently asked his help to insert its informant into Grenada within the next forty-eight hours." Stilwell reportedly called a secret Army aviation unit called Sea Spray at Fort Eustis, Virginia, and asked its commander to get a Hughes 500MD helicopter to Grantley Adams International Air Field in Barbados within forty-eight hours. The problem was that all the unit's 500MDs, "which could skim the surface of the water at night without lights," were in California on a training exercise. But a resourceful officer there, Lieutenant Colonel Michael Foster, arranged to have two 500MDs loaded aboard a Lockheed L-1011 widebodied transport owned by Southern Air Transport, a proprietary company funded by Army special operations, and flown with two pilots to Miami, where the helicopters were unloaded, quickly assembled, and "immediately took off for Barbados [a sixteen-hundred-mile trip!], arriving hours before the Saturday midnight deadline." Emerson related, however, that the CIA's informant, "a wealthy Grenadian landowner who had been away from his home for a long time, suddenly got cold feet and refused to go to Grenada," fearful that "his sudden reappearance would trigger too much suspicion" (Steven Emerson, *Commandos*, New York: G. P. Putnam and Sons, 1988, page 145).

Emerson also wrote that the two Sea Spray helicopters, which "continued to be stationed in Barbados . . . could have been used to prevent one of the worst disasters of the Grenada invasion." Writing of the four SEALs who had "drowned while trying to swim ashore after they parachuted into the rough waters off Grenada," Emerson claimed the helicopters could have been used "to rescue them . . . once the distress call went out." That might have been so had the SEALs ever been spotted by the other SEALs who had parachuted with them, but none of the four was seen in the pitch-black waters. Likely, they were instantly dragged under the waves by heavy, water-soaked parachutes that they couldn't release or unharness because they had failed to put on their life vests and were too laden down with weapons and ammunition that instead should have been stored in their Boston Whalers. Moreover, Emerson failed to note that because Barbados was more than 120 miles west of where the SEALs jumped, the helicopters could not have arrived until an hour after the men were lost.

Yet another account of this mission, in *Best Laid Plans* by CBS Pentagon correspondent David Martin and John Wolcott, national security correspondent for the *Wall Street Journal*, claimed that "in the hours before the operation, the Army's Special Operations Division had tried desperately to infiltrate another [agent]." That was "Col. James Longhofer, [who] flew to Barbados carrying a briefcase filled with $100,000 cash to pay the [only agent the CIA had on Grenada]." Martin and Wolcott wrote that "a civilian transport plane brought in a small Hughes 500D [sic] helicopter to lift the agent to Grenada, but at the last minute the spy got cold feet" (David C. Martin and John Wolcott, *Best Laid Plans: The Inside Story of America's War against Terrorism*, New York: Harper and Row, 1988, page 135).

That story is also unlikely, and Longhofer, now retired in California, says four-fifths of both accounts are wrong. Longhofer is constrained about what he can reveal because he had a dual assignment at the time, working for the CIA's deputy director for operations as well as the Army's Special Operations Division, and he had signed CIA nondisclosure forms that forbid him to this day from disclosing much about his work for Langley. What little is known for a fact is this:

The 500MDs were flown to Barbados in the L-1011 after it refueled in Miami. By the time they were assembled and ready for flight, Longhofer was in the communications center on the seventh floor of CIA headquarters, listening to traffic from Barbados. He could hear the helicopters spooling up (starting their engines) in the background of some conversations he overheard about "flying VIPs." Longhofer got on the radio and told the Sea Spray pilots to shut off their engines, that under no circumstances were they to fly any "VIP missions." The pilots did as he instructed. Whoever the VIPs were (possibly Metcalf and Schwarzkopf trying to get to the *Guam*), they had to make other travel arrangements.

Longhofer did eventually fly to Barbados with a hundred thousand dollars in his briefcase, but not to pay any agent. By then, the agent had already refused to undertake the mission. Longhofer took the money to Barbados "just in case" Delta Force, the SEALs, the Rangers, or other special operations forces needed Sea Spray's support. It was a standard contingency fund to buy aviation fuel, parts, or bribe someone if need be on Barbados, Grenada, or any of its outlying islands. He didn't need to use any of the money and returned with the briefcase unopened.

9   "Fouled up beyond all recognition"—or words to that effect.

10 William H. McRaven, *Spec Ops: Case Studies in Special Operations Warfare, Theory and Practice* (Novato, California: Presidio Press, 1988), page 8.

11 Cole, "Operation Urgent Fury," pages 65, 68; Schwarzkopf, *It Doesn't Take a Hero*, page 258; Colin L. Powell with Joseph E. Serpico, *My American Journey* (New York: Random House, 1995), pages 292 and 430; Caspar Weinberger, *Fighting for Peace* (New York; Viking Penguin, Inc., 1990), page 87.

12 Reagan, *An American Life*, page 457.

13 Remarks to the Reagan Administration Executive Forum, January 20, 1984 (http://reagan.utexas.edu/resource/speeches/1984/12084a.htm).

The Marine, First Lieutenant John P. DeHart, wrote that observation in a letter to author Ben Schemmer while he was aboard the USS *Guam* en route from Grenada to Lebanon. Schemmer, then editor and owner of *Armed Forces Journal International*, decided to print it in the magazine's January 1984 issue with a footnote crediting DeHart. When he saw how nice the material looked in print, he asked his staff to take it to a nearby store specializing in sports trophies and have the owner etch or photo-engrave the clipping onto a brass plaque and for the plaque to be mounted on a small wooden shield. Once he saw how good the whole plaque looked, Schemmer ordered three more of them and called the Pentagon to ask for an early appointment with Defense Secretary Caspar Weinberger. Within an hour, Schemmer was in Weinberger's office with him and then Major General Colin Powell, Weinberger's senior military assistant. Schemmer gave Weinberger the plaque and handed him a duplicate: "Sir, I had this one made for the president. If you think it's appropriate, would you give it to him?" Weinberger read the plaque, smiled, and said he would absolutely do so. Schemmer thought Weinberger was just being his gracious self until, about two hours later, someone in his office told him the White House had called, that the president was on the phone, and that Reagan wanted to speak with him. Schemmer thought it was a prank, good-natured retaliation because he had just chewed out a senior editor, and said to tell the White House operator he'd call back later.

"You don't understand," he was told: "The *President* is on the line!" Schemmer picked up the phone skeptically and found that, sure enough, his staff had put Ronald Reagan on hold. Reagan began thanking him profusely for his Grenada plaque. "Nancy and I just love our plaque," he said, and he wanted to know all about the lieutenant who had broken the nutmeg code. Schemmer told him that Lieutenant DeHart had piloted one of the only two Marine Corps Cobras that was not shot down on Grenada. Reagan wanted to know more. Then more. He thanked Schemmer over and over. At the time, Schemmer didn't realize it, but a tape recording system in his own office was recording the phone call. (One-party-consent recordings are legal in Washington, D.C., and the *Journal* used the system occasionally so as not to misquote people who were willing to speak on the record.) Listening to the tape recording later, Schemmer realized that he had had a hard time getting Reagan to end the conversation. With permission from the White House press office, he duplicated the tape and sent copies of it and the plaque to Lieutenant DeHart in the Mediterranean and to his parents in North Carolina. (Robert B. Sims, special assistant to the president and deputy press secretary for foreign affairs, letter to Captain J. B. Finklestein, USN, special assistant to the secretary of the Navy, January 3, 1984.)

Reagan told the "nutmeg" story in at least six other speeches by October 1984. His audiences laughed in the same places almost each time.

14 Colonel Stephen E. Anno and Lieutenant Colonel William E. Einspahr, Air War College 1988 Research Report, extracted from "Command and Control Lessons Learned: Iranian Rescue, Falklands Conflict, Grenada Invasion, Libya Raid," reprinted by the Naval War College Operations Department.

15 Meyer, Oral History Transcript draft, U.S. Army Military History Institute, October 10, 2001.

CHAPTER 11: TWA 847 AND *ACHILLE LAURO*

1 Although its mission had never changed, by 1983 Brand X had transmogrified into three or five different unit designattions, depending on how one choses to count them:

1977–June 1981	"Brand X" (first a covert cell within the phantom 1701st Mobility Support Squadron, then one within the 437th Military Airlift Wing's combat control team)
June 1981–June 1983	Det 1 MACOS
July 1983–April 1987	Det 4 NAFCOS

2 In the 2002 memoir he co-authored with Tom Clancy and Tomy Koltz, *Shadow Warriors*, retired Army General Carl W. Stiner refers to the Joint Special Operations Command as the "Joint Special Operations Task Force."

3 *Achille Lauro*, an *Encyclopedia Encarta* article (http://encarta.msn.com/index/consciseindex/4D/04D2E000.htm?z=1&pg=2&br=1).

4 Oliver L. North, with William Novak, *Under Fire: An American Story* (New York: HarperCollins, 1991).

5 Weinberger challenges that Moreau "worked with North." In a July 27, 2002 letter to the coauthor he said "Admiral Moreau worked only with the Chairmen of the SCS and with me."

6 When Lieutenant Colonel Tappero brought this to the attention of a Military Airlift Command general officer, he was quickly corrected: MAC did not view this issue in the same light. Memorandum to the authors, May 14, 2002.

7 Weinberger says, "I do not believe North ever had any direct contact with the President—certainly he did not with me, nor did I have vehement objections to any proposal to land at Sigonella." (June 27, 2002 letter.)

8 Warren Berger, "Clear + Present Danger—Touring Ground Zero with Tom Clancy," *Book*, January–February 2002.

9 Retired Army Lieutenant Colonel L. H. Burruss, memorandum to the authors, May 16, 2002.

CHAPTER 12: GROWING PAINS

1 Retired Air Force Major Steven McCleary, memorandum to the authors, February 27, 2002. McCleary had been a member of that unit as a second lieutenant.

2 Brigadier General Duane Cassidy, letter to the author, February 2, 2002.

3 Lest readers be confused by the frequent changes in the unit's name or designation, please recognize that the changes confused us, too—and most of the units we worked with. Here is how the unit officially evolved:

1977–June 1981	"Brand X" (first a covert cell within the phantom 1701st Mobility Support Squadron, then one within the 437th Military Airlift Wing's combat control team)
June 1981–June 1983	Det 1 MACOS
July 1983–April 1987	Det 4 NAFCOS
May 1987–September 1987	1724th Combat Control Squadron
October 1987–March 1992	1724th Special Tactics Squadron
March 1992–present	24th Special Tactics Squadron

4 Locher, *Victory on the Potomac*, page 493.

5 Transcript of hearings before the Senate Armed Services Subcommittee on General Purpose Forces, August 5–6, 1986.

6 Senator William S. Cohen, "A Defense Special Operations Agency: A Fix for an SOF Capability That Is Most Assuredly Broken," *Armed Forces Journal International*, January 1986, pages 38–45.

7 Senator Cohen's conversation with the coauthor, circa August 9, 1986.

8   Like Cohen, Daniel had penned a comprehensive article in *Armed Forces Journal International* calling for major reforms in special operations forces. Daniel had proposed that an entirely separate sixth military service be created (August 1985 issue, pages 70–74). He used the term *sixth service* because he counted the Coast Guard, which reports to the secretary of defense in wartime, as the Pentagon's fifth service.

9   James R. Locher III, memorandum to the author, February 25, 2002.

10 For an authoritative, compelling account of these struggles, see Marquis, *Unconventional Warfare*, pages 117–181.

11 Author's notes from the committee's original transcript of the classified hearing before the House Armed Services Committee Panel on Special Operations, April or May 1984. See also *ibid.*, page 117.

12 I have never expressed to Schemmer my gratitude for never once quipping that this was just another of my failed "rescue" attempts.

13 Benjamin F. Schemmer, *The Raid*, Harper and Row, 1976, revised and expanded by Ballantine Books, published simultaneously with a new hardback edition by the Military Book Club and an audiocassette version by Random House Audio Publishing Group, 2002.

14 The Special Tactics Group and its squadrons later dropped the "17" designators and became the 23rd, 24th, 320th, and 321st Special Tactics Squadrons (the latter two at Royal Air Force Base Alconbury in the United Kingdom and at Kadena Air Base on Okinawa). For the 24th Special Tactics Squadron, that represented the *sixth* unit designation in twelve years for an outfit that had begun as Brand X. In mid-1996, three additional squadrons were formed: the 21st Special Tactics Squadron at Pope Air Force Base, the 22nd Special Tactics Squadron at McChord Air Force Base in Washington, and the 10th Combat Weather Squadron at Hurlburt Field, Florida. We also had a separate detachment of PJs to handle NASA's space shuttle missions.

15 First Lieutenant Dawn D. D. Dennis and Colonel Jeffrey Buckmelter, USAF, "History, 1720th Special Tactics Group, 1 January–31 December 1999," March 5, 2001; Kenneth N. Rose and Colonel Robert W. Neumann, USAF, "History of the 1720th Special Tactics Group, January 1990–December 1991," Volume I, undated.

16 Herbert A. Mason Jr., command historian, "History of the Air Force Special Operations Command, Hurlburt Field, Florida, 1 January 1990–31 December 1991," Volume I, Narrative (formerly classified Secret), undated.

17 *Ibid.*

18 For a superb account of this three-decades-long struggle, see Lt. Col. Joe E. Tyner, USAF, "AF Rescue & AFSOF: Overcoming Past Rivalries for Combat Rescue Partnership for Tomorrow," Center for Special Operations and Low Intensity Conflict, U.S. Navy Postgraduate School, Monterey, CA, undated.

19 All the special operations career profiles are based on a detailed memorandum to the coauthor from George Grimes, deputy public affairs officer, U.S. Special Operations Command, December 22, 1993.

20 McLeary memorandum February 27, 2002.

CHAPTER 13: PANAMA—"JUST CAUSE"

1   Background on the planning for Just Cause and many details of the operation were provided to the authors in a May 20, 2002, memorandum, "Panama," from retired Air Force Colonel Craig F. Brotchie.

2   Malcolm McConnell, *Just Cause: The Real Story of America's High-Tech Invasion of Panama* (New York: St. Martin's Press, 1991), pages 185–186 and 191–193.

3   Robert R. Ropelewski, "Planning, Precision, and Surprise Led to Panama Successes," *Armed Forces Journal International*, February 1990, pages 26–32.

4   McConnell, *Just Cause*, pages 192–193.

5   Thomas Donnelly, Margaret Roth, and Caleb Baker, *Operation Just Cause: The Storming of Panama* (New York: Lexington Books, 1991), page 200.

6   *Ibid.*

7   Ropelewski, "Planning Precision . . ."

8   *Ibid.*

9   Donnelly, Roth, and Baker, *Operation Just Cause*, pages 130–134.

10 Today's aircrews use the ANVIS-9 night-vision goggles, so sensitive that on a night with no moon—and thus no ambient light—they can easily see dust-colored rabbits running through the desert scrub of western Afghanistan, see crows scared into flight by the noise of a helicopter's rotor blades, *and* even see their shadows on the ground.

11 Ropelewski, "Planning, Precision . . . "

12 Retired Chief Master Sergeant Wayne A. Norrad in writen comments to the authors, May 30, 2002.

13 Michael R. Gordon, "Stealth Jet's First Mission Was Marred, Pentagon Says," *New York Times*, April 4, 1990, page A-11. Gordon, apparently, was the only journalist who took the trouble to pace off the ground and actually check how close the bomb craters were to their targets. Had he done so soon after the Pentagon claims of "pinpoint accuracy," his story undoubtedly would have made the front page of the *New York Times* instead of page A-11. Nevertheless, Defense Secretary Cheney was obliged to order an inquiry into the Air Force's original reports on the F-117s' stellar performance.

14 Norad comments.

15 Ropelewski, "Planning, Precision . . . "

16 Staff Sergeant Frank D. Medeiros Jr., after-action report, "Rio Hato Airfield Seizure," and others like it provided by Retired Senior Master Sergeant Cesare A. "Tony" Urenda, a combat controlller from the 1723rd Combat Control Squadron who received the Silver Star for heroism in Vietnam.

17 Details of the SEAL engagement are from April 15, 2002, messages from Retired Navy Commander John Sandoz and retired Navy Captain Rick Woolard, a former Commander of SEAL Team Six. It was forwarded to the authors by retired Army Colonel John M. Collins, a principal author of the forthcoming book, *U.S. Special Operations Forces*.

18 Reuters-CNN, "Panama Seeks Noriega's Extraditions over Killings," April 6, 1999.

CHAPTER 14: "DESERT SHIELD," "DESERT STORM," AND "PROVIDE COMFORT"

1   The trials and tribulations of JSOC's arduous "dialogues" with General Schwarzkopf are based on firsthand accounts of several participants in them, and especially a written memorandum to the authors from retired Air Force Colonel Craig F. Brotchie, May 20, 2002.

2   U.S. Special Operations Command "10th Anniversary History," April 16, 1997, pages 32–41; U.S. Special Operations Command "History," November 1999, pages 34–44.

3   Rose and Neumann, "History of the 1720th Special Tactics Group January 1990–December 1991."

4   Rachelle Marshall, "Special Report: The Kurds' Suffering Is Rooted in Past Betrayals," *Washington Report on Middle East Affairs*, May–June 1991.

5   Dr. (Major) John E. Cantrell, "The Guard's 20th Special Forces Group Provided Comfort to the Kurds," *National Guard*, February 1992, pages 16–19.

6   My son, Chief Warant Officer Second Class Sean T. Carney, III, a Black Hawk pilot, was flying with the 11th Armored Cavalry Regiment to support these operations.

7   Personal vignettes from individual after-action reports compiled by the 1723rd Special Tactics Squadron.

8   Staff of *U.S. News & World Report, Triumph without Victory* (New York: Random House, Times Books, 1992), page 403.

9   Marshall, "The Kurds' Suffering," page 8.

CHAPTER 15: MOGADISHU, SOMALIA—"TASK FORCE RANGER"

1   Tom Donnelly and Katherine McIntire, "Rangers in Somalia: Anatomy of a Firefight," *Army Times*, November 12, 1993, pages 14–16 and 18.

2   Master Sergeant Philip F. Rhodes, "No Time for Fear," *Airman*, May 1994.

3   George Grimes, deputy public affairs officer, U.S. Special Operations Command, memorandum to coauthor Benjamin Schemmer "about events on 3–4 October in Mogadishu, Somalia," November 12, 1993.

4   http://tuvok.au.af.mil/au/database/projects/ay1995/acsc/95-002/chap4/somovr.htm.

5   Grimes memorandum.

6   *Ibid.*

7   Rhodes, "No Time for Fear."

8   Colonel James L. Oeser, memorandum to the author, January 25, 2002.

9   Michael Gordon, "Fateful Decision: Staying to Guard Pilot's Body," *New York Times*, October 25, 1993, page 10.

10 Daniel G. Schilling, "War Stories: 'Ain't No Bull #*@$, There I Was': A Personal Perspective on Heroism and Tragedy," *The [Combat] Controller*, August 2001, pages 17–23.

11 Grimes memorandum.

12 *Ibid.*

13 Wilkinson citation.

14 "A Smile of Gold and a Heart of Steel," *Weekly Mail & Guardian*, August 8, 1996.

CHAPTER 16: HAITI—"RESTORE DEMOCRACY," COMMANDING A STOVE, AND COLLEGE FOR 320 KIDS

1 U.S. Special Operations Command "History," November 1999, pages 49–52.

2 Benjamin F. Schemmer, "Special Books, Special Movies—Special Ops, Special People," *Strategic Review*, summer 1997, pages 62–70.

3 U.S. Special Operations Command Publication 1, *Special Operations in Peace and War*, January 25, 1996, pages 2–25.

CHAPTER 17: AMERICA'S FIRST SPECIAL OPERATIONS WAR—"ENDURING FREEDOM"

1 Jim Garamone, "Rumsfeld Tells Troops to 'Expect the Unexpected,' " American Forces Press Services, February 20, 2002.

2 "2002 Quality of Life Index," *International Living*, January 2002, pages 1 and 4–7.

3 Defense Department Transcript of "Media Availability" by Defense Secretary Rumsfeld's Remarks During Return from India, November 5, 2002.

4 Colonel Robert Holmes, commander, 720th Special Tactics Group, "Special Tactics Mission and Capabilities," briefing for the Air Force chief of staff and major commands, February 2002.

5 Sergeant First Class Kathleen T. Rhem, U.S. Army, "Rumsfeld Lauds U.S. Special Operations Forces in Afghanistan," American Forces Press Service, November 19, 2001.

6 Department of Defense transcript of remarks by Defense Secretary Donald Rumsfeld at the National Defense University, January 31, 2002.

7 James W. Crawley, Afghanistan Commandos' commander to take over Navy SEALS," *The San Diego Union*, May 26, 2002.

8 Gregg Zoroya, "Commando's Fight Abroad Also a Hit at Home," *USA Today*, February 6, 2002.

9 Gerry J. Gilmore, "U.S. Investigators Leaves [sic] Missile Strike Site," American Forces Press Service, February 11, 2002.

10 Carlotta Gall and Craig S. Smith, "Afghan Witnesses Say G.I.'s Were Duped in Raid on Allies," *New York Times*, February 27, 2002, pages A-1 and A-8.

11 Ron Krott, "Bolt Actions Speak Louder Than Words—Canadian Snipers in Afghanistan," *Soldier of Fortune* magazine, August 2002, pages 36–39, 77.

12 Jim Garamone, "Rumsfeld Praises Coalition . . . " American Forces Press Service, June 24, 2002.

13 Associated Press dispatch, "Bush Keeps 'Scorecard' on Terrorist Network," *Naples Daily News*, February 4, 2002.

14 Transcript of February 6 testimony before the Senate Select Committee on Intelligence, Federal News Service, February 7, 2002 (www.nytimes.com/world).

15 Linda D. Kozaryn, "Franks: Al-Qaeda's Safe Harbor Is Gone," American Forces Press Service, February 7, 2002.

16 George Coryell, "Our Secret Warriors," *The Tampa Tribune*, June 16, 2002, pages 1 and 8–9.

17 As told to the author by Brigadier General Richard L. Comar, Vice Commander, Air Force Special Operations Command, April 30, 2002.

18 Transcript of testimony of Deputy Defense Secretary Paul Wolfowitz and Deputy Secretary of State Richard Armitage before the Senate Foreign Relations Committee, June 26, 2002, *op. cit.*

19 "Ground Zero: Solemn Ceremony," *Naples Daily News*, May 31, 2002, page 14-A, quoting voicesofsep11.orgAP.

20 Mark Bowden, *Killing Pablo: The Hunt for the World's Greatest Outlaw.* New York: Atlantic Monthly Press, 2001.

GLOSSARY

AB	air base
ABCC	airborne battlefield command and control center
Abn Div	airborne division
ABW	air base wing
Adm	admiral
AFB	air force base
AFCENT	Air Forces—Central Command
AFRES	Air Force Reserve (s)
AFSOC	Air Force Special Operations Command
AFSOCCENT	Air Force Special Operations Command—Central Command
AFSOF	Air Force Special Operations Forces
AGE	aerospace ground equipment
AGL	above ground level
ANG	Air National Guard
AOR	area of responsibility
APC	armored personnel carrier (s)
ARCENT	Army—Central Command
ARS	Army Rescue Service
ARSOF	Army Special Operations Forces
ARSOTF	Army Special Operations Task Force
ATO	air tasking order
AWACS	Airborne Warning and Control System
BDU	battle dress uniform
BG	brigadier general
Brig Gen	brigadier general

CA	civil affairs
CAG	crisis action group
CAP	combat air patrol
Capt	captain
CCT	Combat Control Team(s)
CDU	central display unit
CENTAF	Central Air Forces
CENTCOM	Central Command
CINC	commander in chief
CMS	chief master sergeant
CMSgt	chief master sergeant
Col	colonel
COMINT	communications intelligence
COMSOCEUR	Commander Special Operations Command—Europe
CONUS	Continental United States
CSAF	Chief of Staff, Air Force
CSAR	combat search and rescue
DCS	deputy chief of staff
DDS	dry dock shelter
DepSecDef	Deputy Secretary of Defense
Det	detachment
DET1MACOS	Detachment One, Military Airlift Command Operations Staff
DET4NAFCOS	Detachment Four, Numbered Air Force Combat Operations Staff
DO	director of operations; deputy for operations
Dr.	doctor
E&E	escape and evade
ELINT	electronic intelligence
EOD	explosive ordnance disposal
ESC	Electronic Security Command
EUCOM	European Command
FARP	foward area refueling (or rearming) point
FARRP	forward area refueling and rearming point
FID	foreign internal defense
FLIR	forward looking infrared
FM	frequency modulated
FOB	forward operating base
FT	fort
Gen	general
GPS	global positioning system
HF	high frequency
HQ	headquarters
IR	infrared
IRCM	infrared countermeasure (s)
IV	intravenous
JCS	Joint Chiefs of Staff

JP-4	jet petroleum
JRCC	joint rescue coordination center
JSOTF	joint special operations taks force
JTF	joint task force
KTO	Kuwait theater of operations
LIC	low intensity conflict
LOS	line of sight
Lt	lieutenant
LtCol	lieutenant colonel
LTG	lieutenant general
LTGen	lieutenant general
Lt (jg)	lieutenant, junior grade
MAC	Military Airlift Command
MajGen	major general
MARCENT	Marines—Central Command
MedEvac	medical evacuation
MG	major general
MRE	meal (s) ready to eat
MSgt	master sergeant
NAS	naval air station
NAVCENT	Navy—Central Command
NCA	National Command Authority
NMC	not mission capable
NMCC	National Military Command Center
NSWC	Naval Special Warfare Command
NSWTG	Naval Special Wafare Task Group
NVG	night vision goggles
OPCON	operations control
OPPLAN	operations (or operational) plan
PJ	pararescueman/parajumper
POW	prisoner of war
PSYOP	pyschological operations
RAdm	rear admiral
RAF	Royal Air Force
RPV	remotely piloted vehicle
RSAF	Royal Saudi Air Force
RWR	radar warning receiver
SAM	surface-to-air missile
SAR	search and rescue
SAS	Special Air Service
SATCOM	satellite communications
SBS	special boat squadron
SBU	special boat unit
SCUBA	self-contained underwater breathing appararus
SEAL	sea-air-land
SecDef	Secretary of Defense
SF	special forces

SFG	Special Forces Group
SFOD-D	Special Forces Operational Detachment—Delta
Sgt	Sergeant
SMSgt	senior master sergeant
SO	special operations
SOAR	Special Operations Avaiation Regiment
SOCCE	special operations contingency communications element
SOCCENT	Special Operations Command—Central Command
SOCEUR	Special Operations Command—Europe
SOF	special operations forces
SOG	special operations group
SOW	special operations wing
SOWT	special operations weather team
SSgt	staff sergeant
STGP	special tactics group
STS/STSQ	special tactics squadron
21AF	Twenty-first Air Force
23AF	Twenty-third Air Force
TACC	tactical air control center
TACON	tactical control
TF/TA	terrain following/terrain avoidance
TFW	tactical fighter wing
TOT	time over target
TV	television
UHF	ultra high frequency
U. K.	United Kingdom
UN	United Nations
U.S.	United States
USASOC	United States Army Special Operations Command
USCINCENT	United States Commander in Chief—Central Command
USCINCEUCOM	United States Commander in Chief—European Command
USCINCSOCOM	United States Commander in Chief—Special Operations Command
USMC	United States Marine Corps
USN	United States Navy
USSOCOM	United States Special Operations Command
UW	unconventional warfare
VAdm	vice admiral
VCR	videocassette recorder
WMD	weapons of mass destruction
WRSK	war readiness spares kit

REFERENCES AND BIBLIOGRAPHY

BOOKS

Beckwith, Charlie A., and Donald Knox. *Delta Force*. New York: Harcourt Brace Jovanovich, 1983.

Bowden, Mark. *Black Hawk Down*. New York: Atlantic Monthly Press, 1999.

————. *Killing Pablo: The Hunt for the World's Greatest Outlaw*. New York: Atlantic Monthly Press, 2001.

Bradlee, Ben, Jr. *Guts and Glory: The Rise and Fall of Oliver North*. New York: Donald I. Fine, Inc., 1988.

Clancy, Tom, with General Carl Stiner (Ret.) and Tony Koltz. *Shadow Warriors: Inside the Special Forces*. New York: G. P. Putnam's Sons, 2002.

Clark, Wesley K. *Waging Modern War*. New York: Public Affairs Press, 2001.

Daugherty, William J. *In the Shadow of the Ayatollah: A CIA Hostage in Iran*. Annapolis, Maryland: Naval Institute Press, 2001.

Donnelly, Thomas, Margaret Roth, and Caleb Baker. *Operation Just Cause: The Storming of Panama*. New York: Lexington Books, 1991.

Emerson, Steven. *Secret Warriors: Inside the Covert Military Operations of the Reagan Era*. New York: G. P. Putnam's Sons, 1988.

Gates, Robert M. *From the Shadows: The Ultimate Insider's View of Five Presidents and How They Won the Cold War*. New York: Simon and Schuster, 1996.

Gormly, Captain Robert A., USN-Ret. *Combat Swimmer: Memoirs of a Navy SEAL*. New York: Dutton, 1999.

Kelly, Orr. *From a Dark Sky: The Story of U.S. Air Force Special Operations*. Novato, California: Presidio Press, 1996.

Kyle, James H., with John Robert Eidson. *The Guts to Try*. New York: Ballantine Publishing Group, 2002.

Lenahan, Rod. *Crippled Eagle: A Historical Perspective of U.S. Special Operations,*

1976–1996. Charleston, South Carolina, and Miami, Florida: Narwhal Press, 1998.

Locher, James R., III. *Victory on the Potomac: The Goldwater-Nichols Act Unifies the Pentagon*. College Station: Texas A&M University Press, 2002.

McConnell, Malcom. *Just Cause: The Real Story of America's High-Tech Invasion of Panama*. New York: St. Martin's Press, 1991.

McRaven, William H. *Spec Ops: Case Studies in Special Operations Warfare, Theory and Practice*. Novato, California: Presidio Press, 1996.

Marcinko, Richard. *The Real Team*. New York: Pocket Books, 1999.

Marquis, Susan L. *Unconventional Warfare: Rebuilding U.S. Special Operations Forces*. Washington, D.C.: Brookings Institution Press, 1997.

Martin, David C., and John Wolcott. *Best Laid Plans: The Inside Story of America's War against Terrorism*. New York: Harper & Row, 1988.

North, Oliver L., with William Novak. *Under Fire: An American Story*. New York: HarperCollins, 1991.

O'Donnell, Patrick R. *Beyond Valor: World War II's Rangers and Airborne Veterans Reveal the Heart of Combat*. New York: Simon and Schuster, 2001.

Powell, Colin L., with Joseph E. Serpico. *My American Journey*. New York: Random House, 1995.

Powell, Jody. *The Other Side of the Story*. New York: William Morrow and Company, Inc., 1994.

Plaster, John L. *SOG: The Secret Wars of America's Commandos in Vietnam*. New York: Simon and Schuster, 1997.

Reagan, Ronald. *An American Life*. New York: Simon and Schuster, 1990.

Schemmer, Benjamin F. *The Raid*. New York: Harper and Row, 1976; Ballantine Books, 2002 (Updated and Revised).

Schwarzkopf, General H. Norman, USA-Ret., with Peter Petre. *It Doesn't Take a Hero*. New York: Linda Grey—Bantam Books, 1992.

Staff of *U.S. News & World Report*. *Triumph without Victory*. New York: Random House, Times Books, 1992.

Waller, Douglas C. *Commandos: The Inside Story of America's Secret Soldiers*. New York: Simon and Schuster, 1994.

Weinberger, Caspar W. *Fighting for Peace: Seven Critical Years at the Pentagon*. London: Michael Joseph, 1990.

———— with Gretchen Roberts. *In the Arena: A Memoir of the 20th Century*. Washington, D.C.: Regnery Publishing, Inc., 2001.

Wetterhahn, Ralph. *The Last Battle: The Mayaguez Incident and the End of the Vietnam War*. New York: Carroll and Graf Publishers, Inc., 2001.

The World Factbook. Washington, D.C.: Central Intelligence Agency, 2000.

MONOGRAPHS

Colonel William G. Boykin, USA. "Special Operations and Low-Intensity Conflict Legislation: Why It Was Passed and Have the Voids Been Filled?", U.S. Army War College, April 12, 1991.

HEARINGS

Senate Armed Services Subcommittee on Sea Power and Force Projection, August 5–6, 1986.

REPORTS

Commander, Joint Contingency Task Group. "The Son Tay Prisoner of War Rescue Operation, Parts 1 and 2," Office of the Chairman of the Joint Chiefs of Staff, Washington, D.C., 1970.

Ronald H. Cole. "Operation Urgent Fury: Grenada," Joint History Office, Office of the Chairman of the Joint Chiefs of Staff, Washington, D.C., 1997.

Joint Military Operations Historical Collection. "Chapter III, Operation Urgent Fury," Office of the Joint Chiefs of Staff, Washington, D.C., July 15, 1997.

John M. Collins. "Special Operations Forces: An Assessment, 1986–1993." Congressional Research Service Report for Congress, June 30, 1993.

Technical Sergeant Randy G. Bergeron. "Desert Shield/Desert Storm: Air Force Special Operations Command in the Gulf War," June 2000.

Herbert A. Mason, Command Historian. "History of the 1720th Special Tactics Group, 1 January 1990–31 December 1991," Air Force Special Operations Command, Vol. 1, narrative, undated.

Kenneth N. Rose and Colonel Robert W. Neumann, USAF. "History of the 1720th Special Tactics Group, January 1990–December 1991," Volume I, undated.

First Lieutenant Dawn D. D. Dennison and Colonel Jeffrey Buckmelter, USAF. "History, 1720th Special Tactics Group, 1 January–31 December 1999," March 5, 2001.

Colonel Robert Holmes, Commander, 720th Special Tactics Group. "Special Tactics Mission and Capabilities," unclassified version of Briefing to MAF/CAF [Mobile Air Force/Combat Air Force], January 2002.

ACKNOWLEDGMENTS

The authors are especially indebted to the following individuals who shared their written works (many of them unpublished) or personal recollections. Most of them carefully reviewed various drafts of our manuscript to ensure accuracy, balance, and proper credit to many previously unsung heros.

Colonel Craig F. Brotchie
Colonel Jeffrey Buckmelter
Lieutenant Colonel L. H. Burruss
Senior Master Sergeant Rick Caffee
General Duane A. Cassidy
Colonel John M. Collins, USA-Ret.
Master Sergeant Bart Decker
Lieutenant Colonel John P. DeHart
George Grimes
Colonel Robert Holmes
Captain Wade Ishimoto
Chief Master Sergeant Nick Kiraly
William Kloman
Major John Koren

Chief Master Sergeant Michael I. Lampe

The Honorable James R. Locher III

Earl F. Lockwood

First Sergeant Kenny Longfritz

Technical Sergeant William "Calvin" Markham

Herbert A. Mason

Senior Master Sergeant James McClain

Major Steven L. McCleary

Chief Master Sergeant Wayne Norrad

Lieutenant Colonel G. W. T. "Digger" O'Dell

Colonel James Oeser

Senior Master Sergeant John Pantages

Major General Robert B. Patterson

Senior Master Sergeant John Pighini

Thomas Quinn

Colonel Craig D. Rith

Lieutenant Commander Edie Rosenthal

Staff Sergeant Daniel G. Schilling

Captain Denise Shorb

Colonel Charles Tappero

The Honorable Caspar W. Weinberger

Lieutenant Billy White

INDEX

ABOUT THE AUTHORS

Col. John T. Carney Jr., the founding father of Air Force Special Tactics, was the first commanding officer of any such unit. Originally a six-man team known as Brand X, this elite unit now comprises a group of seven squadrons deployed worldwide. In 1996, Carney was presented the U.S. Special Operations Command Medal for his outstanding contributions to the revitalization of special operations, and, in 1997, he was inducted into the Air Commando Hall of Fame. He lives in Tampa, Florida.

Benjamin F. Schemmer is a West Point and Army Ranger graduate, and a former paratrooper. He is the author of *The Raid*. He has written for *The Washington Post* and *Los Angeles Times* and has long been a frequent lecturer at military command, staff, and war colleges. He lives in Naples, Florida.